ROGER MARTIN DU GARD

The Novelist and History

ROGER MARTIN DU GARD

The Novelist and History

By DAVID L. SCHALK

Cornell University Press
Ithaca, New York

Copyright © 1967 by Cornell University

CORNELL UNIVERSITY PRESS

First published 1967

Library of Congress Catalog Card Number: 67–14083

PRINTED IN THE UNITED STATES OF AMERICA
BY KINGSPORT PRESS, INC.

To the Memory of Robert Larchar

Preface

All translations in the text, unless otherwise indicated, are the author's own. Editions Gallimard has kindly given permission to quote from copyrighted material.

The author would like to thank the following people for their generous assistance: Mme Félix Sartiaux, Messrs. Denis Boak, Clément Borgal, Léon Epsztein, Nathanael Greene, H. Stuart Hughes, Brian Pocknell, Emile Poulat, and Réjean Robidoux.

Elisabeth Schalk's dedication and perseverance in the task of preparing the manuscript have been exemplary.

The author would also like to thank Harvard University for a traveling fellowship to France in 1961–1962, the Department of Humanities at Massachusetts Institute of Technology for a research grant in the summer of 1965, and the staff of Cornell University Press for prompt and careful attention to all matters dealing with publication.

D. L. S.

Cambridge, Massachusetts
June 1966

Contents

ROGER MARTIN du GARD

The Novelist and History

CHAPTER I

The Novel as History

The value of the novel for historical study is widely recognized, if rarely discussed analytically. Three broad claims have been made regarding the usefulness of the novel to the historian. They all find illustration in critical commentary on the work of Roger Martin du Gard.

The simplest use that a historian can make of a novel is in obtaining background information about the social and intellectual atmosphere of an epoch, information which might be lacking or not so well presented in a historical text. This documentary quality, which no historian would question, is well illustrated in the fiction of Roger Martin du Gard. After listing several histories of the Dreyfus crisis, Roger Soltau remarks: "The atmosphere of the period is vividly reproduced in Roger Martin du Gard's wonderful half-play, half-novel, *Jean Barois*, and in Anatole France's *Histoire contemporaine*." [1]

A novel has historical value in another and more complex sense. A great novel is read and understood differently in each successive generation. This seems to occur regardless of the intentions of the author and whether or not the period treated is contemporaneous with the date of the writing. The

[1] *French Political Thought in the Nineteenth Century* (New Haven: Yale University Press, 1931), p. 334.

1

analysis of such shifts in interpretation has great interest for the historiographer, though it has usually been limited to an appreciation of how the understanding of the past shifts with the changing present. Carl Becker has pointed out that each generation rewrites its own history, playing new tricks on the dead, tricks necessary for its peace of mind.[2] The historian may or may not be conscious of the fact, and he may or may not admit it, but there is always an intrusion of the "climate of opinion" [3] upon his objectivity. In the reading of literature this phenomenon appears in the same general pattern as in the reading of history; a moral force or an inspiration, grounds for optimism or pessimism, perhaps an appeal to action, are found and made relevant to the problems of the moment. Seen in this light, the novel is history in a second sense, which can conveniently be termed "historiographical."

Roger Martin du Gard's works, essentially dead objects, have undergone a striking evolution, which has continually altered their meaning and value. Despite their author's opinion to the contrary, novels like *Jean Barois* and *Les Thibault*, though set in a specific historical epoch and placed in a rigid social and geographical framework, continue to retain their contemporaneity. Martin du Gard is in error, or at least is outnumbered, when he asserts in his *Journal* nine months after the catastrophe of June 1940, that he has been bypassed by events, that he will have nothing to say which can be of interest to the men of the new epoch.[4] Writing in 1948, the

[2] *Everyman His Own Historian* (New York: Crofts, 1935), pp. 252–253.

[3] Carl L. Becker, *The Heavenly City of the Eighteenth-Century Philosophers* (New Haven: Yale University Press, 1932), p. 5 and ch. i, *passim.*

[4] Roger Martin du Gard, *Souvenirs autobiographiques et littéraires,* in *Oeuvres complètes,* I (Paris: Gallimard, Bibliothèque de la Pléiade, © 1955), page c. (The original publication dates of materials collected

critic Jean Larnac can see in Jacques Thibault's death, which occurs in *L'Eté 1914,* published in 1936, an anticipation of the generation of the Resistance.[5] In 1946 the Goncourt prize-winning novelist Roger Ikor asserts that the irrational violence so necessary during the war years must now be eliminated and that action must be taken in the name of reason, of what for him is most human in man. Therefore *Les Thibault* has, he feels, a special applicability to his time.[6] Nine years later Albert Camus concludes his important preface to the Pléiade edition of Martin du Gard's *Oeuvres complètes* by terming him our "perpetual contemporary."[7] Throughout the essay Camus emphasizes the relevance of Martin du Gard's work to the present day. For Camus his themes "rejoin our *actualité.*"[8]

The contrast between Martin du Gard's opinion of his *actualité* and the opinions of others can be further illustrated. In 1949 Martin du Gard declares: "What I am writing seems to me extraordinarily *inactuel.* . . ."[9] Yet in 1956 Maurice Nadeau refers to the "profound *actualité*" of Roger Martin du Gard's work,[10] in 1957 Pierre Daix to the "ever-renewed *actualité*" of *Les Thibault,*[11] and in 1958 Françoise Giroud to

---

in the *Oeuvres complètes* are given in the bibliography; all are © Editions Gallimard, 1955. Henceforth, following his own custom, we shall abbreviate Roger Martin du Gard as R. M. G., and the two-volume edition of his works as *O.C.*)

[5] *La Littérature française d'aujourd'hui* (Paris: Editions sociales, 1948), p. 86.

[6] "L'Humanité des Thibault," *Europe,* June 1946, p. 28.

[7] *O.C.,* I, xxix.

[8] *Ibid.,* p. xiv.

[9] *Souvenirs, O.C.,* I, cxxvi.

[10] "Les Souvenirs de Roger Martin du Gard," *France observateur,* January 19, 1956, p. 12.

[11] *Réflexions sur la méthode de Roger Martin du Gard* (Paris: Editeurs français réunis, 1957), p. 86.

the "striking *actualité*" of Roger Martin du Gard.[12]

The Marxist critic Pierre Daix explains in some detail why *Les Thibault* appears to him to have immediate relevancy to burning issues of the day. Daix writes in 1957: "This novel of the First World War, completed as the second was beginning, seems thus directly written for the post-war period which we are experiencing; against those who, immediately following the moment of victory, began to prepare us for a new between-two-wars.[13] Daix finds parallels between the capitulations of the Social-Democrats during the summer of 1914 which are described in *Les Thibault* and current French policy toward Algeria.[14]

In an article written after Martin du Gard's death in August 1958, Daix further clarifies his thought, asserting that Martin du Gard's works are not merely descriptions of the past: "Without my having willed it [i.e., one presumes, despite political differences] it was the work of Roger Martin du Gard which illuminated and overwhelmed with its truth the hesitating and obscure mass of directed information, of partial truths, and of official lies, of that summer when Maurice Audin disappeared." [15] There is more than resem-

---

[12] F. G. [Françoise Giroud], "Qui est donc ce Martin du Gard," *L'Express*, August 28, 1958, p. 11. Cf. also J. Ries, "Roger Martin du Gard," *La Revue socialiste*, November 1958, p. 242, on the "constant *actualité*" of *Jean Barois*. For Jean Tortel, writing in the *Cahiers du Sud*, November 1958, p. 263, our problems today are the same as those of Jean Barois and Jacques and Antoine Thibault. *Les Thibault*, though set in a specific period in the past, "is our contemporary history, forty years after the death of Antoine."

[13] *Réflexions*, p. 32.

[14] *Ibid.*, pp. 47–48.

[15] "Roger Martin du Gard," *Les Lettres françaises*, August 28–September 3, 1958, p. 5. Maurice Audin, lecturer at the Faculté des Sciences of the Université d'Alger, was arrested June 11, 1957, by paratroopers and tortured; he disappeared under scandalous conditions

blance, Daix believes, between the adventure of a Jean Barois or a Jacques Thibault and contemporary events. There is identity: "identity on a superior level, on the level of the meaning which a human life can assume, when it is seen through the *interrogations* and the determinations of Jean Barois, of Jacques, of Antoine Thibault, . . . and the *interrogations* and the determinations of a Henri Alleg." [16] Again one must conclude that an author's personal opinion is not necessarily correct or influential, for Martin du Gard stated in a note of December 30, 1943, that he was contemporary only with the past. "That which I could think, that which I could now say, does not respond to any of the *interrogations* which present themselves to us today, nor to those which will present themselves in the future, to the young men who will survive the present disasters." [17]

At the time of Martin du Gard's death, a number of other commentators made specific reference to the profound contemporary relevance of his work. Pierre Abraham felt that for those who might be questioning themselves as to the necessity and urgency of their public action, *Jean Barois* was a book to read.[18] For Roger Stéphane, *Jean Barois* was not dated, and he found in his own day "filiations" with characters in the novel: "I have even recognized, in the words of a young nationalist addressed to Jean Barois, phrases which one can read every day in the newspapers glorifying the para-

which have never been elucidated. In 1962 his case was finally juridically closed and officially forgotten, by the legal procedure of *non-lieu*. See Laurent Schwartz, "Les 'Oubliés' de la guerre d'Algérie," *Le Monde*, June 1, 1962, p. 7.

[16] "Roger Martin du Gard," p. 5 (italics mine). Martin du Gard was to become personally involved in the Henri Alleg case.

[17] *Souvenirs*, O.C., I, cxix (italics mine).

[18] "Roger Martin du Gard," *Les Lettres françaises*, August 28– September 3, 1958, p. 5.

chutists." [19] On the cover of the August 28, 1958, issue of *L'Express,* an issue which also contains an obituary article and selected passages from Martin du Gard's works, there is a photograph of a young African girl. Under the caption, "A Young Woman of the A.O.F." (Afrique Occidentale Française, now of course nonexistent and replaced by independent nations), there is a citation from *Les Thibault:* "The only hope which I retain is that maybe it will not be absolutely necessary that there be, in every country, bloody revolution." [20]

There have been references indicative of the continuing timeliness of Martin du Gard even after the flurry of obituary articles in the summer of 1958, for example in the January 24, 1962, number of that excellent and often profound satirical journal, *Le Canard enchaîné.* One of the weekly prize winners in a contest of apropos quotations sent in the following excerpt from *Les Thibault:*

All the governments protest, with the same force and the same appearance of sincerity, that they do not want war. Why don't they instead prove it, by showing themselves to be less intransigent? They speak of nothing but national honor, of prestige, of inalienable rights, of legitimate aspirations. . . . They all seem to be saying: "Yes, I want peace, but a peace which is to my own profit." [21]

The contest winner believes that the passage relates closely to the current attitude of the four "greats" toward the problem of Berlin.

[19] "Roger Martin du Gard," *France observateur,* August 28, 1958, p. 5.

[20] The passage is from *L'Eté 1914* (© Editions Gallimard, 1936), in *O.C.,* II, 163. *L'Eté 1914* is Part VII of *Les Thibault* (11 vols.; Paris: Editions Gallimard, 1922–1940).

[21] Also from *L'Eté 1914, O.C.,* II, 337.

Similarly, in a doctoral thesis which was defended successfully at the Sorbonne in 1962 and published in 1964, Father R. Robidoux suggests that today *L'Eté 1914* draws a large part of its force, its capacity to sway the reader, from the fact that "the reality in which we live—just as the reality of the time in which Martin du Gard was writing—reveals itself to be in strict conformity with the reality described by the novel."[22]

It seems clear that the documentary quality of the novel sustains, while the historiographical quality lends itself to, historical analysis. Yet the novel appears to possess still another attribute which merits the historian's attention and perhaps his envy. This is a deeper significance, which shades over into the metaphysical and is usually formulated rather dogmatically, without explanation or definition. It can be described as "suprahistorical," and it is the aspect which will most concern us. In literary criticism and elsewhere one often finds the assertion that the novel offers insights into or intuitions about the real meaning of the historical epoch it treats, insights and intuitions which the work of history cannot provide. Thomas Mann may be referring to himself when he speaks of "the sensitive function of the literary man to discern and to define the will of the times, the changes and transitions of the spiritual, ethical and social life. He does this with a precision which is the result of acute powers of perception and of nervous reaction, and he registers these reactions even when outward circumstances, as in these days [1940] make them difficult of recognition to less penetrating eyes." [23]

[22] Réjean Robidoux, *Roger Martin du Gard et la religion* (Paris: Aubier, 1964), p. 297.

[23] "Freedom and Equality," in *Freedom: Its Meaning*, ed. Ruth N. Anshen (New York: Harcourt Brace, 1940), p. 68.

Though by no means a uniquely French phenomenon, this heightened perceptivity seems most prevalent among French literary figures. One is not surprised at Herbert Luethy's semiserious complaint that in France, a country with enormous literary production per capita, literature has replaced political economy, sociology, statistics. "All the publications of the Statistical Office reveal less about present-day [1955] France than do the works of Balzac." [24] Balzac himself is reported to have terminated a long conversation on politics and the fate of the world by remarking, in an attempt to shift discussion to his novels, "And now let us return to serious things." [25]

As early as 1925, when only three of the eight parts of *Les Thibault* had appeared, the critic Georges Heitz asserted that to comprehend the generation of 1890, future students would refer to *Jean Barois;* for a deeper understanding of the decade before the First World War, they would read *Les Thibault,* just as in 1925, "to comprehend the century just past, we go directly to the *surest* sources, Balzac and the Goncourts." [26] Similar citations, dogmatic in their claims but not immediately enlightening, could be multiplied at will concerning Roger Martin du Gard.[27]

[24] *France Against Herself*, tr. Eric Mosbacher (New York: Frederic A. Praeger, 1955), pp. 72–73.

[25] Albert Camus, *L'Homme révolté* (Paris: Gallimard, 1951), p. 321. For a slightly different version of this famous anecdote, see André Gide, *Journal, 1889–1939* (Paris: Gallimard, Bibliothèque de la Pléiade, 1951), p. 801.

[26] "Deux Romanciers d'aujourd'hui: Roger Martin du Gard et Henry de Montherlant," *Le Monde nouveau,* January 15, 1925, pp. 25–26 (italics mine).

[27] Three are especially striking: (1) Henri Peyre, *The Contemporary French Novel* (New York: Oxford University Press, 1955), p. 39, writes that Martin du Gard stands as "the most faithful imaginative portrayer of the conflicts that tore France between the

There seems to be general agreement that in his major novels, Martin du Gard, "the chronicler of France's great transitions," [28] is making an immense effort to describe and explain three major crises in modern French history.[29] One of his characters, Dr. Philip, indicates the nature of these crises, when, on August 1, 1914, he lists the three somber dates which have marked his existence:

The first was when I, as a pious and provincial child, discovered one evening, in reading the four Gospels from start to finish, that they were a tissue of contradictions. . . . The second was when I became convinced that a vile person, by the name of Esterhazy, had committed a foul deed, and that instead of condemning him,

Dreyfus Affair and World War I, the two great events in the history of French conscience in this century. No history of the Third Republic has yet succeeded in bringing to life the significance of these French crises as have the novels of Martin du Gard." (2) Jean Prévost, "Roger Martin du Gard et le roman objectif," *Problèmes du roman*, ed. Jean Prévost (Lyon and Paris: Confluences, 1943), p. 96, declares that *Jean Barois* has become a classic in Martin du Gard's lifetime, and that "there is no better place to study Frenchmen of the years 1880–1910." (3) Jean Paulhan, "Roger Martin du Gard," *Nouvelle Nouvelle Revue Française*, October 1958, p. 577, writes, "In the future one will read about the Dreyfus Affair in *Jean Barois*, the 1914 war in *Les Thibault*, the 1940 war in the *Colonel de Maumort*." (Henceforth the *Nouvelle Nouvelle Revue Française* will be abbreviated as *N.N.R.F.*, and the *Nouvelle Revue Française* as *N.R.F.* Quotations from *N.N.R.F.* are used by permission of Editions Gallimard, Paris.)

[28] Pierre Dominique, "Martin du Gard," *Dictionnaire des contemporains*, ed. Jean Galtière-Boissière (*Crapouillot*, No. 9, 1950), p. 133. (The French reads, "le chroniqueur des grandes coupures de la France.")

[29] That is, above and beyond the more common novelistic goal of the portrayal in depth of individual characters. The question as to which aim was or should have been central in Martin du Gard's work is of major importance and will be discussed in detail further on, especially in Chapter IV.

the authorities persisted in torturing in his place a person who had done nothing, but who was Jewish. . . . The third took place just a week ago, when I saw the broad outlines of the game of billiards. . . . When I understood that the people were going to pay the costs of this match.[30]

Jean Barois can be viewed as dealing with the first two of these crises, *Les Thibault*—especially the seventh part, *L'Eté 1914* —with the third.

The key question which confronts us is: Wherein lies the supposed superiority of these novels to a historical treatment? And more generally, what do critics mean when they claim that the novel is the surest source of information about a given historical period? Certainly the "traces of construction"[31] are among the characteristics present in a work of history which would be eliminated in a novel, even a novel adhering closely to historical facts. With the historian the marks of his effort, of his painstaking reconstruction, are visible—both within the text and in addenda such as footnotes, bibliography, and appendices. (The twelve footnotes in *Jean Barois* are indeed exceptional.) In contrast to the work of history, the novel, as Claude Roy says of *Les Thibault*, "flows with the happy or melancholy ease of life itself."[32]

Any work of history is obviously pedagogic and has a thesis, whether openly declared or not, which is inherent in it and has guided the choice of topic and sources. There is, on the other hand, universal critical consensus that too much didacticism, too much ideology, destroy irreparably the artistic value of a novel. Our question must be modified: How, we must ask, does the novelist escape didacticism and at the same

[30] *L'Eté 1914*, O.C., II, 597.
[31] Claude Roy, "Roger Martin du Gard ou le Massif Central," *Libération*, February 28, 1956, p. 2.
[32] *Ibid.*

time retain the ability, which has been so dogmatically claimed for him, to surpass the historian at his own task? In the first place, the demand that an artist begin in complete freedom from all preconceptions is probably impossible to fulfill. Perhaps the best any novelist can do is to disguise with great skill (and this may well be one of the measures of that elusive attribute, talent) the fact that he builds from an idea, probably a moral idea, that his method is deductive, not inductive.

In the case of Roger Martin du Gard, some helpful clarification of this problem is offered by the Belgian critic Nelly Cormeau. She feels that Martin du Gard has successfully banished any pedagogic conceptions from *Jean Barois*, that the novel does not contain what she terms "ideology openly developed." Such ideology would tend to dissipate or at least intrude upon the "*romanesque* illusion" in a work of literature and would divide it into "two bodies." [33] Mme Cor-

---

[33] *Physiologie du roman* (Brussels: La Renaissance du Livre, 1947), pp. 142, 147. Critical opinion is divided as to whether Martin du Gard was able to remain really objective in *Jean Barois*. The posthumously published "Projets de préface pour *Jean Barois*," *N.R.F.,* December 1959, pp. 1123–1128, proves decisively that Martin du Gard had strong agnostic and anticlerical convictions, and it is a mark of his literary skill that they have not always been detected. In these outlines Martin du Gard with great scrupulousness formulates warnings for people who have kept their religious faith. After he had finished writing *Jean Barois*, he realized that "this book is partial" (p. 1128). There is a fairly strong implication in these "Projets" that Martin du Gard would not have been disappointed if Catholics were to read *Jean Barois* to the detriment of their faith. Even today Catholic censorship reserves his works for "mature and cultivated readers" (*Livres et lectures,* [April 1959], p. 204). Abbé Charles Moeller believes that *Jean Barois* must be closely analyzed and carefully dealt with by Catholic apologists, for it "profoundly disturbs those readers who are not fully aware of the true image of Christian life" (*Littérature du vingtième siècle et Christianisme,* II [Paris: Casterman, 1957], 167).

meau suggests that the conflict between religion and atheism which so marked the end of the nineteenth century is in itself a very poignant drama, but for her it is literature which brings this episode in intellectual history to life. This conflict of ideas would never have taken on a "sharpness" and "living authority" if its own rhythm had not been linked with the life cycle of a single man, Jean Barois.

Ideas and problems are here blended with the vital forces of an individual whose character, history, slightest movements we know; they are the direct emanation of one human experience. Better yet, transformed into attitudes and acts they are the real substance of the man, the manifestation of his vitality. They lose their general aspect, and present themselves only as dramatic forces, motivating emotions and human behavior.[34]

When there is a purely abstract discussion in Martin du Gard's novel, the ideas pass from the theoretical to an individual plane and appear to be an inherent part of the personalities of the different characters, part of their "interior necessity." They represent within the novel's development a step which is "bursting with life and of an irresistible urgency." [35] Only through an informing, an injection of dramatic content into the ideological and moralizing sections of a work, can these sections attain a real vitality. Mme Cormeau uses the term "transposition" to describe this phenomenon, and I find it an excellent choice. The same transposition is present when Martin du Gard treats in his novels more strictly

[34] *Physiologie du roman*, p. 147. Cf. Brian S. Pocknell, "The Nature and the Limits of Realism in the Works of Roger Martin du Gard," (unpublished Master's thesis, University of Manchester, 1959), p. 81. Pocknell carries Mme Cormeau's idea even further, arguing that Jean Barois himself serves as a link between the real world and the world of fiction, with the fictitious "enhancing, crystallizing, the real."

[35] *Physiologie du roman*, pp. 147–148.

"historical" material (that is, political, social, and economic history, as opposed to the history of ideas). Glado de May describes *Les Thibault* as "a slice of history transposed onto the plane of art."[36]

The reader's comprehension and appreciation of major political events are enhanced when these events are viewed from the perspective of one or a limited number of individuals. In his review of *L'Eté 1914*, François Porché discerned an effort on Martin du Gard's part to combine two elements of pathos: "on the one hand, the terrible correlation which, after a certain fact, as after the pulling of a switch, inexorably led the world towards the cataclysm; on the other hand, the agitations, the conflicts, the supremely passionate *élans* of a few particularized destinies on the brink of the abyss."[37] Historical events, continues Porché, which have in themselves the immobility that is the condition of things past, are "brought into the present, made alive, at the same time that they are elucidated, commented upon, by the diverse reactions of the individual consciences in which they are reflected."[38]

[36] "*Les Thibault,* monument social," *Glanes,* November–December 1948, p. 31.

[37] "Chronique littéraire," *L'Echo de Paris,* December 7, 1936, p. 4.

[38] *Ibid.* Other critics have similar ideas: (1) Heitz, "Deux Romanciers d'aujourd'hui," p. 25, after praising Martin du Gard's characterization, asserts that "the entire society relives by the evocation of individuals." (2) Pocknell, "Realism in the Works of Martin du Gard," p. 145, argues that it is through the reactions of fictitious characters to external forces that the movement of history is felt. Jean Barois himself "reflects the conscience of a nation" (p. 81). The novel is "devoid of the cold, historical atmosphere of a chronicle of the Third Republic" and "profits from the human content which rules the tone of the novel, if it cannot rule the events" (p. 47). (3) Pierre-Henri Simon, *L'Esprit et l'histoire* (Paris: Armand Colin, 1954), p. 55, describes the process in this fashion: The questions which

The root of the claim of "suprahistoricity" seems thus to lie in the novelist's ability to personalize ideology and history. This in turn permits the working of the psychological process of identification. A realistic treatment of character is necessary to bring to life the society in which the novelist's cast moves. If the reader cannot identify with one or more of the characters, his appreciation, his sense of participation will invariably be lost.[39]

In order for the reader to empathize so strongly with a character that he is able to re-experience the past, it would seem necessary for the author first to come directly into contact with the events he is depicting. If this occurs, the resultant type of novel is often described as a *témoignage* and is viewed by many critics as different from, and sometimes inferior to, the "pure" novel. The problem of the *témoignage*, of whether or not it is more than a glorified form of journalism—a *reportage* sustained by emotional force and a certain degree of literary talent—must be resolved by the biases of the individual critic. There is, however, an important question of definition which is brought up by the use of the word *témoignage*.

Roger Martin du Gard cannot be considered a *témoin* in the modern sense, as Camus and Sartre are in their novels and

---

Martin du Gard is led to ask in his *Les Thibault* about the movement of history and its relation to human will are not developed extrinsically in the novel, but are always joined, "according to an impeccable novelistic technique, to the crises of conscience and options of the characters." The different characters "represent the different [possible] individual responses to the facts of war and revolution."

[39] I do not of course mean to imply that all valid fiction must involve the process of identification. But I would argue that a high degree of sophistication is required before one can accept and derive benefit from modern novels in which identification is difficult if not impossible.

other writings, as Jean-Jacques Servan-Schreiber is in his *Lieutenant en Algérie* (1957) or Henri Alleg in his unforgettable *La Question* (1958). (There is a curious parallel between the contemporary meaning and the use by the early Christians of a word equivalent to *témoin* to describe those whom we today would term martyrs, those who had voluntarily suffered and died during the persecutions, thus "bearing witness" for Christ.) [40] Martin du Gard himself was too young to be involved actively in the Dreyfus controversy, and during the dramatic month of July 1914, he was not present in Paris.[41] By his own admission he had never seen Jean Jaurès in the flesh.[42] He had moreover, great difficulty in treating contemporary subjects and seemed always to need the cushion of objectivity provided by the passage of time before he could write about a given epoch. Yet in the critical literature I have discovered more than twenty-five references to Martin du Gard as a *témoin* or as the creator of a *témoignage* of his era. This apparent paradox can be resolved by clarifying the definition of *témoignage*. Léon Blum, who played a considerable role in the Dreyfus Affair and should have been a good judge, praised "that astonishing *Jean Barois* in which the Dreyfusist atmosphere, the Dreyfusist soul are re-created without any directly received impressions—Roger Martin du Gard was too young—through the intuition of art alone: for, more powerful in this respect than science, art reconstitutes life." [43]

[40] André Piganiol, *L'Empire Chrétien* (Paris: Presses Universitaires, 1947), p. 373.

[41] R. M. G., *Souvenirs*, O.C., I, xlvii; Jean Schlumberger, *Eveils* (Paris: Gallimard, 1950), p. 248.

[42] René Lalou, *Histoire de la littérature française contemporaine*, II (Paris: Presses Universitaires, 1953), 720.

[43] Léon Blum, *Souvenirs sur l'Affaire* (Paris: Gallimard, 1935), p. 131.

The *témoignage* in Roger Martin du Gard's works is thus related to his art, is internal, bound up with the development of his characters and with their relation to the evolution of historical events. It is not external, as is implied by ordinary modern usage—the direct consequence of the overwhelming effect of contemporary events on the life of the individual writer. This distinction does not of course preclude an intense vicarious emotional involvement with the historical materials out of which Martin du Gard reconstituted life. As Claude Roy puts it, "Every great novel is in its essence a *reportage of the past;* every great reportage is . . . in its essence an *involuntary novel.*" [44]

The professional historian would be quick to point out the subjective nature of transposition and identification and would probably argue that these phenomena bear no real relation to his craft. He would at the very least demand that the novels under consideration remain faithful to the history of the period they treat. Roger Martin du Gard's works are quite adequate in this respect.[45] His early training at the Ecole des chartes stood him in good stead, and all his life he

---

[44] *Descriptions critiques,* I (Paris: Gallimard, 1949), 66 (italics his).

[45] Numerous critics and scholars have checked Martin du Gard's works to verify his accuracy. Very rarely have they discovered errors. For example, in the opinion of Pierre Rain, then professor at l'Ecole Libre des Sciences Politiques, the conversations of the international group of socialists at Geneva, which Martin du Gard imagined, "go beyond mere resemblance, and bear the stamp of truth" ("L'été 1914," *Sciences politiques,* March 1937, p. 35). Professor Rain notes (p. 38) that though Martin du Gard probably did not consult the diplomatic correspondence which was published at about the same time as his novel, he attributes to the fictional diplomat Rumelles "statements which a historian cannot criticize." The very few examples of Martin du Gard's deliberate tampering with the facts of history will be discussed later, as they are of the utmost significance for the understanding of the psychological and socio-political aims of his art.

relied upon the methods acquired there, sometimes even criticizing himself for being a slave to them, for being overly conscientious and devoting too much time to documentation.[46] Martin du Gard's suprahistoricity is of a dual nature. Not only does his treatment of the Dreyfus crisis and the outbreak of the First World War cause these episodes to come alive for the reader through the processes of identification and transposition, but a study of his work also provides the historian with insights into the period in which he was writing his masterpiece, *Les Thibault*. He was deeply representative of his epoch and his nation, even though—or rather because—his artist's antennae were not always as immediately sensitive as Thomas Mann considered desirable. A new level of interaction between history and literature emerges from an examination of Martin du Gard's reactions to the pressures of contemporary events. The development of a historical consciousness during the years in which he was writing *Les Thibault* (1920-1939) forced him into two courses of action: to change artistic plans for this novel series which deals with the period 1904-1918 and to become politically involved, a step which he was psychologically and emotionally deeply opposed to taking.

[46] *Souvenirs, O.C.*, I, xlvii-xlix. Martin du Gard's own feelings as to the value of his *chartiste* education were divided. Cf. Robert Laulan, "Roger Martin du Gard et la formation chartiste," *Mercure de France*, March 1959, pp. 550-551. Laulan collects the major references in Martin du Gard's published correspondence and other writings which deal with his experiences at this school. It is possible to exaggerate the negative effects on Martin du Gard; if it had really been in his nature, he probably would have followed his own advice more faithfully: "It is necessary to *smother the chartiste* and revive the *poet* that I was at fifteen" (letter to Pierre Margaritis, February 6, 1918, Martin du Gard's italics, published in the Martin du Gard memorial issue of *N.N.R.F.*, December 1958, p. 1127).

CHAPTER II

Early Career: Jean Barois
and the Dreyfus Affair

"Jean Barois IS *the Dreyfus Affair, and no
document can equal it for a general understanding of that Affair.*" [1]

Martin du Gard's first major novel, *Jean Barois*, and its
intimate relationship with the Dreyfus Affair cannot be discussed in a vacuum. A certain amount of background material must be presented, including a brief examination of
Martin du Gard's early life and first literary efforts, and, in
an attempt to pinpoint the significance of *Jean Barois*, a few
remarks on other novels which deal with the Dreyfus crisis.
This will facilitate an evaluation of *Jean Barois* and of the
rather extravagant statements which have been made about
it, such as the one quoted as an epigraph to this chapter.

Roger Martin du Gard was born on March 23, 1881, just
outside Paris, into a family which had been in the legal pro-
fession for many generations, and which had never before

[1] André Perrin, "Roger Martin du Gard et *les Thibault*," *Le Mois*,
January 10, 1937, p. 165.

produced an artist. He took pains to emphasize in his *Souvenirs autobiographiques et littéraires* that the particle *du* does not indicate noble origins.[2] Despite his family background, Martin du Gard sensed his literary vocation early and began at a tender age to compose tragedies in verse and, a few years later, short naturalistic tales, "in an unimaginably bad taste."[3] When he passed his *baccalauréat,* his father offered him a rifle so that he could join in hunting expeditions as every member of the *haute bourgeoisie* should. Young Martin du Gard, however, stated a preference for a Larousse dictionary, which he did not receive for six months, until his furious father had calmed down.[4] There is also some evidence that Martin du Gard, while still quite young, attained a social consciousness. His distant cousin, the critic and commentator Maurice Martin du Gard, never friendly with him for religious, political, and perhaps personal reasons, reports the following detail which he finds amusing: While still living with his family, Roger, feeling guilty about his privileged status in French society, refused to let the family servants into his room, made his own bed, cooked his own eggs, and even shined his own shoes.[5]

In November 1900, after some desultory studies at the Faculty of Letters of the Sorbonne, culminating in his failing

[2] *Souvenirs, O.C.,* I, xxxix.

[3] *Ibid.,* p. xlii.

[4] Henri Chaperon, "Roger Martin du Gard (Souvenirs)," *Bulletin de la société littéraire des P.T.T.,* June 1959, p. 10.

[5] "Roger Martin du Gard," *La Revue des deux mondes,* October 1, 1958, p. 472. The conservative Catholic nationalist Maurice could never understand Roger's attitudes and regretted that he found him unchanged just before his death, obsessed by "some sort of need to find fault with his social class, his country, even with his race, for it was against the whites that he loved the blacks" (p. 465).

the examination for the *licence,* Roger Martin du Gard entered the Ecole des chartes.[6] This was not out of any singular devotion to paleography and archival studies, but rather, as he once wrote of a young *chartiste* whom he saw as a mirror image of himself: "He had entered the School just as one enters under a *porte cochère* during a rainstorm: to wait." [7]

Never was Martin du Gard's attention diverted from his goal of becoming a novelist. This is clearly indicated in a letter to his mentor and former professor, the defrocked priest Marcel Hébert. From the context of their important correspondence, the letter can be dated about August 20, 1901, and was sent from the family home in Sancergues (Cher). Martin du Gard felt that he was passing through a serious crisis: "This is due to two circumstances which I shall in strict confidence explain to you: (1) The fact that I have for the first time read the Bible seriously, with doubts to enlighten. (2) I have come to the country to write a novel . . . yes, a love novel, the story of a young couple." [8] He goes on to summarize his plans, demonstrating both youthful idealism and a curious maturity. More than four years away from his own marriage, he foresees the kinds of problems which would beset a French intellectual with liberal ideas when he married. In the projected novel the husband was to make a resolution to help his wife rid herself of old-fashioned prejudices and "give the woman a new morality,

---

[6] Réjean Robidoux, *Roger Martin du Gard et la religion* (Paris: Aubier, 1964), p. 51. Robidoux's checking of the records at the Ecole des chartes, thus correcting an error in the Pléiade edition chronological table, is typical of his fine scholarship.

[7] See *Souvenirs, O.C.,* I, xlviii. The reference is to the character Bernard Grosdidier in *Devenir!, O.C.,* I, 17.

[8] Communicated by M. Emile Poulat.

based upon the theories of evolution. . . . The title is self-explanatory: '*La Chrysalide*.' " In a letter from the same series dated September 17, 1901, he more openly asserts his anticlericalism: "I am separating myself from the Catholic cult." [9] This is a striking admission of the linkage Martin du Gard probably made in all his works. Moral, ideological problems (his loss of faith, in this case) are closely identified with artistic projects (*La Chrysalide*). This early effort did not come to fruition, and it is not yet known whether the manuscript still exists.

Except for a year of military service in 1902–1903, Martin du Gard remained at the Ecole des chartes until February 1906, when he successfully defended his thesis, married a devout Catholic, Hélène Foucault, and left Paris for a long holiday. His thesis, an archeological study of the ruins of the famous Norman abbey of Jumièges, was published in 1909 and favorably reviewed in the *Mercure de France*.[10] Whether it harmed or aided his art, Martin du Gard's *chartiste* training did enable him to produce a solid volume of archival research.

Art was always the foremost of his concerns, and during his honeymoon in 1906 he prepared the outline of a long novel, a biography of a country priest, which he intended to entitle *Une Vie de saint*. After eighteen months of labor, he abandoned the project, following the advice of a friend to

[9] See also Albert Houtin, *Un Prêtre symboliste, Marcel Hébert* (Paris: F. Reider, 1925), pp. 138–139. Houtin cites another letter of September, 1901, which Martin du Gard had authorized him to publish. Here Martin du Gard refuses to consider Hébert's plea that he remain in the church, speaking out firmly against the abuses he finds therein: "What need is there to remain in a collapsing house crying out '*au secours?*' "

[10] Charles Merki, "Archéologie, Voyages," *Mercure de France*, August 6, 1910, p. 701.

whom he had read the manuscript. Discouraged and depressed, Martin du Gard spent the winter and spring of 1908 attending lectures on psychiatry at several Paris hospitals. Fear of failure eventually saved him from what might have become a career of dilettantism. He had the idea that if he could himself produce a portrait of a total *raté*, he would be saved from his protagonist's destiny. Thus *Devenir!* came to be written in the summer of 1908. In contrast to his usual habits, Martin du Gard dashed off a rough draft in a few weeks, without notes or a detailed outline. The novel was accepted for publication at the author's expense in the fall of 1908, and Martin du Gard felt able to settle down again to a more extensive work involving years of preparation and note-taking. He writes about *Devenir!*: "I have always considered *Devenir!* as an improvisation caused by circumstance, as a sort of exorcism, destined to conjure away the depression which I was under after the failure of *Une Vie de saint*. I hesitated a long time, after the war, before I decided to allow the publication of a new edition of this work of my youth." [11]

Nevertheless, the novel is not without interest. The critical reception was in general favorable,[12] and this, along with the encouragement of friends, helped Martin du Gard to persevere in a novelist's career. A study of the evolution of his literary talent toward the full maturity of *Les Thibault* or *Confidence Africaine* would devote considerable attention to *Devenir!* The novel is, however, almost entirely concerned with the presentation of character, with the semitragic yet

[11] *Souvenirs, O.C.,* I, li–lii. Albert Camus remarks that in *Devenir!* Martin du Gard had once and for all to get rid of certain complacencies of style, "as with adolescent acne" ("Préface," *O.C.,* I, x).

[12] See Rachilde, "Les Romans," *Mercure de France,* August 16, 1909, p. 696: "a pretty book, well written, *spirituel,* and well composed." See also Jean Lionnet, "Les Livres," *Revue Hebdomadaire,* October 2, 1909, pp. 115–117.

inexorable destiny of the innocuous hero, André Mazarelles. Social, political and historical questions receive little consideration in *Devenir!* [13] The action in the novel cannot be precisely dated; Jean Cocteau, who was born in 1889, recognized himself as one of the youthful characters,[14] and the story contains a humorous reference to the resemblance of André Mazarelles's father to President Loubet [15] (President of the Republic from 1899 to 1906). There are also a few satirical remarks about the *bourgeoisie bien-pensante*.[16] Brian Pocknell finds only "shadowy reflections" of the real world in *Devenir!* and no sense of the novel's evoking a moment in history. The realism of the work is limited "by the faintness of many of the outlines. Lack of precision in the references to the problems of the day deprive the problems of their impact." [17] Such a novel may well have aesthetic qualities, but for the historian it is of little interest.

Even though he considered *Devenir!* to be a minor work, Martin du Gard did successfully "exorcise" his fear of failure and began another long and serious work of broad scope. This time it was to be *Marise*, the biography of a woman. And once again, but when he was still in the note-taking stage, he realized that he was at an impasse. He simply did

[13] Cf. Denis Boak, *Roger Martin du Gard* (Oxford: Clarendon Press, 1963), p. 16.

[14] Jean Cocteau, "Devenir, ou l'âme exquise de Roger Martin du Gard," *N.N.R.F.*, December 1958, p. 994.

[15] *O.C.*, I, 13.

[16] For example, Martin du Gard writes about André's father: "He had himself no conscience, or sense of justice; he accepted completely, as eternal truths, the stagnant opinions of his milieu" (*ibid.*, p. 14). See also p. 11, on the banal dose of religious faith implanted in the children of the wealthy *bourgeoisie bien-pensante*.

[17] "The Nature and the Limits of Realism in the Works of Roger Martin du Gard" (unpublished Master's thesis, University of Manchester, 1959), pp. 41–42.

not have an adequate knowledge of the female personality. Without undue suffering he destroyed most of the manuscript, saving only a fragment, which he retouched and published as a novella, *L'Une de nous* (1910).

The young publisher Bernard Grasset brought out the novella, at Martin du Gard's expense, though agreeing to publish his next novel without charge. In later years Martin du Gard regretted publishing *L'Une de nous,* finding it to be "of a superannuated 'naturalism,' and of a deplorable sentimentality and bad taste." [18] When, during the First World War, Grasset wrote asking Martin du Gard what should be done with the remaining stocks, the reply was to have them pulped. There are a few copies of the work extant. (It was not, along with two other short stories published in limited editions, reprinted in the Pléiade edition of 1955, which has the misleading title *Oeuvres complètes.*) One can readily understand Martin du Gard's later aversion for *L'Une de nous.* It has none of the subtlety of *Jean Barois* and is a *roman à thèse,* a bitter and open attack on religion, not a flanking movement. Martin du Gard has "loaded the dice too heavily in favor of his own view and disregarded all considerations of objectivity." [19] For this reason *L'Une de nous* will be discussed in Chapter VI, in dealing with Martin du Gard's ideological and political involvement.

In 1910, Martin du Gard decided to leave the hectic intellectual atmosphere of Paris and retire to his parents' home in the provinces. Isolating himself almost completely from the currents of Parisian literary activity, he labored for three years on another long novel, provisionally entitled *S'affran-*

[18] *Souvenirs, O.C.,* I, lii.
[19] Boak, *Roger Martin du Gard,* p. 25.

chir. To Marcel Hébert he wrote, "I am preparing something very important, on a really fine subject, the need for religion which is a part of human nature." [20] In a letter of May 11, 1911, he defined his aims more explicitly. The novel would be built around the life experience of one man and would utilize a scenic method, close to that of the theatre: "a series of frescos, of tableaux, made as alive as possible by an almost scenic form; . . . which I am seeking to realize, and which would give to the novel all the precious uniqueness of the theatre, while allowing it to retain the nuances, the half tones, a greater ease in liberating itself from the too-narrow conventions of works to be 'played.' "

The book was completed in the spring of 1913, and the manuscript turned over to Bernard Grasset. Though held by his obligation to publish the work, Grasset strongly advised against it. In a letter he described the novel as a "dossier" and indicated that he felt it to be a total failure: "I defy the reader to go beyond Page 100." [21] Dismayed by the negative verdict of one of the most intelligent young publishers of the day, Martin du Gard had the good fortune to meet an old schoolmate, the publisher Gaston Gallimard. The rest is an episode in literary history. André Gide and Jean Schlumberger read the manuscript, the novel was published in November 1913, with the title *Jean Barois*, and Martin du Gard joined the group of the *Nouvelle Revue Française*. The resultant association with Gide was one of the most important literary friendships of the century, and the appearance of their correspondence of over a thousand letters, far-ranging in subject and unsparing of personalities (one of the reasons

[20] Letter of October 15, 1910.
[21] Quoted in R. M. G., *Souvenirs, O.C.,* I, lv.

why it has not yet been made public) will be a major literary event.[22]

Martin du Gard received letters praising *Jean Barois* from Le Dantec, Alain, Suarès, Péguy, and others. The critics took notice after Gustave Lanson's quite favorable review in *Le Matin* of December 24, 1913. Paul Souday brought the book to the attention of the readers of *Le Temps* on January 7, 1914.[23] Roger Martin du Gard was established as a novelist of significance.

Jean Barois, "the portrait of an age," [24] has had an exceedingly wide influence. Numerous commentators who feel

[22] See *ibid.*, p. lvii. For the account of the fascinating relationship of these two so different men, see especially R. M. G., *Notes sur André Gide*, O.C., II, 1355–1423. There are many references to Martin du Gard in Gide's *Journal*, and several important ones in his *Journal des faux-monnayeurs* (Paris: Gallimard, 1927). *Les Faux-Monnayeurs*, Gide's only full-length novel, is dedicated to Martin du Gard. Of the many articles on the relationship, the most comprehensive is Jean Pénard, "Aspects d'une amitié: Roger Martin du Gard et André Gide," *Revue des sciences humaines* (January–March 1959), pp. 77–98. In English, see the chapter "Gide and Martin du Gard" in David Tylden-Wright, *The Image of France* (London: Secker and Warburg, 1957), pp. 58–91. My translations from R.M.G.'s *Notes sur André Gide* by permission of Viking Press Inc., publishers of *Recollections of André Gide*, by Roger Martin du Gard.

[23] Martin du Gard made a curious error which was picked up and repeated in all the commentaries that followed the publication of his *Souvenirs* in 1955. He thought that Souday's review was the first to appear, and that once this article, by "the official arbiter of letters, the redoubtable mentor of the *Temps*," was out, "the game was won!" (*Souvenirs*, O.C., I, lvii). Surely it was the article by the very distinguished Lanson which provided the initial impetus. Oddly, Lanson in his column disregards almost entirely Alain Fournier's *Le Grand Meaulnes* and devotes all his attention to *Jean Barois*.

[24] From the title of Eugen Weber's perceptive essay, "The Secret World of Jean Barois—Notes on the Portrait of an Age," in *The Origins of Modern Consciousness*, ed. John Weiss (Detroit: Wayne State University Press, 1965), pp. 79–109. The fact that Weber, one

it to be the best work available on the Dreyfus crisis have already been cited. Emmanuel Berl, speaking for the generation which came of age around 1914, thinks that the work transformed many people into "Dreyfusards after the fact" (*Dreyfusards à retardement*).[25] Jean Schlumberger informs us that more than forty years after its publication, the majority of the students in one of the *grandes écoles* named *Jean Barois*, when asked what book aided them most in the attainment of their "moral autonomy."[26]

The dramatic nature of the Dreyfus case lends itself to novelistic treatment, and the Affair finds its way into the works of most of the French authors who lived through it. Many of them were personally involved in the controversy and tried to translate their experience into art. The way the Affair has been reflected in literature has been rather thoroughly studied, and two books have been written on the Dreyfus Affair and the French novel. In her study Mme Cécile Delhorbe describes *Jean Barois* as the best known of the "Dreyfusist novels."[27] Brief mention of some of the other novels in which the Affair plays a role will clarify the significance of *Jean Barois*, primarily by pointing up sharp differ-

---

of the more astute American writers on contemporary France, should choose this topic is in itself significant.

[25] Cited in Roger Giron, "M. Roger Martin du Gard, témoin irrécusable de son temps," *Toute l'Edition*, December 26, 1936, p. 6. For Pierre Brodin, two generations later, *Jean Barois* has "hardly aged and retains all its emotional power" (*Présences Contemporaines*, II [Paris: Nouvelles Editions Debresse, 1955], 263).

[26] *Oeuvres*, II (Paris: Gallimard, 1958), 31.

[27] *L'Affaire Dreyfus et les écrivains français* (Paris: Editions Victor Attinger, 1932), p. 312. Mme Delhorbe mentions several other "Dreyfusist novels," which have not passed the test of time and are largely forgotten today.

ences. (To be sure, anti-Dreyfusist writers were deeply affected by the Affair, and Mme Delhorbe has chapters dealing with Barrès and the neomonarchists Charles Maurras and Léon Daudet.)

Emile Zola's personal role in the Dreyfus Affair was considerable, as any history of the period will document. His polemical writings on the Affair were collected into a volume, *La Vérité en marche*. But when he tried to transpose what was effective and powerful as propaganda into a novel, the results were fairly disastrous. The novel, entitled *Vérité*, was posthumously published in 1903, and is the last completed volume of a proposed four-volume saga, parts I and II being *Fécondité* and *Travail*. These works are widely considered to be Zola's poorest, and in any case, while important in the study of his later intellectual evolution, they have little relevance for the historian. According to Zola's plan, a dynasty was to develop from the hero of a previous novel, Pierre Froment, and his wife Marie. Their four sons were to be named, with blatant biblical parallelism, Mathieu, Marc, Luc, Jean. The hero of *Vérité* is Marc—the bringer of truth. The crime is the rape and murder of a child, and the accused, Simon, is a schoolteacher who happens to be Jewish. The whole country is shaken as in the Dreyfus case, with Simon-ism, anti-Simonism, and so forth. There is however, only "a very superficial resemblance between the heroes of *Vérité* and the characters in the Dreyfus Affair. The true author of the crime of which Simon is accused is Brother Gorgias, member of a teaching order. He resembles Esterhazy only in his shouting." [28]

In Georges Duhamel's ten-volume *roman-fleuve*, *La Chronique des Pasquier*, there is no reference to the Dreyfus

[28] *Ibid.*, p. 71.

crisis until Volume II, where it is mentioned in passing. The work is closely oriented around the Pasquier family circle, and when in Volume III there is a more extensive reference to the Dreyfus Affair, it is in relation to divisions within the family. When the word *bordereau* comes up by chance during a family conversation, there is a moment of nervous and irritated silence. The narrator, Laurent Pasquier, explains:

Each time that a word having the slightest relationship with the Dreyfus Affair entered into our discussions, it seemed that immediately a chasm opened beneath our feet and divided the family: on the one side, Cécile and myself, both Dreyfusards with a frenzy, on the other side, Ferdinand, Joseph, and as an occasional reinforcement, our father. At the price of much supplication, my mother had obtained an agreement that "the Affair" would be banned from our familial discussions. Nevertheless, a name sometimes, or even an idea, an intonation, some sort of vague wind would traverse our bickerings, and our spirits would immediately stiffen up like insects in position of combat.[29]

Such a remark would interest the historical sociologist, since similar situations most probably existed in many French families. However, it stands alone, and its very formulation indicates how Duhamel always turns his attention toward the familial plane. The Dreyfus Affair occurs somewhere vaguely in the outside world and serves only to increase tensions and divisions already present.

One can read of the theft of eighty thousand bales of hay and of the unjust condemnation of Pyrot in Anatole France's marvelous satire of the Dreyfus case and the modern world in general, *L'Ile des pingouins* (1908). France's famous short

[29] III: *Vue de la Terre promise* (Paris: Mercure de France, 1934), 16–17. (The other reference is in II: *Le Jardin des bêtes sauvages*, 257.)

story, *Crainquebille*, is also viewed by critics as a transposition of the Affair.[30] France's intellectual evolution toward a position which makes support of Dreyfus possible is carefully traced by Mme Delhorbe. He had begun a long work, a four-volume novel series, *L'Histoire contemporaine*, before the Dreyfus case really "broke." The first two volumes were published in 1897, but in the last two (1899, 1901), the Affair attains considerable importance. As in *L'Ile des pingouins*, the tone is very satirical. France's Dreyfusist sentiments are clearly manifested; the Duc de Brécé, one of the leading anti-Dreyfusists in the novel, blames the agitation for Captain Dreyfus on miscellaneous enemies of France, including Jews and Germans. He explains: "And what unheard-of audacity to dare to question the decree of a military tribunal! For in the last analysis it cannot be admitted that seven French officers could be in error." [31] A minute later the Duke sees some pheasants, and is "overwhelmed by an instinctive and profound desire to kill." [32] Continuing with some violently anti-Semitic remarks and a general attack on the Enlightenment, the Duke narrates with pride the story of his ancestor, a certain *Nez-d'Argent*, who under Charles IX hanged 636 Huguenots. Another character proclaims, "I am republican, Jacobin, terrorist . . . and a patriot. . . . I admit that one has the right to guillotine generals, but I cannot accept challenging the decisions of our military justice." [33]

The last two volumes of *L'Histoire contemporaine* are packed with delightfully humorous adventures, with royalist

---

[30] Renée Riese Hubert, "The Dreyfus Affair and the French Novel —From Fact to Fiction," Ph.D. dissertation, Columbia University, 1951, p. 17.

[31] III: *L'Anneau d'améthyste* (Paris: Calmann-Lévy, 1956), 375.

[32] *Ibid.*, p. 376.   [33] *Ibid.*, p. 437.

plots and counterplots. The tone is for the most part lightly ironical, though it does at moments rise to a really bitter denunciation of the anti-Dreyfusists, of clericalism, and more generally, of human hypocrisy and stupidity. It must be emphasized that France was writing in the heat of the Dreyfus crisis, that his novel was not organized around the Affair, but rather that the Affair was integrated into a previously existing plan for a satirical work of broader scope, dealing with many aspects of modern life. Also, in 1899 and 1901 France could not benefit from the ten-year perspective which Martin du Gard had when he began *Jean Barois*. He could not have witnessed the transformation, which so distressed Charles Péguy, of the *mystique* of the original supporters of Dreyfus into the *politique* of the *Combiste* republican parliamentarians.[34]

The Dreyfus Affair is a frequently recurring theme in Proust's *A la Recherche du temps perdu*, starting with Volume VI, the first part of *Le Côté des Guermantes*. No discussion, no matter how superficial, of the role of the Dreyfus Affair in the French novel can fail to consider Proust's great work. The major characters all take strong positions, often but not invariably dictated by their social status and religious and racial background. Young Robert de Saint-Loup is an ardent supporter of Dreyfus; this leads him into violent arguments with his fellow officers, slows down his military career, and prevents him from getting into the Jockey Club.[35]

[34] Charles Péguy, *Notre Jeunesse* (Paris: Gallimard, 1933), pp. 26–28 (originally published in the *Cahiers de la quinzaine*, 1910).

[35] *A la Recherche du temps perdu*, VI–VII (Paris: Gallimard, 1920–1921): *Le Côté de Guermantes*, Part I, pp. 127–128, 131; *Le Côté de Guermantes*, Part II, p. 71, where M. de Guermantes remarks emphatically, "When one's name is the Marquis de Saint-Loup, one is not a Dreyfusard, what more can I say!"

Robert's firm stand may have something to do with his love affair with the Jewish actress Rachel, though this is not explicitly stated. The narrator, Marcel, is quite careful to hide his own sentiments as he objectively describes those of his characters. However, a close scrutiny of the text uncovers two indications of his Dreyfusist position. Marcel's father, a personal friend of Prime Minister Méline, was convinced of Dreyfus' guilt, and did not speak to his son for eight days when he learned that he had followed "a different line of conduct." [36] Later the narrator offhandedly notes that he was involved in several duels during the high period of the Affair, but no details are given.[37]

It seems apparent that the insertion of the Dreyfus Affair into Proust's novel is primarily for artistic purposes, to deepen perceptions into the inner nature of the characters and, as a consequence, the society in which they move. References to Picquart, Esterhazy, Dreyfus crop up on almost every page, because the Affair was a subject of conversation in the salons which Proust is describing. On account of her Dreyfusism, Mme Sazerat, who used to be an anti-Semite, now receives M. Bloch *père* with pleasure in her salon.[38] The character who is perhaps most affected by the Dreyfus Affair is Charles Swann. Swann assures Marcel that all the Guermantes are at heart anti-Semitic. Marcel observes, with a touch of sadness and irony, that Swann's Dreyfusism has made him, once the wisest and wittiest man of the world, rather naive and illogical. Swann now classifies people according to whether they are Dreyfusist (thus intelligent) or not (thus stupid). He puts "all his admirations and all his disdains to the test of a

---

[36] *A la Recherche*, VI, 185.
[37] *Ibid.*, IX (Paris: Gallimard, 1921–1924): *Sodome et Gomorrhe*, Part I, p. 16.
[38] *Ibid.*, VII, 137.

new criterion, Dreyfusism." [39] He has forgotten his past criticisms of Clemenceau and now sees Barrès as a man with no
talent. The Prince de Guermantes makes a real turnabout
and becomes a Dreyfusist, owing to his contact, while taking
les eaux, with two charming princesses who are pro-
Dreyfus.[40]

Through Proust's references to the Dreyfus case the reader
gains insights into the personalities of Swann and the Prince
and an indication of the capriciousness of the highest society,
which believes seriously in nothing. I would argue that one
derives immensely valuable psychological and sociological insights from reading Proust, but that for the historian his work
is of less direct relevance. After all, Proust's goal was to
escape, or to go beyond, time. My point is illustrated, with
specific reference to the Dreyfus case, in the last volume of
A la Recherche du temps perdu. The narrator gives his view
of what the novelist's task should be; there is an "interior
book" which the writer must unlock, and no one can aid him
or collaborate with him in this effort.

Yet how many have turned away from writing this book, how
many tasks have been assumed, in order to escape this [all-
important] one. Every event, whether it be the Dreyfus Affair,
whether it be the war, has furnished writers with other excuses to
avoid deciphering this book; they wanted to assure the triumph
of justice, to remake the moral unity of the nation, and did not
have the time to think of literature. But all this was nothing but
excuses, because they had no genius, or had lost their genius (that
is to say their instinct). For instinct dictates our duty, and
intelligence furnishes us with pretexts to evade it.[41]

[39] *Ibid.*, IX, 243.   [40] *Ibid.*, IX, 180–181.
[41] *Ibid.*, XV (Paris: Gallimard, 1927): *Le Temps retrouvé*, Part II,
p. 23. I do not mean that Roger Martin du Gard was never attracted
to a similar goal. He was, and in 1918 would have been in full agreement with Proust's statement

In *Jean Barois* the Dreyfus Affair takes on a role of far greater significance than in any of the novels just discussed. The Affair is the focal point, the center of the novel, the highest point in the curve of the hero's life, the moment when his life is integrated into his historical epoch. For, far from being the dossier which Bernard Grasset criticized, *Jean Barois* is rigorously constructed, and all the historical material, including the fairly detailed treatment of the Dreyfus crisis, has a specific purpose.

Jean Barois is written in a form which, while not completely original with Martin du Gard, has rarely been used with such success—that of the dialogue novel. Occasional letters and other documents, and also brief, concise descriptions of scene and character, give variation to the dialogue. With its rapid changes of scene and its use of the close-up, the novel has been praised for its cinematographic qualities.[42] The dramatic intensity of a cinema-like technique, combined with the "pull to the present"[43] exerted by a realistic dialogue, makes such a form an ideal one in which to present complex historical and philosophical subject matter. There are three main divisions in the novel, coinciding with the hero's youth, his mature years (the years of his "liberation" and involvement in the Dreyfus Affair), and his decline and death. The study of a life cycle, with the return essentially identical to the starting point, is worked out with great intricacy. The

[42] Cf. Pocknell, "Realism in the Works of Martin du Gard," pp. 46, 170, 190; Henri de Régnier, "La Vie littéraire," *Le Figaro*, July 31, 1928, p. 2. Other critics such as Pierre Brodin and Henri Clouard also mention this, and Maurice Martin du Gard felt that if Roger had been young in 1931, he would have begun his career by writing for the cinema ("Le Théâtre," *Les Nouvelles littéraires*, November 21, 1931, p. 8).

[43] Grant E. Kaiser, "Roger Martin du Gard's *Jean Barois*, an Experiment in Novelistic Form," *Symposium*, Summer 1960, p. 138.

most obvious example is of course Barois's reconversion to the Catholic faith, after having been a leading freethinker. Whereas in *Devenir!* there was no temporal precision, in *Jean Barois* the date is immediately given. It is 1878, and the action is set in the little town of Buis-la-Dame in the department of the Oise. Young Jean Barois, age twelve, thus born in 1866, has just returned from a pilgrimage to Lourdes with his grandmother. (The importance of these dates, which must be emphasized here, will become apparent in the discussion of the third part of the novel, when the action essentially "drops out" of historical time.) The boy is in danger of developing a fatal case of tuberculosis, which is hereditary in his family. The pilgrimage has weakened rather than ameliorated his condition. An atmosphere of oppressive religiosity has extinguished his will to live; he feverishly anticipates the next world.

Dr. Barois, Jean's father, tries to counter his son's indifference to his physical condition by stressing that he can cure himself if he only wills it: "Our entire existence is a combat; life is the victory which endures." [44] The reader's sense of the conflict between the two influences is skilfully heightened when Dr. Barois has to shout to make himself heard above the church bells, which are tolling the elevation of the Host. Jean is eventually convinced by his father and recovers completely, though there is a danger of recurrent susceptibility to tuberculosis. On his deathbed, Dr. Barois warns his son of this, emphasizing that he must not overexert himself after the age of forty.[45] We mention this detail since it is yet another deterministic factor in making Jean's eventual collapse more plausible.

[44] *O.C.*, I, 216. My translations from *Jean Barois* by permission of Viking Press Inc.
[45] *Ibid.*, p. 256.

As a young man, Jean develops religious doubts, and
Martin du Gard presents a dialogue between his hero and the
Abbé Joziers, the first of many such discussions with several
different priests. The theology contained in these confronta-
tions has been treated in detail elsewhere, especially in
Father Robidoux's admirable (and almost always impartial)
study of religious and moral themes in Martin du Gard's
works.[46] What is significant for our purposes is the fact that
Jean's questioning nature develops early, that he has a tendency to demand absolute coherence from a doctrine which he
then adopts absolutely. Since the problem of evil is not satis-
factorily explained for him by Catholic apologetics, he already
fears that he will become a freethinker.

Jean Barois goes to Paris to study medicine and natural
sciences and there his faith is more and more troubled. His
need for absolutes is ever-apparent, as he experiences "a sort
of vertigo with these first contacts with Science, when one
begins to distinguish for the first time some of the great laws
which order the universal complexity!" [47] He has some hope
that a new friend, the Abbé Schertz, will help steady his
wavering faith; he regrets that he is obsessed with religious
questions, but he cannot control his need for rational explanation. The discoveries of modern biblical criticism now con-
front him, yet at the same time he feels he must have a
religion: "I need it, I need it, as I need to eat or to sleep." [48]
If he loses his faith, his whole life will be based upon an "ab-

---

[46] Besides Robidoux's work, already cited, see in particular Robert
Jardillier, "Le Problème de la foi chez R. Martin du Gard, l'auteur
de *Jean Barois*, et J. Malègue, l'écrivain de *Augustin ou le maître est
là*," *Arts et livres*, September 1946, 86–101, and Charles Moeller, *Littérature du vingtième siècle et Christianisme*, II (Paris: Casterman,
1957), 165–216.

[47] *O.C.*, I, 228.   [48] *Ibid.*, p. 237.

surd contradiction." Yet, because of the unity of Catholic doctrine," if one rejects even a fraction, one loses the whole!" [49] Anxious to keep Jean in the church, though pushed further than he would like by his arguments, the Abbé Schertz finally outlines a "symbolist compromise." Critics have often remarked that this position is close to that taken by Marcel Hébert, who was eventually forced to leave the church because of his modernism, and to whom *Jean Barois* is dedicated. Jean momentarily clings to this compromise—symbolic acceptance of doctrine—as "the only chance for an equilibrium which remains for me." [50]

Jean is on his way to becoming a professor of natural sciences when news arrives that his father is seriously ill and that pressure is being applied to him to return to the Catholic faith. Jean's reaction is one of "dull animosity," [51] indicating how far he has progressed on the path to atheism. He goes to Buis to be at his father's bedside, and there meets again his childhood sweetheart.[52] At this time a marriage is arranged. When Jean learns that his father has confessed and taken communion, he tries to hide his disappointment by forcing a joyous smile. Dr. Barois, now a mere shadow of his former energetic self, tells his son with an edge of fear in his voice, "You know, my boy, they can say what they like. . . . It's a

---

[49] *Ibid.*, p. 238.   [50] *Ibid.*, p. 246.   [51] *Ibid.*, p. 249.

[52] There is here a very interesting love-death identification. Jean and Cécile make the first gestures of love while waiting for the dying doctor to awaken so that they can see him once more (*ibid.*, p. 254). This is but one of innumerable examples of perceptions in Martin du Gard's works which suggest, I believe, that they could be studied with profit by a critic with a psychoanalytic viewpoint. (Since this writing, Armand Descloux has published a work entitled *Psychanalyse du docteur Thibault de Roger Martin du Gard* [Paris: Editions universitaires, 1965].)

terrible X." [53] Martin du Gard's equation of fear and physical weakness is patently clear here, as it will be in the case of Jean Barois himself.

Following the advice of the Abbé Scherz, Jean decides to go ahead with his plans to marry the devout Cécile Pasquelin, and not to forewarn her of his doubts as to the validity of Catholic doctrine. Two years pass, and in the next part of the novel, aptly entitled "The Chain," the real break has come in Jean's religious life. He has clung desperately to Schertz's symbolic interpretation, but to no avail, and is now an atheist. His wife is sincerely distressed, even horrified, by his unbelief. Jean is also disillusioned with her; he feels that he has stupidly engaged his entire life because he was sure that intense happiness would be his. "I was in advance resolved to find everything perfect," [54] he says, demonstrating that the intransigent quality so remarkable in his character also applies to his personal life. Refusing to disavow the transformist Darwinian doctrine he has presented to the students in his biology courses, Barois resigns from the Catholic Collège Wenceslas. In conjunction with this step, he resolves to leave his wife and daughter, and all that is symbolized by the country town of Buis, and go to Paris alone. Though he is a sincere and honest man and is pained by the suffering he causes his wife ("And it is not even your fault: *you could not have acted differently*"), [55] he cannot help but feel exhilarated at the thought of leaving for Paris. He senses "a new intoxica-

---

[53] *Ibid.*, p. 257.   [54] *Ibid.*, p. 280.

[55] *Ibid.*, p. 295 (italics his). This is a fine example of the force of Martin du Gard's belief in determinism and of the justice with which he treats all his characters. It has been noted that there are no real villains in Martin du Gard's work. Almost all his characters are truly *hommes de bonne volonté*.

tion, the violent desire for a liberty just at hand, a furious appetite to live again!" [56] On the twentieth of May 1895, he is able to write to a friend that he now has his freedom: "I embrace it, I possess it, I initiate myself passionately into it, I shall cling to it forever!" [57] The irony of these remarks will become apparent.

The expansion of the novel from a personal and familial to a historical plane is now possible. Brian Pocknell is quite right, I believe, when he asserts that the inclusion of historical material is not the main issue in *Jean Barois*. Martin du Gard's primary aim was not to reconsider the Dreyfus case and evaluate it as a historian would.[58] Nevertheless, it is 1895 and not 1885 or 1905 when Jean Barois arrives alone in Paris, with the givens of his character, education, beliefs which have just been summarized. His involvement in the Dreyfus Affair will be a natural and inevitable result of these factors, just as Frédéric Moreau's joyous participation in the February days of 1848 is the result of his set of givens, which Gustave Flaubert presents with such exquisite meticulousness in *L'Education sentimentale*.

These generalizations can be tested by a close analysis of

---

[56] *Ibid.*, p. 312.   [57] *Ibid.*, p. 315.

[58] "Realism in the Works of Martin du Gard," pp. 47–48. Though I have found no verification in Martin du Gard's own writings, I think Father Robidoux is justified in stating that "the original intention of Martin du Gard was to describe the life of a man, and it is not until now . . . through the necessity of 'incarnating' his character in a living world, that the book assumes the quality of a historical novel, and, as a consequence, of a novel of ideas. In the author's mind, History would intervene only when it illuminated the individual destiny of the hero, Jean Barois" (*Roger Martin du Gard et la religion*, p. 118).

the second part of *Jean Barois*, dealing with the hero's mature life. Martin du Gard mentions for the first time the statue on Barois's mantelpiece, which will be a recurrent symbol throughout the rest of the novel. This is a copy of Michelangelo's "Slave," [59] and there is an ironic contrast intended between the figure of the slave, silently and hopelessly struggling throughout eternity, and Jean Barois, who is described as being at the peak of his strength, happy, youthful-looking. In his manner and bearing are visible "emancipation, certainty, a passionate confidence in the future." [60] He and a group of freethinking friends decide to found a review, *Le Semeur*. The meeting in which they outline plans for the review is powerfully described by Martin du Gard. A strong enthusiasm, a spontaneous humanism and faith in progress, bind the group together. There is also a feeling that religion is suffering from a general "anemia" and must be replaced by a new social morality. The great enemy will be the *bien-pensants*, whose negative potential is taken more seriously by Barois than by the others: "Ah, one must *have been a part of*

[59] *O.C.*, I, 317. This statue is intimately related to Martin du Gard's life and work; the copy owned by Marcel Hébert surely influenced him. (See Houtin, *Un Prêtre symboliste*, p. 203, and R. M. G., *In Memoriam*, *O.C.*, I, 575.) As early as 1937 a friend reported seeing a large copy of Michelangelo's statue in Martin du Gard's apartment on the Rue du Dragon (Camille Cé, "Souvenirs familiers sur Roger Martin du Gard," *Le Figaro*, November 11, 1937, p. 5). When Martin du Gard was lying very ill, he had the statue brought into his bedroom, so that, unlike Jean Barois, he would not give way to what he called " 'the weakness' of his hero" (Jean Delay, "Dernières Rencontres," *Le Figaro littéraire*, August 30, 1958, p. 5).

[60] *O.C.*, I, 316. When the statue is mentioned again in the novel, Jean has greatly changed. He is ravaged by fever, by doubts as to the validity of his lifework, by fear of dying (pp. 533–534). A bit later, he points to the figure, which can never raise its arm: "*Perhaps I have been like him for years, and possessed only the image* [simulacre] *of freedom*" (p. 538, italics his).

them to comprehend that unchangeable mass, that inert power which they still are!" [61]

The group decides to dedicate the first issue of *Le Semeur* to Marc-Elie Luce, a distinguished philosopher and an independent member of the Senate, a man who belongs to no organized group, who is often said to be modeled after Scheurer-Kestner, vice-president of the Senate at the time of the Dreyfus crisis.[62] Luce is honored by the dedication and associates himself with the young review. His constant emphasis is on tolerance and on the necessity for the free development of divergent tendencies within the progressive movement *Le Semeur* synthesizes. Thus his only worry is that *Le Semeur* become too aggressive, too sectarian. Barois counters this position with a typical remark: "I believe that a young and powerful doctrine is, by its very nature, intolerant. A conviction which begins by admitting the legitimacy of an opposing conviction condemns itself to inactivity; it is without force, without effectiveness." [63]

In June 1896, the *Semeur* group meets, and the first mention of the possible innocence of Captain Dreyfus brings forth a reaction of incredulity, though of interest. From his friend Woldsmuth, a strange character who spends his entire lifetime

---

[61] *Ibid.*, p. 333 (italics his).

[62] Victor L. Brombert, *The Intellectual Hero* (New York: J. B. Lippincott, 1961), p. 112. Martin du Gard has vigorously denied that any such identification can be carried very far: "I give you my word that *not one of the characters in the book is a portrait*" (letter of July 30, 1916, to Mme Henriette Charasson, cited in her "Autour de Roger Martin du Gard," *La Dépêche tunisienne*, September 20, 1958, p. 6, italics his). Nevertheless, Luce is the character whose ideological position can be most closely related to that of Martin du Gard himself. Luce is the only character in the novel who succeeds both in his life and in the manner of his dying. He is perhaps too perfect, overidealized; such a character becomes impossible in *Les Thibault*.

[63] *O.C.*, I, 339.

in a laboratory, trying to find the chemical formula which will re-create life, Barois gets more information on Dreyfus. He also meets the chemist's niece, Julia, who will play a significant role in Barois's evolution, though she appears only briefly in the novel. Barois begins to be convinced of Dreyfus' innocence and agrees to arrange a meeting between Luce and Bernard Lazare, an actual historical figure, one of the early Dreyfusist leaders. Martin du Gard gives extensive historical detail at this point, quoting from Lazare's writings on the Dreyfus case.[64]

The interview between Luce and Bernard Lazare is carried on off stage in the novel, thus sparing Martin du Gard the difficulty of a firsthand description of a historical figure, which always leads to problems for a novelist. Luce tells of this meeting in a letter to Barois, and Martin du Gard acknowledges that he drew directly upon Péguy's *Notre Jeunesse* for the portrait of Bernard Lazare.[65] Luce is deeply affected by what he learns but wants to use his senatorial connections to get full information on the case before committing himself to the Dreyfusist cause. By July 1897, Luce has become absolutely certain of Dreyfus' innocence, though he has grave doubts as to whether a demand for revision of the original trial of 1894 would be worth the bitter strife it would stir up in French society. The general staff of the army, and thus the government of the Republic, would be compromised. Barois has none of these qualms: "It is not for us to hesitate!" In Barois's immediate taking of sides Luce senses a private sentiment: "There is in you a sort of *personal satisfaction*, rather like revenge."[66] Luce's—or rather Martin du Gard's—acute perception here shows how logical and inevitable it is for Barois, whom the reader has known since his

[64] *Ibid.*, pp. 358–363.   [65] *Ibid.*, p. 365.
[66] *Ibid.*, p. 369 (italics mine).

pious provincial childhood, to become an important partici-
pant in one of the major crises of the Third Republic.

Despite his keen sense of the dangers involved, Luce feels
obliged to side with Barois: "Each of us must consent to his
own life, and mine forbids me to be silent." [67] With joy and
pride Barois agrees to risk the failure of his painfully created
review. This is the beginning of the period of "superhuman
exaltation," the period of *mystique* so nostalgically evoked
by Péguy in *Notre Jeunesse*. A special edition of *Le Semeur*
is printed and is quickly sold out, causing tensions to rise in
Paris. Martin du Gard departs from strict historicity here,
since no important periodical came out for Dreyfus as early
as the summer of 1897.

By January 1898, *Le Semeur* has moved to new offices, and
Julia Woldsmuth has joined the staff. Martin du Gard dis-
creetly tells us that she and Barois are lovers.[68] In these trying days Barois has her companionship and support. On one
occasion, just after he has been giving generously of his
energy and his courage to the others, whose spirits are flag-
ging and who admire him greatly for his qualities of leadership, Julia "spontaneously drew near Barois and took his arm;
he did not seem to realize this." [69]

The Zola trial is an excellent example of how Martin du
Gard skilfully blends history into a novelistic treatment. Actual testimony from the trial record is used, but Martin du
Gard is careful never to allow Zola to speak in the novel.
While waiting for his case to begin, "he slowly looked over
the crowd which hated him, and his glance slowed down,
rested an instant upon the group from *Le Semeur*." [70] After
the adjournment of the trial, while a riot is going on outside,
Zola is pictured as leaning against a pillar of the Palais de

[67] *Ibid.*, p. 370.   [68] *Ibid.*, p. 379.   [69] *Ibid.*, p. 403.
[70] *Ibid.*, p. 381.

Justice, very pale, waiting to escape from the angry nationalist crowd. "He noticed Luce, then Barois, and shook hands
with each of them, brusquely, without a word." [71] Even Luce
is discouraged by the brutality of the crowd. Barois is portrayed in an extremely favorable light at this time. With his
dynamism and courage, he restores the enthusiasm of the
others, reminding them that their defeat is only temporary,
that truth must win out in the end.

On August 31, 1898, the *Semeur* group learns of the arrest
of Colonel Henry, suspected of falsifying the documents
which led to Dreyfus' arrest and conviction. This in itself is
exciting news, but when Woldsmuth enters with a newspaper announcing Henry's suicide, there is "a savage cry of
triumph, a long shout, a veritable delirium." [72] This is the one
point in the novel where Martin du Gard deliberately deviates
from the historical record. In actuality, the announcement of
Henry's suicide was not given to the papers until the following day. What is the purpose of this intentional error?
Knowing Martin du Gard's aversion to all varieties of sec-
tarianism,[73] I find Cécile Delhorbe's explanation most plausible. She suggests that the reason Martin du Gard makes his
heroes pass through this moment of savagery is "without a
doubt to make us see what happens even to humanitarians

---

[71] *Ibid.*, p. 400. As Brian Pocknell has put it, "Zola's very silent
presence is perhaps the safest and most convincing method of
mingling real people with fictitious characters lest their real personality belie their fictitious one" ("Realism in the Works of Martin
du Gard," p. 64).

[72] *O.C.*, I, 409.

[73] See, for example, Martin du Gard's Nobel Prize speech in *Les
Prix Nobel en 1937* (Stockholm: Imprimerie Royale P. A. Norsted
and Söner, 1938), p. 67. Martin du Gard speaks of himself as one who
is "*sans parti pris*," a man who doubts and hesitates, a man who has
always struggled against the fascination of partisan ideologies.

when they make war, and when, for them, for many months, the problem of good and of evil has reduced itself to a single question: will there or will there not be a revision of the Dreyfus case?" [74]

The victory represented by Henry's suicide is the high point in the novel, and from this moment, even though it is not immediately apparent, decline sets in on both personal and historical levels. There is another jump, of a year, to August 6, 1899, the day before the beginning of the retrial at Rennes. Barois is under great pressure but is happy and confident. The very calling of the Rennes trial he views as a victory for his faction, and he is optimistically planning a special issue of *Le Semeur* to celebrate the clearing of Dreyfus' name. From Paris the scene shifts to Rennes, and by means of letters and other documents written by Barois reporting the trial, the reader is informed of the situation there. By the fifth of September Barois has lost his confidence and enthusiasm. No longer is he certain that the judges will vote for Dreyfus' innocence. Too many lies have been scattered about: "Confronted with all this smoke, we are without weapons; no struggle is possible." [75] The second conviction of Dreyfus, this time a ten-year sentence—guilty with extenuating circumstances—is announced by a telegram from Barois to Luce. After two years of violent effort, the Dreyfusists are near exhaustion, and the members of the *Semeur* group who have been at Rennes, dejected, enervated, and unable to stop talking about the Affair, take the train the same night for Paris. Everyone realizes that because of his poor health Dreyfus must compromise with absolute justice and accept a pardon, rather than return to prison and continue the struggle in this fashion.

[74] *L'Affaire Dreyfus et les écrivains français*, p. 318.
[75] *O.C.*, I, 423.

There is never more than a paralleling of historical and individual tragedy in *Jean Barois*. The hero is not broken, is not overwhelmed by this defeat, as is clearly indicated by his telegram to Luce: "Long live Justice, despite everything! The Affair continues!" [76] But the historical defeat is a factor in Barois's decline, and Martin du Gard with perfect timing adds yet another factor which makes the hero's ultimate collapse even more inevitable, and which at the same time reacts upon the historical material, bringing it to life. When Jean Barois returns to Paris, he finds that Julia has deserted him for another member of the *Semeur* group. This is a severe blow to Barois: "A bitter, personal, unhealthy suffering was *grafted onto that other suffering*, onto that vast discouragement which had exhausted him." [77] In describing Barois's grief, besides giving an excellent example of what critics like Nelly Cormeau term transposition, Martin du Gard points out more clearly what he has hinted at before—that a complete man must have the support and companionship of a woman, if he is to compete effectively in the outside world. Barois may seem to recover and will continue his activities, even becoming a highly respected leader of the freethinking movement, but he can never be as strong as he was during the great days of the Affair when Julia was at his side.

The Dreyfus Affair continues on its course. In a speech at the 1900 exposition, Luce, in a passage recalling once again Péguy's *Notre Jeunesse*, proclaims that "a crowd of partisans whose existence we had not even suspected has come and mixed in with the group of active thinkers which until now we formed. . . . They have invaded the liberated spaces which our effort at social purification had uncovered. And today, so soon after the victory, it is they who occupy, as masters, the terrain." [78] Luce makes Péguy's distinction be-

[76] *Ibid.*, p. 428.   [77] *Ibid.*, p. 432 (italics mine).
[78] *Ibid.*, p. 435.

tween a "handful of *dreyfusistes*," and an "army of *dreyfusards*." [79] He portrays Barois as the inspiration for all, and
Le Semeur as the focal point of liberal opinion.

"Several years" pass, as precision strangely begins to slip
out of Martin du Gard's dating. Barois seems to be at the peak
of his strength and popularity; he is giving courses and publishing books. He prepares an important lecture on "The
Future of Unbelief," which he gives on a Sunday before a
large and enthusiastic audience. Barois declares in his lecture
his firm belief that the Catholic Church is doomed to total
dissolution. Religious feeling has no place "in truly modern
minds. . . . The present current is indisputably oriented
toward a world without God, toward a truly scientific conception of the universe!" [80]

Only a few months later Barois is involved in a serious
carriage accident, which has Pascalian overtones (his servant
is even named Pascal), and which ironically prefigures a
traumatic experience in Martin du Gard's own life, to be
discussed in Chapter IV. When Barois sees that a crash is inevitable, he cannot help repeating the prayer of his childhood,
"Hail Mary, full of grace. . . ." Then he loses consciousness,
to awaken in his apartment. Terrified by this demonstration
of weakness, he immediately sets down a testament, in which
he denounces any possible future reversion to Catholicism.
This document has been termed "one of the most forceful
statements of naturalist faith to emerge from the imaginative
literature of the years just preceding the outbreak of the First
World War." [81] The whole testament is of extreme interest,

[79] *Ibid.*, p. 436.   [80] *Ibid.*, pp. 444–445.

[81] H. Stuart Hughes, *Consciousness and Society* (New York: Alfred
A. Knopf, 1958), p. 31. One of Martin du Gard's probable sources has
been identified as the testament at the end of Ernest Renan's *Souvenirs
d'enfance et de jeunesse* (Paris: Calmann-Lévy, 1893), pp. 375–378.
Marcel Hébert, after reading *Jean Barois*, was moved to write to his
old pupil: "Luce is admirable. I reread his death scene several times.

but perhaps the most relevant passages are the following:

I do not believe in an immortal and substantial human soul.

I do not believe that matter is in opposition to mind. The soul equals the sum of psychic phenomena, as the body equals the sum of organic phenomena. . . .

. . . I know that my personality is nothing but an agglomeration of particles whose disintegration will bring about total death.

I believe in universal determinism, that our dependence upon circumstance is absolute. . . .

Good and evil are arbitrary distinctions. . . .

I believe that though all the phenomena of life have not yet been analyzed, they shall someday be analyzed.[82]

Five years now pass, and a compression of time in the story is already beginning, for the date should be at least 1910. Yet there are two precise indications that it is no later than June 1908, making Barois forty-two. The age of his daughter Marie is given as thirteen, and reference is made to the ceremony of the transfer of Emile Zola's ashes to the Pantheon. The old *Semeur* group meets, and bitter denunciations are made against the ceremony as no more than a theatrical

---

May I so die! I've always been afraid of the evil forces of the subconscious and the entourage. Save this letter, and if these forces succeed, publish my protest and absolute denial" (unpublished letter of September 20, 1913). This letter did not satisfy Hébert, and he decided to make his sentiments public in his own "Testament spirituel," *Coenibium*, March 31, 1914, pp. 32–34. Though Hébert always believed in some sort of spiritual Entity and was far from Jean Barois's materialistic determinism, the influence of the novel is clear, both from the date of the article and from the content of Hébert's message: "Is it not too pretentious to write a spiritual testament? . . . If I do so, it is with the knowledge that sickness could reduce me to the state of a human rag doll, who can be made to say whatever is wanted. My friends will thus find in these lines the summary of my convictions, written in full consciousness and complete liberty."

[82] *O.C.*, I, 454–455.

performance and against the utilization of a great name for the political ends of the *Dreyfusards*.[83] Given the date, Barois must be exaggerating when he tells his comrades, "We all seem to have come together for a specific reason, to expose and display our middle-aged disappointments (*les déceptions de nos cinquantaines*)." [84]

The era of fatigue, disillusion, and decline has set in for Barois and for his *Dreyfusiste* friends. *Le Semeur* has lost a number of subscribers because Barois has protested in its columns against the extremes of antimilitarism and of *Combiste* anticlericalism, and against the application, which he finds unjust, of the law of separation of 1905. Though he is discouraged and in poor health, Barois has by no means lost concern for changes in contemporary French society. He is still in Paris, has not yet retreated to Buis, where he rejoins his wife, reconverts to Catholicism, and eventually dies. Barois has not become Jean again, as he does in the concluding section of the novel. (It is curious, and has never, to my knowledge, been noted by the critics, that all during his active life, whenever Barois speaks, he is simply "Barois." As if to give a sign of his deep pity and sympathy for his character, Martin du Gard addresses him as "Jean" at the end of the novel.) Already in 1908 the signs of his impending decline are many. He tells Luce that he is losing faith in his old linear conception of life, that he has more and more the sense of a line's bending and gradually curving back toward its beginning: "The ring is going to close upon itself." [85]

---

[83] *Ibid.*, pp. 464–467. Present at the ceremony were Fallières, President of the Republic, Clemenceau, Prime Minister, and the whole Council of Ministers. "Gaston Doumergue delivered the funeral elegy on Emile Zola. There is not a single word worth remembering in that speech prepared for the occasion" (Armand Lanoux, *Bonjour Monsieur Zola* [Paris: Club des Librairies de France, 1954], p. 533).

[84] *O.C.*, I, 467.   [85] *Ibid.*, p. 464.

Other factors besides the tubercular lesions which threaten once again to become active will be necessary to drive Barois home to Buis. On the personal level the most important development is the entry of his only child into a nunnery. One of the reasons why Luce, unlike Barois, is able to remain firm in his agnosticism and die an "exemplary" death, loyal to the end to the principles which have guided his life, is the fact of his large family.[86] Barois has not been granted this form of perpetuation. On the social and political levels, Barois is alienated from the new generation which is growing up around 1910. He has, furthermore, come a long way from his youthful intransigent atheism of 1895 and has no empathy with his young assistant, Dalier, who has never had a religious crisis in his life, who can assert, "With me, atheism is innate. My father, my grandfather were atheists." [87]

On the other side of the political spectrum, the new conservative, nationalist generation which has grown up since the Dreyfusist "victory" completely repels him. This is the generation represented by Agathon and the Action Française, by Psichari and the Catholic revival. Barois has an interview with Grenneville and Tillet, two young nationalists who have been identified as Henri Massis and Alfred de Tarde. Massis and Tarde wrote under the pseudonym of Agathon and produced a very significant document on the state of mind of the youth of France just before the First World War. The new prestige which the young authors give to the word "war" perhaps best exemplifies their attitudes.[88] Jean Barois

---

[86] See *ibid.*, pp. 342, 522. His last words are "My children, they are so beautiful!"

[87] *Ibid.*, p. 501.

[88] Agathon, *Les Jeunes Gens d'aujourd'hui* (Paris: Plon, 1913), p. 32: War is a young, new word "adorned with that seduction which

is shocked by their fictional counterparts, by the violence of
their attitudes, by their cult of action, by their manifest dis-
respect for their elders, by their refusal to engage in rational
discussion. Also, they are Catholics of a special kind; Catholicism provides them with a rigid body of dogma to sustain

---

the eternal bellicose instinct has regenerated in the hearts of men.
These young men impute to it [war] all the beauty of which they are
enamoured and which they lack in their daily existence. War is
especially, in their eyes, the occasion for the noblest human virtues,
. . . energy, self-mastery, self-sacrifice for a cause which surpasses us."
There is an irony here in that if one calculates Martin du Gard's time
scheme carefully, one discovers that in actuality, at the same moment
these young nationalists in the novel are having the discussion with
Barois, they are fighting in the war they so desired (and which turned
out not to be the kind of war they wanted). Martin du Gard's
personal distaste for this group is apparent, both in his private
correspondence and in *Jean Barois*. He wrote Marcel Hébert on
October 27, 1912, that he had been highly pleased by Romain
Rolland's *Buisson ardent*, because it took to task much of the new
generation. Martin du Gard found it very disagreeable, "at thirty, not
to feel oneself in communion of thought and effort with the majority
of one's contemporaries, to run counter to one's time. Nonetheless, I
cannot subscribe to any of their postulates." Massis reacted as one
would expect. See Agathon's review, "Leur Jeunesse—A propos de
Jean Barois," *L'Opinion*, January 17, 1914, pp. 77–78. Massis, who was
elected to the Académie Française in 1961, remained bitterly hostile to
Martin du Gard right up until the latter's death in 1958. Of the many
articles by Massis, see especially, "Les Idées et les faits (Lectures—Du
côté d'Agathon—II)," *La Revue universelle*, January 15, 1935, p. 219:
"Through the voice of Jean Barois, who incarnated the passions, the
beliefs, the freethinking and rationalist frenzy of the *Dreyfusard*
University, . . . the fears [of this group] were translated." For Massis
this Sorbonne of Gabriel Séailles, Charles Seignobos, Emile Durkheim
and others "put in deliquescence all that had made the force and nerve
of our people" (p. 220). It is still too early to tell whether Barois (and
surely Martin du Gard is speaking here) is correct in asserting that
this rightist swing of the pendulum will ultimately have only a
"documentary interest" (*O.C.*, I, 516). For a contemporary evaluation
of this generation, see Hughes, *Consciousness and Society*, pp. 338–344.

their "will for action." [89] An inevitable conflict of generations has set in, and no dialogue is possible.

Barois's disease takes a turn for the worse, just at the moment his daughter takes her final vows. It may be that Martin du Gard is implying an identity between sickness and a return to the Catholic faith. The doctor tells Marie, "Yes, even after forty years of dormancy, it is common; old lesions are revived." [90] In any case, Marie's entry into the convent is intimately linked with Barois's decision to resign his position as editor of *Le Semeur*.[91] When he meets his wife at the ceremony and sees his daughter for the last time, he makes the further decision to return to his grandmother's house in Buis and to live out his remaining years there, with his wife. From then on the steps in Barois's physical and moral disintegration are rapid and inevitable—moral, of course, only from an atheist's viewpoint, but clearly this is Martin du Gard's position. The contrast between Luce's honorable death—"*en confiance*," [92] without deviation from his principles—and Jean's frightful agony is apparent. Luce's death has been seen as the point in the novel at which Martin du Gard's objectivity really gives way.[93] Jean dies very soon after Luce, and, as Denis Boak succinctly points out, "Barois is never able to escape his environment and heredity, and thus his end in the Church he had fought is, paradoxically enough, itself an illustration of [scientific] determinism." [94] Jean dies in the room which had witnessed his father's deathbed conversion. His widow finds the testament Barois wrote after his accident and, with the silent, perhaps culpable, assent of the attending

[89] *O.C.*, I, 512.   [90] *Ibid.*, p. 518.   [91] See *ibid.*, p. 520.
[92] *Ibid.*, p. 554.
[93] Pocknell, "Realism in the Works of Martin du Gard," p. 83.
[94] *Roger Martin du Gard*, p. 48.

priest, drops it into the fireplace. Thus ends the novel, with the cycle completed.

Clément Borgal, correcting René Lalou's original estimate of 1915, shows that the earliest possible historical date for Jean Barois's death is 1918.[95] In his letter to Marcel Hébert of May 11, 1911, Martin du Gard outlined the plan for a novel which would embrace a period of more than sixty years.[96] This would have made Barois's death occur in 1926! Though Martin du Gard made some efforts at compression in the final version of the novel, the disturbing question remains: Why should this story, so tightly linked with historical events, dated with such precision, essentially fall out of history and end in the future? We must remember that *Jean Barois* was completed in 1913. War, even if threatening, did not to many appear inevitable. In 1914 only a few old men could remember war. Governments faced "incalculable resistance" [97] to any military adventure, resistance which had grown up since 1870. No one could say exactly how new and untried forces, international socialism in particular, would react to a war situation. At such a time it seemed possible that a man like Jean Barois—and this is a measure of his freedom—could retire to the country and finish out his destiny. He is destroyed by the multiple determinisms of his character and environment, after having his destiny *pushed on* but not vitally altered by a period of contact with historical actuality. In this sense Jean Barois is a privileged hero, who has many relatives among the heroes of nineteenth-century literature.

[95] *Roger Martin du Gard* (Paris: Editions Universitaires, 1957), p. 113. Lalou's estimate is in his *Roger Martin du Gard* (Paris: Gallimard, 1937), p. 28.

[96] Unpublished letter previously cited on p. 25.

[97] Stephan Zweig, ". . . 1914 et aujourd'hui," Bracke [A. M. Desrousseaux] tr., *Le Populaire*, December 20, 1936, p. 4.

There is an evolution in Jean Barois's participation in history when it is compared to the behavior of Stendhal's Fabrice del Dongo at Waterloo. The hero of *La Chartreuse de Parme* has no comprehension of what is happening around him, wanders on and off the battlefield, and remains basically unaffected by his experience.[98] Already in Gustave Flaubert's *L'Education sentimentale*, a temporary paralleling of historical and individual destinies is possible. The prime example of this occurs when Frédéric Moreau, Flaubert's sadly ineffective hero, returns to Paris immediately after the final disaster which closes the long series of pitiful setbacks in his personal affairs. Napoleon III's *coup d'état* of December 1851, with all that it implies for the shattering of liberal hopes, has just taken place. Frédéric sees his friend Sénécal, once a utopian socialist, now a uniformed government agent, coldly shoot down their old friend Dussardier, the simple, good-hearted democrat, who is agitating in one of the sporadic and feeble demonstrations against the new regime.[99]

In *Jean Barois*, especially at the moment of the Rennes verdict, there is the same sort of paralleling. But never is there an intersection, an ultimate confrontation. The summer of 1914 will, however, make possible a new relationship between historical events and individual destinies.

[98] For a comparison of Jacques Thibault and Fabrice del Dongo, see Borgal, *Roger Martin du Gard*, p. 118.

[99] (Paris: Louis Conard, 1923), p. 599.

CHAPTER III

Years of Optimism and Productivity

Roger Martin du Gard did not immediately turn to the writing of another novel after his initial success with *Jean Barois*. In the months that preceded the outbreak of the First World War his full attention was diverted toward the theatre, which had always been a "temptation" for him.[1] This was the period of Martin du Gard's association with Jacques Copeau and his recently founded Théâtre du Vieux-Colombier, a period of intense activity and great promise, during which a total renovation of the French theatre was projected. One of the first results of Martin du Gard's entrance into the *N.R.F.* literary circle had been his meeting with Copeau in October 1913. The two men (Copeau called him Jean Barois[2]) spontaneously felt a deep sympathy for each other and became fast friends immediately. Martin du Gard, with a singular devotion, gave unsparingly of his time and energy, and could be seen regularly checking coats at

---

[1] Cf. R. M. G., *Souvenirs, O.C.*, I, lviii: "When I began to write, my taste for the theatre was still so strong that I could not entirely rid myself of this attraction. Instinctively, I searched for a compromise" (i.e., the utilization of the dialogue form in *Jean Barois*.)

[2] *Ibid.*, p. lxiv. On the remarkable depth and warmth of this friendship, see the whole section, "Ma Dette envers Copeau," pp. lxii-lxxiv, and Martin du Gard's "Hommage à Copeau," *Les Nouvelles littéraires*, February 10, 1949, p. 1.

the Vieux-Colombier.[3] He also produced a play dedicated to Copeau, *Le Testament du Père Leleu*.[4] This robust peasant farce was first performed in 1914 at the Vieux-Colombier and attained a considerable success, entering the repertory of the Comédie Française in 1938.[5]

One can exaggerate the degree of Martin du Gard's temptation by the theatre, though during the war he did plan a whole series of farces on modern themes. After Copeau's return to France from America in 1919, Martin du Gard aided in re-establishing the Théâtre du Vieux-Colombier.[6] However, Martin du Gard's posthumously published correspondence with Pierre Margaritis shows that he was thinking seriously about his next novel even before the armistice of November 1918.[7] Copeau himself had greatly changed during the long years of "exile." Martin du Gard broke away from the theatre in the spring of 1920, as soon, one can assume, as he felt the obligations of friendship fulfilled, and returned to what he termed his "real vocation, the novel." [8] Jacques Copeau, in an article paying homage to his old friend at the time of Martin du Gard's Nobel Prize (1937), praises his

---

[3] Jacques Copeau, *Souvenirs du Vieux-Colombier* (Paris: Nouvelles Editions Latines, 1931), p. 27.

[4] The play is reprinted in *O.C.*, II, 1,129–1,163.

[5] For details on this play and other aspects of Martin du Gard's theatrical interlude, see especially Clément Borgal, *Roger Martin du Gard* (Paris: Editions universitaires, 1957), ch. iv, "Intermezzo."

[6] The extent of Martin du Gard's commitment is amply demonstrated by the fact that he wrote an article on Jacques Copeau in the *N.R.F.*, December 1, 1919, pp. 1,113–1,118. While this is not, as certain writers have asserted, Martin du Gard's only article, it is clear that he must have felt quite strongly about the Vieux-Colombier in order to have broken his habitual silence and published something other than fiction.

[7] R. M. G., "Consultation littéraire: Lettres à Pierre Margaritis," *N.N.R.F.*, December 1958, p. 1,132 (letter of September 1, 1918).

[8] R. M. G., *Souvenirs, O.C.*, I, lxxviii.

exemplary dedication to the Vieux-Colombier just after the war, noting that Martin du Gard even took up housekeeping in a little apartment near the theatre. "If I emphasize Martin du Gard's prolonged contact with the Vieux-Colombier, it is not because I wish to derive glory from this fact. Nor is it because I wish to linger over precious memories. But I think that this contact had importance for the author of *Les Thibault*, that it had salutary effects upon him, because it detached him from the theatre." [9]

When Martin du Gard began *Les Thibault* in 1920, he had of course experienced another interlude besides that of the Vieux-Colombier, and one of immensely greater significance. In June 1914, Martin du Gard spent a week in the country with one of his new friends from the *N.R.F.*, Jean Schlumberger, and Germany was a topic of their conversations, but, writes Schlumberger, "on a singularly irrelevant plane—the only one in which we had any competence—that of the sweeping away of the eternal misunderstandings." [10] They even planned to write a book on the myopia of French policy toward Germany.[11] Given Martin du Gard's hopes for a peaceful settlement of the Franco-German rivalry, which he held as late as June 1914, it is surprising that he could have been so pessimistic in 1911, at the time of the second Moroccan crisis. In a most revealing letter of September 18, 1911, he wrote to Marcel Hébert:

I must admit that for some days now the atmosphere surrounding these negotiations is stifling. Those who, like myself, have deep affections and an aim in life, and a neck to risk which

[9] Jacques Copeau, "Sa Vie," *Marianne*, November 18, 1937, p. 4.
[10] *Eveils* (Paris: Gallimard, 1950), p. 248.
[11] R. M. G. and Jean Schlumberger, "Martin du Gard et Schlumberger se racontent leur guerre," *Le Figaro littéraire*, June 17–June 23, 1965, pp. 7–8 (five previously unpublished letters).

they find precious, are following with anguish the evolution of attitudes. There is a slow and progressive intoxication of bellicose nationalism, which is little by little invading all classes, almost all the parties, the majority of Frenchmen. Are you also witnessing this incredible modification of outlook? I am making some inquiries in the region. Everybody is ready and waiting. In the isolated corner in which I find myself at the moment, the lowliest day laborer has reread his military papers, and somber but submissive, waits for developments.[12]

There is an interesting repetition of this detail in *L'Eté 1914*, when Antoine Thibault, nervous, but refusing to accept his brother's impassioned claim that war is threatening, first recalls where he put his *livret militaire*, then checks it to find when and where he is to be mobilized.[13] In fact, Antoine's overall reaction resembles the one Martin du Gard is describing here in 1911.

Martin du Gard goes on in the letter to note his surprise at the absence of either panic or resistance:

The passivity of September leaves in a stormy wind. It's a cruel blow. I am obliged to admit that I had more illusions. I could not imagine that the menace of a war would be received with this fatalistic calm, and, it must be said, this courage of inertia. . . . Are we still so far, so far, from our goal? Is it necessary that every *élan* be cut short, every effort toward progress be turned into a mockery by events? Whatever the outcome of the present crisis may be, I am convinced that it will have the greatest and most deplorable reaction upon our internal policies. Never have these clouds of dry powder produced anything good. France is making warlike noises, which is the most evil omen. At least let us hope that these noises will intimidate the other and spare us the shame, in 1911, of so many potential funerals.

[12] Communicated by M. Emile Poulat. Any further citations of letters to Marcel Hébert will be from this unpublished collection, unless otherwise indicated.

[13] *O.C.*, II, 129, 303.

When potentiality became reality, Martin du Gard did not flee to Switzerland. Unlike his hero Jacques Thibault and unlike Romain Rolland, he accepted his military duty, though he may have regretted this decision. Maurice Martin du Gard, reporting a conversation which took place in August 1919, stresses Roger's great admiration for Rolland, "who, he said, had saved honor during the war." [14] From the second day of mobilization (August 3, 1914), Roger Martin du Gard served as a noncommissioned officer in a motorized supply group assigned to the First Cavalry Corps. His unit was in constant movement, and the nature of his tasks placed him in close contact with the Front. He was not discharged until February 1919.

The war was a terrible gap in Martin du Gard's productive life, from his thirty-third to his thirty-eighth year, a gap which merits our attention. Here and there one can uncover indications of his state of mind and of his reactions to events. On November 3, 1914, he wrote a long letter to Marcel Hébert describing his war experience, giving a general picture of the slaughter and misery he saw around him:

How sad this all is, what a disillusionment for me that all this "could have been possible!" I shall have great difficulty recovering from this blow; one can hope for nothing from the human race when one has seen what I see almost daily, the savagery of everyone, the best accepting, without profound internal revolt, this law of the strongest, the only law which counts today. . . . One cannot tolerate hearing it said everywhere [when one is in regular contact with French soldiers] that we are engaged in the struggle of civilization against barbarism; on both sides there is the same vileness, the same cruelty, the same instincts revived; it is two barbarisms locked in struggle. What will come of it?

In 1915 a ray of light appeared on this dismal scene. A

[14] *Les Mémorables, I (1918–1923)* (Paris: Flammarion, 1957), p. 94.

friend sent Martin du Gard a pamphlet by the nationalist Henri Massis. Massis reprinted Romain Rolland's famous article, "Au-dessus de la mêlée," which had originally appeared in a Geneva newspaper in 1914. Massis included Rolland's article only in order to refute it, and it was by means of this reverse twist that a piece of pacifist writing was able to reach Martin du Gard on the battlefield. He was deeply affected, and wrote off immediately to Rolland: "This brochure reached me this morning. I glanced at the article by Massis. I turned rapidly to yours. . . . Ah! what a burst of fresh air, finally, finally! I have been transformed by it, made youthful, more than ever avid to experience the future." [15]

By 1915 the war had assumed a nightmareish quality for Martin du Gard; he viewed it as a senseless, needless interruption which would be followed by a return to the peaceful Europe of the nineteenth century, a Europe fundamentally unchanged, though probably more capable of undertaking reforms in a socializing direction.[16] This would be a world in

[15] Romain Rolland, *Journal des années de guerre, 1914–1919* (Paris: Albin Michel, 1952), p. 504, letter of Roger Martin du Gard to Rolland, August 25, 1915. In his correspondence with Marcel Hébert there is an echo of this significant break in the monotony of Martin du Gard's wartime existence, though here he is less impassioned. In a letter of August 31, 1915, he describes Rolland's article and his enthusiasm for it, but remarks: "This great appeal, which will be classic one day, which will be his greatest glory, his great act of courage, has encountered an almost total and unanimous incomprehension—I tremble in speculating on what must be done upon our return in order to go against the current . . . I ask myself if my generation, so decimated, can do it."

[16] By 1915 he thought it "reasonable" to envisage an "honorable peace" negotiated with Germany. Since a military solution was impossible, since he himself observed the tremendous slaughter a "victorious" offensive entailed in order to capture a few feet of ground, he proposed a diplomatic solution. This would prove that

which Martin du Gard could continue to write novels, in which a privileged hero such as Jean Barois could live out his destiny. Jacques Copeau summarizes Martin du Gard's attitude perfectly when he notes that the war did not interrupt their friendship: "For Roger as a soldier denied that the war had the power to change anything in the world! Each of his letters affirmed that the war was only a *suspension*, a *parenthesis*, and we would, after its termination, find again and take up again things where we left them. Such was our expectation." [17]

In February 1919, when Martin du Gard finally returned to France from the occupied Rhineland, he was returning to a victorious country, a country whose regime had withstood the stresses of a decimating war. In France it was reasonable to formulate literary projects on prewar models. Martin du Gard did not have the perspective of Thomas Mann, who could write in the foreword to *The Magic Mountain*, published in 1924:

The exaggerated pastness of our narrative is due to its taking place before the epoch when a certain crisis shattered its way through life and consciousness and left a deep chasm behind. It

---

"war is a plague which one must avoid at any price" (Martin du Gard to Jean Schlumberger, letter of June 14, 1915, in *Le Figaro littéraire*, June 17–June 23, 1965, p. 8). The two writers disagreed so strongly over this point that they stopped corresponding for three years and did not renew their friendship until after the war. While I do not think Maurice Martin du Gard a completely reliable source of information, and while his book telling of the conversation was not published until 1957, it is worth mention that Maurice quotes Roger as exclaiming during an evening spent together in August 1919: "It's splendid, what we're going to live through. This postwar period! What a revival! The wind blows from the East! It brings liberty!" (*Les Mémorables*, p. 95).

[17] "Sa Vie," p. 4 (italics mine).

takes place—or, rather, deliberately to avoid the present tense, it took place, and had taken place—in the long ago, in the old days, the days of the world before the Great War, in the beginning of which so much began that has scarcely left off beginning.[18]

Serenus Zeitblom, the narrator in Thomas Mann's later *Doctor Faustus,* explains perhaps as well as anyone why a German could have this conception of radical change. He has a premonition as early as 1914 that an epoch is ending, the epoch of liberalism and the growth of the idea of freedom.

No wonder the disintegration of defeat increased this feeling to its highest pitch, no wonder either that in a defeated country like Germany it occupied the mind far more than among the victorious nations, whose average mental state, precisely on account of victory, was much more conservative. They by no means felt the war as the massive and decisive historical break which it seemed to us. They saw it as a disturbance, now happily passed, after which life could return to the past out of which it had been thrust. I envied them. *I envied in particular France*, for the sanction which, at least apparently, had been vouchsafed by the victory to its conservative bourgeois intellectual constitution; for the sense of security in the classic and rational, which it might draw from its triumph.[19]

Now that the background against which Roger Martin du Gard established his plans for artistic production after the war has been described, a more extensive analysis of these plans can be made. We are fortunate to have a series of eight letters to his close friend, Pierre Margaritis, dated from January 18 to September 14, 1918, and published in the Martin du Gard memorial edition of the *N.N.R.F.* Their importance has been rightly recognized by critics; the germ of

[18] H. T. Lowe-Porter, tr. (London: Penguin Books, 1960), p. xi.
[19] H. T. Lowe-Porter, tr. (London: Secker and Warburg, 1959), p. 353 (italics mine).

the *Thibault* series is visible in them. Martin du Gard writes of his preoccupation with problems of the day:

> I feel myself attracted (*and the war has done nothing but push me further along this route*) toward works of ideas, toward a work with a thesis, philosophical. Or, more exactly, I feel the attraction of stuffing my literary work, novel or theatre, with ideological speculation. I am preoccupied with all the great contemporary problems, and I am proud of this fact.[20]

He explains how he labors constantly over his documentation, clipping and filing away innumerable articles. Crammed with all the great issues of the early part of the century, *Jean Barois* is a sort of encyclopedia.

Every so often, however, Martin du Gard has a moment of serious doubt, when there comes to him, "like a thunderbolt, the intimate and dizzying revelation" that he is "*on the wrong track*."[21] On such occasions he feels that he has been lying to himself and with infinite effort forcing himself in a false direction. His true talent then appears to him to lie in deep analysis of character, in sensitive perception of human emotion, in imaginative work full of imagery and intrigue. In short, he feels that he is a novelist, and not a thinker, not a sociologist. It seems likely that in one of these moods Martin du Gard would have subscribed completely to Marcel Proust's pronouncement against the artist's involvement and concern with external political issues. In *Jean Barois* he has come to prefer the human qualities, the rare scenes of "pure sentiment." He now finds the novel's strength in the portrayal of "the aging of Barois, and not so much the aging of his intelligence, the senile evolution in the domain of ideas, as the

---

[20] R. M. G., "Consultation littéraire: Lettres à Pierre Margaritis," *N.N.R.F.*, December 1958, p. 1,118 (italics mine).
[21] *Ibid.*, p. 1,119 (italics his).

tragic aging of the man, in his body and in his heart, his physical collapse, that mortal anguish in the face of disease." [22] It is noteworthy that Martin du Gard is referring here to the nineteenth-century aspect of *Jean Barois*, the fact that the hero has the privilege of being able to return to Buis to complete his tragic destiny, after his period of historical-ideological activity.

Martin du Gard would now like to build a novel on this traditional basis alone. He wants to turn his back on ideology, though he fears it may be too late, that he may no longer be capable of doing so. His dossiers, his philosophical and scientific texts, must be put away: "I am gripped by the desire to close resolutely my door on these sounds of the crowd, to concentrate on individuals." [23] It does not seem to occur to Martin du Gard that some kind of *mélange* (which is eventually achieved in *Les Thibault*) is possible. There is a reminiscence of the youthful intransigence of his fictional creation, Jean Barois, when he writes, "I cannot dodge the issue any more. I must choose for or against: for it is necessary to give of oneself *without division*. Whether it be of 'ideas' or of 'sentiments,' the work demands, from the very beginning a *total* giving." [24] The proposed title of the "colossal novel" he intends to write is *Le Bien et le mal:* "I see it as a pure novel, a voluminous and constantly rebounding tale, a swarming of living beings, gripping like the spectacle of life itself." [25]

Why, when Martin du Gard settled down after the First

[22] *Ibid.*

[23] *Ibid.*, p. 1,121. Cf. p. 1,131: "The day when I allow this gift [for creating live and vital characters] to bloom and flourish without smothering it under the crawling plants of ideologies, I shall perhaps create works which will endure."

[24] *Ibid.*, p. 1,122 (italics his).

[25] *Ibid.*, p. 1,132.

World War to write a novel, did he not adhere to this eloquently and passionately stated program? Why does ideology creep back in, even, to some degree, into the first volumes of *Les Thibault?* A good deal of attention will be given to this important question. Perhaps one of the reasons is that Martin du Gard's correspondent, Pierre Margaritis, died in a military hospital of Spanish influenza on October 30, 1918, just a few weeks after writing the last of the published letters in the series. *Les Thibault* is dedicated to his "fraternal memory." His premature death "destroyed the powerful work [he was a brilliant young musician] which was ripening in his tormented and pure heart." [26] One can presume that the war which had snuffed out this life, this talent, would be extensively treated in *Les Thibault*, and that consequently a whole series of problems which go beyond the individual would have to be dealt with in the novel.

In the spring of 1920, after the interlude with Jacques Copeau and the Vieux-Colombier, Martin du Gard retired to the country and worked out a detailed plan for *Les Thibault*. Quite suddenly the idea of writing the story of two brothers came to him: "two beings with temperaments as different, as divergent, as possible, but fundamentally marked by the obscure similarities which are created, between two people of the same blood, by a very powerful common atavism. Such a subject offered me the opportunity for a fruitful doubling: I

[26] Pierre Margaritis also served as an important inspiration for the character of Jacques Thibault. "At about the age of fifteen, Pierre Margaritis ran away from home and, under orders from his father, was sent for some time to a reform school near Tours" (Jacques Brenner, *Martin du Gard* [Paris: Gallimard, 1961], p. 22). This fact would surely be an added incentive for Martin du Gard to concentrate on the First World War, since if he were to maintain the parallel, Jacques would also be prematurely destroyed in the conflict.

saw in it the possibility of simultaneously expressing two contradictory tendencies in my nature: the instinct of independence, of evasion, of revolt, the refusal of all conformity; and that instinct for order, for measure, that refusal of extremes, which I owe to my heredity." [27]

Gide encouraged Martin du Gard to continue with the project, finding it perfectly suited to his talents. The work was planned to cover a period of some forty years, and after a few months Martin du Gard was able to return to Paris with a dozen well-ordered dossiers, each dossier dealing with a single character. From the material in these dossiers the novel was to be constructed. One detail which is of great interest is the fact that, according to the original outline, only Jacques was to be killed in the First World War. Antoine would return unscathed and marry Jenny, aiding her in the upbringing of Jean-Paul, Jacques's son. These characters will become familiar as the discussion progresses. What matters for the moment is that Martin du Gard already had in mind a complicated domestic intrigue which would involve Jean-Paul at the age of twenty.[28] A simple calculation based on the chronology of the novel shows that Jean-Paul was born in 1915. In 1920, then, Martin du Gard was so sure that the political future of Europe would be a stable one, that he could take his story as far into the future as 1935.

In 1922 the first two parts of the novel were published by Gallimard, *Le Cahier gris* in April and *Le Pénitencier* in May. In October of the following year the two volumes of Part III, *La Belle Saison*, appeared. A gap of almost five years intervened before the publication of the fourth part, *La Consultation*.

[27] R. M. G., *Souvenirs*, O.C., I, lxxviii.
[28] This information is from Martin du Gard's discussion of his decision to change *Les Thibault*, in *ibid.*, p. xcv.

This break was not due to any doubts on Martin du Gard's part as to the artistic value of his vast project. His father had died in April 1924, and his mother a year later, after a lingering illness which required his full attention. Around 1925 he decided to purchase the splendid property of Le Tertre in Bellême (Orne) from his father-in-law. A great deal of repair and restoration of the chateau was necessary before Martin du Gard could move in with his family and feel secure about his library, his working materials, his whole pattern of life.[29] It is rumored that every time he moved from a residence, a truck was necessary to transport his notes. The habit of hoarding dossiers must have been stronger than the wish to escape them expressed in the Margaritis correspondence. Martin du Gard devised a very complex system of handling his vast quantities of material so that he could work with the utmost efficiency, and he even had a specially equipped chair.[30] By the autumn of 1926 he was definitely installed at Le Tertre and ready to settle down to serious writing. *La Consultation* appeared in April 1928, *La Sorellina*

---

[29] Most of these biographical data come from the chronological index at the beginning of *O.C.* For a discussion of this gap in the production of *Les Thibault*, see Borgal, *Roger Martin du Gard*, pp. 74–75. Louis Martin-Chauffier describes Le Tertre in "Huit Jours chez Roger Martin du Gard," *Vendredi*, November 19, 1937, p. 1. Martin du Gard received talented young authors with a prodigious hospitality and a rare generosity—but visitors observed the rigid rules as far as working hours were concerned. Probably one of the most important intellectual experiences for Martin du Gard during this quietly productive decade was the time he spent at the Pontigny summer sessions. Organized by Paul Desjardins, these ten-day discussion periods brought together the intellectual elite of Europe. For Martin du Gard's own account, especially of his friendship with the young Malraux, see *Souvenirs, O.C.*, I, lxxv–xcii.

[30] Louis Martin-Chauffier, "Roger Martin du Gard," *Fémina-Illustration*, April 1956, p. 100.

in May of the same year, and in March 1929, *La Mort du père,* which carried the action down to December 1913. Nothing more was to be heard of the Thibault family until November 1936.

In the early volumes of *Les Thibault* it would appear, from a cursory reading, that Martin du Gard was able to write the kind of novel of character and sentiment he had outlined in his letters to Pierre Margaritis. The date of events is not given until Part IV, *La Consultation,* and only then can calculations be made which show that the action begins in the late spring of 1904. From the outset the emphasis is quite clearly on individuals, and ideology has been pushed into the background—but perhaps not as far as Martin du Gard would have liked! When only two volumes were out, Henri Massis asserted that he detected a kinship between *Jean Barois* and *Les Thibault,* that the ties between the two works, while not readily apparent, were profound. Massis thought that Martin du Gard's rationalist *Sorbonnard* anticlerical ideology was as visible in *Les Thibault* as in *Jean Barois.* He contended that Martin du Gard was neither realistic nor objective and asserted that his convictions distorted reality, that Martin du Gard bitterly hated the bourgeoisie which had nurtured him and the priests who had educated him: "He is taking vengeance through his books." [31] Much of what Massis claimed may

[31] Henri Massis, "Le Romantisme de l'adolescence," *La Revue universelle,* September 15, 1922, p. 753. After Martin du Gard's death, Massis published a letter he had received when this article first appeared. In it Martin du Gard, whether completely sincere or not, registered surprise at Massis' reaction: "The article inspired by my first two volumes is by far the most intelligent devoted to them. But it is so false! It's unbelievable. You assign to me preferences, theories, a 'philosophical position,' a hundred diabolical intentions which I never had. . . . Intelligence leads you astray, and your own *parti-pris. But no; I tell a story, Sir, and that is all"* (cited in Henri Massis, "Roger Martin du Gard, l'Abbé Hébert et Monseigneur Duchesne," *Le Bulletin des lettres,* October 15, 1958, p. 333, italics his).

well be true, his personal antipathy perhaps giving him a keener perceptivity. Most critics, however, were not so quick as he to detect the ideological base of *Les Thibault*, or felt that Martin du Gard had made an admirable effort to be objective, struggling against his own prejudices. Martin du Gard must have been pleased by Georges Heitz's review of 1925, which emphasized the impartiality of *Les Thibault*. It was Heitz's opinion that Martin du Gard was solely concerned with the presentation of character, that "without any doctrine, without a theory, he [was] in the process of giving the novel a stable form, perfect, having its end in itself." [32] The truth is surely somewhere between the extremes of Heitz and Massis; the ideology is latent, but it does not predominate in the early volumes.

At the beginning of *Le Cahier gris*, Dr. Antoine Thibault and his father Oscar are searching for young Jacques Thibault. With dexterity and an economy of words Martin du Gard sets the scene and fills in necessary detail. (The fact that Oscar Thibault writes *chroniques* for the *Revue des deux mondes* tells us much about his background and character.) Jacques is not at school and his preceptor, the Abbé Binot, informs M. Thibault of the discovery of a gray notebook. Binot, the only priest portrayed in a definitely negative light by Martin du Gard, feels that Jacques has been led astray by a dangerous comrade, "of whom, alas, there are many in the state schools." [33] Rather gleefully, the Abbé narrates how he found Jacques reading such tabooed works as Rousseau's *Confessions* and Zola's *La Faute de l'abbé Mouret*. The confiscation of the gray notebook has left no doubt in Binot's mind that Jacques is involved in a homosexual relationship with a Protestant schoolmate, Daniel de Fontanin. When the Abbé

[32] "Deux Romanciers d'aujourd'hui: Roger Martin du Gard et Henry de Montherlant," *Le Monde nouveau*, January 15, 1925, p. 21.
[33] *Le Cahier gris* (© Editions Gallimard, 1922), in *O.C.*, I, 583.

told Jacques of his discovery, the youth had a nervous crisis and threatened suicide. (Jacques is as death-haunted as a character in one of Malraux's novels. He threatens suicide six times in the first volume alone, witnesses the violent death struggle of a great work horse strangled in its traces, and tells Daniel that he once saw two dead men in the morgue. Jacques's obsession with death and his encounters with it are frequently recurring themes throughout the novel.) It soon becomes apparent that Jacques and Daniel have run away. The main theme of *Le Cahier gris* is this adolescent *fugue* and the effects it has on the Thibault and Fontanin families.

Oscar Thibault notifies the police immediately. He favors the most severe treatment of the runaways and the "sustaining of paternal authority."[34] Refusing to believe that there is a homosexual basis to Jacques's and Daniel's friendship, Mme de Fontanin takes a contrasting attitude; she will not, furthermore, read the incriminating notebook, since it would be an invasion of the boys' privacy. Her immediate aim is to locate her libertine husband Jérôme, a man of great charm and little morality.[35] Her thirteen-year-old daughter, Jenny, who knows more about the boys' escape than she will disclose, becomes very ill, and the reader is presented with the first of many sickroom scenes in *Les Thibault*. Such scenes have all the accuracy of a medical text, and have been highly praised, not only by critics, but also by doctors.[36]

---

[34] *Ibid.*, p. 601.

[35] There is a leitmotiv, an odor of "half-evaporated" *eau de toilette*, which always indicates Jérôme's rather disquieting presence (*ibid.*, pp. 602, 655).

[36] See, for example, Pierre Mauriac, *La Médecine et l'intelligence* (Bordeaux: Delmas, 1949), pp. 178–185; Gilberte Alméras, *La Médecine dans "Les Thibault" de M. Roger Martin du Gard*, M.D. thesis (Paris: P. Fournié et Cie, 1946); and Michel Laparade,

In part following the method of multiple presentation of events used in *Jean Barois* rather than adhering to a strict narrative, Martin du Gard inserts fragments from the gray notebook into his text—enough to show that the relationship between Jacques and Daniel is strictly platonic. There is much talk of visiting foreign countries, of the unapproachable Ideal, of a dedication to Art—in sum the typical romanticism of intelligent adolescents.[37]

The boys get as far as Marseilles and try unsuccessfully to board ship for Africa. Though smaller in size than Daniel, who knows that his mother will forgive him and is ready to give up the adventure, Jacques is portrayed as the organizer of the flight and as a passionate, dynamic, tough boy. He is filled with bitterness against "schools in general, the Abbé, his *lycée,* the proctor, his father, society, universal injustice." [38] Jacques threatens to kill himself if Daniel abandons him, and Daniel, terrified, agrees to keep on, "submissive to the extraordinary fascination of Jacques." [39] I have mentioned these details in order to emphasize that a Catholic nationalist critic like Massis is unfair or at least incomplete when he argues that all Martin du Gard is doing in this novel is pleading for progressive education and making a virulent attack on the Catholic clergy, in particular the clergy in its teaching role.

Réflexions sur quatre médecins de roman, M.D. thesis (Bordeaux: Imprimerie René Samie, 1948). For the Martin du Gard selection in his anthology *Readings I've Liked* (New York: Simon and Schuster, 1943), Clifton Fadiman chooses the scene of the operation in *La Belle Saison.*

[37] One is reminded of the "literature of evasion," in which the destination is so frequently Africa, as in Gide's *Paludes, Les Nourritures terrestres,* and *L'Immoraliste.* Though no specific destination is given, Rimbaud's *Bateau ivre* would of course be another famous example.

[38] *O.C.,* I, 633.   [39] *Ibid.,* p. 634.

Massis feels that Martin du Gard is implying that if only Jacques had been given more liberty, he would have developed in a healthy fashion.[40] This theory does not, of course, explain why Daniel, too, went wrong, since he was surrounded by maternal affection and given complete freedom. And Martin du Gard from the very beginning portrays Jacques as one who has rebellion in his inmost nature, as one who could never be at ease in any society.[41] His unhappy experience at the Catholic school certainly aggravates these already-present tendencies, but it is not the decisive factor in creating them.

When the boys are caught and brought home, Daniel, knowing he will not be punished, is inwardly relieved, though he puts up a brave front for the sake of appearances. Jacques is at first very rebellious, then breaks down and cries. He is greeted with genuine affection by his brother Antoine, but faces the prospect of severe punishment by his father. There is irony in the fact that Oscar Thibault, who as a leader of the Catholic *grande bourgeoisie* has been occupied with charities for many years, especially with problems of juvenile delinquency, has already set up a "model penitentiary" for wayward youth. Forcing back the emotion which comes to him spontaneously when Jacques is brought into his presence,

[40] Massis, "Le Romantisme de l'adolescence," p. 759.

[41] This theme reappears frequently throughout the novel. It is perhaps most explicitly stated in *La Mort du père*, O.C., I, 1,319: "At no time in his life, and in no place, had he ever felt right, belonging, on his true soil at last—like Antoine. Nowhere had he been in his element—not in Africa, or Italy, or Germany—not even in Lausanne. And beyond mere separation from his environment he felt trapped [*traqué*]. By his family, by society, by the conditions of life. . . . Trapped by something which he could not grasp, which seemed to come from himself" (*La Mort du père* [© Editions Gallimard, 1929], Part VI of *Les Thibault*).

Oscar determines to break his spirit by incarcerating him in the reformatory which he himself has founded.

It is apparent that Martin du Gard is not completely objective in *Le Cahier gris*. The portrait of Oscar Thibault could be seen as a cruel caricature, and the Abbé Binot is most unsavory. A Catholic writer obviously would have handled similar characters and events very differently. Nonetheless, the change in tone from *Jean Barois* does exist. There is much less emphasis on history and ideology, a narrowing of focus. Martin du Gard would seem to have concentrated his energy and talent upon the early chapters of a fresh reading of Marcel Proust's "interior book."

This impression is not challenged in Part II, *Le Pénitencier*. Nine months have passed since Jacques left Paris to enter the reformatory, making the date about April 1905. Antoine, a brilliant young doctor of twenty-four, is coming to doubt the justice of his father's decision to lock up Jacques. The volume centers upon Antoine's efforts, aided by the Abbé Vécard, Oscar's confessor and a very sympathetically drawn priest, to remove Jacques from his prison, and upon Jacques's gradual rehabilitation after his physically and morally debilitating experience. Adolescent sexuality is one of the major themes, and a more detailed study is also made of Antoine's character, heretofore only sketchily presented. Antoine's determination to obtain Jacques's release is his first "movement of filial revolt." [42] Against his father's orders, he pays a visit to the reformatory at Crouy.

The account of this visit is one of the finest examples of Martin du Gard's artistry. Antoine's shifts in mood—from suspicion to anger at himself for having imagined that Crouy might be a real prison rather than a reformatory in the best

[42] *Le Pénitencier* (© Editions Gallimard, 1922), in *O.C.*, I, 679.

sense of the word, to suspicion again—and his "decision" to return for a second look after "accidentally" missing the train back to Paris are treated with great skill by Martin du Gard. Antoine is finally able to persuade Jacques to describe the miserable reality of his life at Crouy. The older brother is completely taken aback by the younger's insistence that he would rather remain in the penitentiary than return to the oppressive atmosphere of his family. Antoine, with his habit of quick and forceful determination, therefore decides to take care of Jacques himself, to obtain his father's permission to set up housekeeping in an apartment downstairs from the one presently occupied by the family. Back in Paris, he breaks in on his father, "feeling already the paralysis of the desire to win." [43] A bitter argument ensues, and Oscar Thibault's "massive immobility" gives way only under the prodding of the very able Abbé Vécard, who has also become convinced that Jacques must be brought home immediately.

When Jacques arrives in Paris, dazed and unsure of himself, Antoine feels that he has strength and will enough for them both. He emphasizes the superior force of the Thibault family, and assures Jacques that he can catch up quickly in his studies: "The Thibaults can will. And it is for this reason that the Thibaults can attempt anything. Surpass the others! Assert yourself! This must be so. This strength, hidden in a race, must finally produce results! It is in us that the Thibault tree must finally bloom. The blossoming of a long line!" [44] The conclusion of the novel will make Antoine's words seem hollow and ironic. In the scene with Jacques at the reformatory, it would seem, Martin du Gard is already unconsciously preparing for the fate he will, in the final version of the novel, reserve for Antoine. He writes of Antoine, "His desires

[43] *Ibid.*, p. 721.   [44] *Ibid.*, p. 764.

were always so imperious that he never doubted of their realization; and, in fact, he had up to the present always brought to a successful conclusion whatever he had wished for with real obstinacy." [45]

Benefiting from the freedom Antoine permits him, Jacques does progress rapidly in his studies and seems to adapt himself to his new situation. The remainder of the volume deals with Jacques's first sexual experience, and with the re-establishment of contact with the Fontanin family, despite Oscar Thibault's express prohibition. In the delicately written account of adolescent awakening, the concern is entirely psychological; further commentary is not needed here.[46] The visit to the Fontanins, which Antoine decides upon after discovering that Jacques is in correspondence with Daniel, merits some attention, since it foreshadows much that is of significance in the novel. The contradictions and complexities which are inherent in Jacques's nature and which make any stability, any kind of adaptation, impossible for him, are manifest in his confusion when Antoine gives in to his request to see the Fontanins. He is "disoriented at having won his cause without a struggle. He [has] the impression that he is the dupe of some machination which he [has] not perceived." [47] An instant later he is ashamed of his doubts; yet he still asks himself if he really has such a strong desire to see his friend.

During the visit to the Fontanins, there is a hint of the possibility of a future love affair between Jacques and Jenny.[48] At this time, however, Jenny is overtly hostile, since

[45] *Ibid.*, p. 716.

[46] The love-death linkage, a recurrent theme already found in *Jean Barois*, is also present. Lisbeth Frühling, Jacques's first lover, comes directly from attendance upon her aunt's coffin into his arms (*ibid.*, pp. 808–813).

[47] *Ibid.*, p. 781.   [48] See *ibid.*, pp. 799, 807.

she blames Jacques for the episode of the flight to Marseilles. Antoine, who has had an ambiguous rapport with Mme de Fontanin from the very beginning (which, however, never goes beyond mutual admiration), opens his heart to her, explaining both his respect for his father and the total lack of any common ground between them. Mme de Fontanin approves of Antoine's going against Oscar's wishes, since she has for the older man "an instinctive and ferocious antipathy. The interdiction of which her son, her home, and thus herself were the object, seem[s] to her to be odiously injust and motivated by the vilest possible reasons." [49] She is even more delighted when Antoine tells her that he has left the Catholic church. He says that he has always been attracted to Protestantism, though, Martin du Gard informs us, he had never thought about Protestantism before knowing the Fontanins.[50] Under the influence of Mme de Fontanin's strong and attractive personality, Antoine, during their conversation, goes into a deeper self-analysis than is his habit and demonstrates a certain haziness of thought, one of the characteristics of this man who is so deeply committed to action—at least as long as action is possible for him. With pride he explains to her that he is a practical person:

I don't say that science explains everything, but it does verify, and for me, that is sufficient. The *hows* interest me enough for me to renounce the vain search after the *whys*. . . . As far as morality is concerned, I am not at all preoccupied with it. . . . You see, I love my work, I love my life, I am energetic, active, and I think that I have demonstrated that this activity is in itself a rule of conduct. In any case, up to the present, I have never found myself hesitating about what I had to accomplish.[51]

[49] *Ibid.*, p. 795.   [50] *Ibid.*, p. 797.
[51] *Ibid.*, p. 796 (italics his).

This happy state of certainty is not to last. Even before certain painful decisions which his medical career will force him to make, and before his disastrous encounter with history, the experience of love, "will drastically shake up the principles and the conventions with which he had surrounded himself like a suit of armor." [52]

La belle saison could describe the period which was later looked back on as *la belle époque*, France under the presidency of Fallières (1906–1913). And in *Les Thibault*, Part III, *La Belle Saison*, the characters enter a period of optimistic beginnings which shades into a rich and vital noontide of experience. The particular *belle saison* is the summer of 1910. The central theme is love: Antoine's love for the opulent Rachel, Jacques's pure, timid, and somewhat narcissistic passion for Jenny de Fontanin, and the more disturbingly sensual attraction he feels for Gise, a mulatto girl brought up in his family, who in turn loves him with an animal-like devotion. Other characters, including Daniel de Fontanin and many less important figures, are involved in love affairs and marriage plans.

Jacques Thibault is now twenty and seems fairly well integrated into bourgeois society, though he enjoys spilling out to Antoine or to himself a generalized antipathy against his life and his surroundings, "against his already laid-out existence, against morality, the family, society!" If only he could escape, he imagines, he could at last find "that interior equilibrium which he accused others of making impossible for him!" [53] He will not, however, burn his bridges and leave

---

[52] Robert de Ribon, "La Vie littéraire—*Les Thibault*, par M. Roger Martin du Gard, III et IV," *La Revue Hebdomadaire*, March 1, 1924, pp. 111–112.

[53] *La Belle Saison* (© Editions Gallimard, 1923), in *O.C.*, I, 818.

Paris. Obviously Jacques's lack of balance is not entirely caused by others, but is an inherent part of his nature. His reactions upon learning that he has been admitted to the Ecole Normale Supérieure with an excellent grade are highly ambivalent—both relief and further *angoisse,* a sense of being ever more securely trapped by his environment.

A group of his friends persuades him and Antoine to dine at an exclusive night club in honor of the occasion. The scene at the night club gives Martin du Gard another opportunity to display his artistic powers. The gaiety, the music, the violence, a certain atmosphere of decadence, a masterful seduction by the very Gidian character Daniel de Fontanin— all are presented with great force and a sure mastery of the novelist's craft. (It is significant that the character who explicitly adopts the Gidian doctrines expounded in *Les Nourritures terrestres* plays a relatively minor role in Martin du Gard's work.)[54]

Antoine never arrives at the celebration. He is called away on an emergency accident case and by chance encounters Rachel, the victim's neighbor, a mysterious, exotic woman, who is to become his mistress. Antoine immediately sets about making his diagnosis; "he almost never thought without be-

---

[54] Jacques admires Gide's work but reacts strongly against the philosophy it presents. For in it Daniel "found all his excuses." Jacques senses the powerful appeal of the doctrine but finds it "redoubtable" (*ibid.,* p. 820). Cf. the oft-cited passage which treats Daniel's discovery of Gide and the exaltation he derives from finding a philosophy which justifies his own penchants (*ibid.,* pp. 829–830). One could probably study with profit the subtle influence of Gide on Martin du Gard and vice versa, particularly in the domain of literary technique. See, for example, Martha O'Nan, "Form in the Novel: André Gide and Roger Martin du Gard," *Symposium,* Spring–Fall 1958, pp. 81–93. Martin du Gard's own conclusion, given in his *Notes sur André Gide, O.C.,* II, 1,417, places quite severe limits upon any Gidian influence in his work.

ginning at the same time to act, . . . for he was always impatient to make a decision." [55] Martin du Gard shows a skill perhaps never surpassed in his description of the emergency operation Antoine performs.[56] The operation is carried out under the most primitive conditions, and Antoine is not a little exalted and proud of his superior ability and his command of the situation. He has just the time to think, "I am a marvelous chap." [57] Rachel and the young doctor who assist Antoine are greatly impressed with his performance, and he feels "the intoxication of the leader." [58]

The next morning Antoine's affair with Rachel begins, an affair which is to transform and enrich his existence, to round off the contours of his surprisingly immature personality, to cut into his self-assurance. His dependence upon her grows very quickly; she teaches him to laugh and reinforces his energies and his dedication to medicine—though apparently not his philosophical abilities. At one moment he feels himself to be completely the master of his destiny and cannot understand how anyone could deny the existence of free will. An instant later, speaking of his vocation, he says, "One always thinks that one has chosen. Actually it is circumstances." [59]

The idea of the briefest absence from Rachel becomes impossible for him to bear, and he even imagines that he could abandon his organized bourgeois professional existence, and go away with her. However, when he proposes a new life together, she merely laughs and appears incredulous, and to salvage a bit of dignity, he pretends that he was joking.[60]

[55] *O.C.*, I, 870.
[56] The ligature of a femoral artery. Cf. Alméras, *La Médecine dans "Les Thibault,"* pp. 53–59.
[57] *Ibid.*, p. 871.   [58] *Ibid.*, p. 879.
[59] *Ibid.*, pp. 896–897. On the change in Antoine see also pp. 1,005, 1,024.
[60] *Ibid.*, p. 1,029.

Finally, in November of 1910, she leaves him for another lover who is in Africa, one who surely represents the aspect of her life which Antoine cannot adopt. There is an air of fatality about Rachel's departure. A month before she takes the steamer from Le Havre, Antoine realizes that his happiness is going to end, that he will be alone: "There is nothing, absolutely nothing, to do about it. He understood this without her having told him, long before he knew why, before he even began to suffer from it, and as if he had always been prepared for it." [61] He does not even try to understand her motives and feels no jealousy, only "the sentiment of his impotence, of their irresponsibility, of the weight of life itself." [62] He even briefly contemplates suicide; he has come a long way from the superbly confident Antoine who could always satisfy his wishes.

In tracing out this revolution in Antoine's personality the form of *La Belle Saison* was not followed. In the volume Martin du Gard jumps rapidly from scene to scene, treating first one character, then another, developing simultaneously a multiplicity of intrigues of lesser or greater importance. We must now turn to Jacques and briefly discuss his activities during *la belle saison*. The day after his success at the Ecole Normale he goes to the family summer home in the wealthy residential area of Maisons-Laffitte, where the Fontanins also have a place. Antoine joins the family for dinner that evening, and Oscar Thibault takes his two sons aside and explains to

---

[61] *Ibid.*, p. 1,037. It certainly looks as though Martin du Gard believes stable relationships to be impossible, and T. W. Hall appears correct in stressing his pessimism in matters of love ("Roger Martin du Gard's Philosophy of Life as Viewed Through His Treatment of the Theme of Love," unpublished Ph.D. dissertation, University of Maryland, 1958).

[62] *O.C.*, I, 1,041.

them a project he has been formulating. He wants them to
sign papers and adopt the name Oscar-Thibault. His deep
emotion as he presents the plan is obvious; he does not want
his sons to be "confused with all the other Thibaults of
France." [63] Antoine, fresh from his victory over death and
his "conquest" of Rachel (it is unclear in the text who conquers whom), finds Oscar's proposal amusing. This reaction
distressed Jacques, who has "the impression that his brother
touched his heart with dirty hands." [64] Jacques usually avoids
judging his father, since his judgements are invariably negative, but this time he is "painfully struck" by the anguish
which shows through his father's "need for perpetuation."
He himself, despite his twenty years, is unable to "imagine
death without a sudden weakness." [65]

That same evening Antoine and Jacques make a visit to the
Fontanins' delightful summer home, and Jacques meets Jenny
again. The relationship between the two is at this time,
superficially at least, one of coldness and conflict.[66] Some
time later they meet at tennis, and their habitual discourtesy
to each other finally breaks down, after she defeats him
soundly. From then on the deep feelings they have actually

[63] *Ibid.*, p. 913.   [64] *Ibid.*, p. 914.   [65] *Ibid.*

[66] Martin du Gard has frequently been criticized for a lack of
ability to create lifelike women characters. Such criticism may in part
be due to a misunderstanding of his aims. In the case of Jenny, Martin
du Gard has created a definite psychological type: intelligent, in-
trospective, competitive, good at repartee with a tendency to be
cutting. She makes Jacques seem like an idiot (*ibid.*, p. 921). She also
has an aversion for physical contact; when her cousin Nicole tries to
embrace her, she cries out involuntarily, since "she could not tolerate
anyone's touching her" (*ibid.*, p. 922). She has never learned to dance.
I think that because of his own particular set of qualities, Jacques
would be attracted only toward such a person, who in many ways is
a reflection of himself, and who would exaggerate the narcissistic,
homosexual element present in any love.

had for each other come more and more to the surface.[67] They both like to believe that they are different from and misunderstood by others. Both have a thirst for purity, and they find a subject of common interest in Jenny's brother Daniel, whom they criticize for his immoral behavior. Both disapprove of Daniel's penchant for citing Walt Whitman, whom they find impure. They think simultaneously how much they resemble each other; [68] the element of narcissism is very strong in their love.

Eventually faced with the reality of Jacques's love when, with great timidity and delicacy, he makes a declaration, Jenny is torn by violently ambivalent feelings. She complains bitterly to her mother about the Thibault family, and in so doing reveals enough for her mother, always very perceptive, to comprehend the true state of her sentiments. Even while trying to comfort her daughter, Mme de Fontanin realizes with her habitual prescience that there is nothing she can do: "She saw spread out before Jenny her ineluctable destiny, and henceforth neither her fears nor her tenderness nor her prayers could tear her child from its grasp." [69]

This, however, is all that is seen of Jacques and Jenny in

[67] The themes of love and death are again intertwined. As Jacques and Jenny are walking, they see, in a brutally realistic scene reminiscent of the scene of the work horse in *Le Cahier gris*, a dog run over by a car. This leads the conversation to the subject of death (see *ibid.*, pp. 955–956).

[68] *Ibid.*, pp. 958–959. She: "How we resemble each other." He: "How she resembles me!" Cf. R. M. G., *L'Eté 1914*, *O.C.*, II, 322. When Jacques finds Jenny again, he tells her of his feeling for Gise, that he had wanted it to be pure, but that it is no longer pure and fraternal. He loves Jenny, however, "as a sister." The distance between incest and narcissism is not great. Cf. *ibid.*, II, 557, 573, for further hints of the incestuous aspect of the love affair between Jacques and Jenny. (They sleep together on Daniel's bed.)

[69] *La Belle Saison*, *O.C.*, I, 990–991.

La Belle Saison. We do not learn what happens to them with the arrival of autumn, as we do with Antoine. The volume ends with Antoine's return to Paris after having made his adieux to Rachel in Le Havre.

The jump from November 1910, and the Le Havre railroad station, to the Thibault house in Paris three years later is abrupt, though not necessarily unjustified artistically. Some critics have contended that Part IV of *Les Thibault*, *La Consultation*, has no real importance as far as the overall development of the novel is concerned. Others find this naturalistic "slice of life," in the form of a close description of fourteen hours of Antoine's working day, most relevant, and praise it as a marvel of realistic writing. While our primary concern is not with artistic value, a compromise view could be suggested; the volume is necessary to make many transitions and to fill in detail, though perhaps some of the scenes are extraneous to the development of the story, designed to permit the exercise of Martin du Gard's virtuosity. As the critic Henri Bidou puts it, Martin du Gard as successfully brings off such scenes as a great chef tosses off *crêpes*.[70]

It is only in this volume that a precise date is given— Monday, October 13, 1913—and one can work back and date the action of the previous volumes. Monday is the day Antoine holds doctor's hours, and each of the little vignettes of his conferences with patients shows him making an accurate and brilliant diagnosis and provides insights into the psychology of medicine. Antoine is now a busy and important doctor with his own practice, and he seems more personally involved in his cases than before. He had formerly tended to take a technical, experimental view of illness. What had mattered was the diagnosis and correct treatment of the malady,

---

[70] "Parmi les livres," *Revue de Paris*, September 1, 1928, p. 207.

84 *Roger Martin du Gard*

and the sufferings of the patient were irrelevant. Now the presence of pain always calls forth in him an "involuntary emotion."[71] He has developed an interest in nervous and mental disorders, and in general has a much greater sensitivity. These changes, like so many others, he attributes to the influence of Rachel.

Early in the day Antoine stops in to see his father, who is now very sick and does not have long to live. Antoine is playing the painful game of convincing his father that he is really feeling better. A nurse is trying to force the old man to eat, and Antoine is struck by the change in his father, by what has become of "that inflexible authority, against which his entire youth had clashed! Previously this despot would have thrown out the importunate nurse without explanation; today weakening, disarmed. . . . At such moments, the physical ravages appeared even more manifest than when Antoine measured under his fingers the decay of the bodily organs."[72] In *La Belle Saison*, Martin du Gard had already begun a gradual revision of the original negative portrait of Oscar Thibault. Now, under the pressure of pain and fear, Oscar's humanity comes more and more to the surface.[73]

At this time Antoine's *patron*, Dr. Philip, is introduced into the novel. Philip, one of the most favorably drawn of all Martin du Gard's characters, can be seen as the spokesman for the author's own views. He is in the grand tradition of medical figures in French literature, reminding one in particular of the great Dr. Larivière in *Madame Bovary*. Antoine

[71] *La Consultation* (© Editions Gallimard, 1928), in *O.C.*, I, 1,052. See pp. 1,106, 1,114 for further references to Antoine's growing compassion and humanity.

[72] *Ibid.*, p. 1,062.

[73] This is another example of the quality of justice in Martin du Gard, which has already been remarked upon in the discussion of this treatment of Jean Barois's devout wife.

and Philip go together to examine a patient, a small child who is in great pain, and whose case is clearly hopeless. Philip feels that Antoine is too honest and abrupt in his handling of the patient's family. Dr. Héquet, the child's father, is a colleague, a surgeon, who "must in effect *know* that there is no hope at all. But, as a father. . . . You see, the graver the hour is, the more one plays hide and seek with oneself." [74] Philip's words take on a tragically ironic meaning when, in *Epilogue*, he makes another diagnosis and Antoine is the patient; the reader cannot help but feel that at some level, conscious or unconscious, Martin du Gard was in these early volumes preparing for the change in his plan for the novel series which was not to take place until 1931. Remarks like these take on a richness of meaning which they would not have, if Antoine were to survive the war.

In *La Consultation*, among the patients Antoine treats during his office hours, is a character who provides an important link with the later volumes of *Les Thibault*. The diplomat Rumelles arrives in official garb directly after a luncheon at the Serbian embassy. During the dramatic weeks of July 1914, the ambitious but fundamentally weak Rumelles will be a source of information for Antoine and thus for the reader. Rumelles shows an "inoffensive mania" for predicting a general European war, speaking of this contingency as "the moment to show oneself *à la hauteur*." Antoine translates this ambiguous phrase, which could mean "to go to fight," as "to climb to power." [75] Despite himself, Antoine is interested by Rumelles's dire predictions, by his comments on the dangers of Austria's violent ambitions, which have up to the moment been checked by her ally Germany. Then, Rumelles points out, there is France's *politique cocardière*, which

[74] *O.C.*, I, 1,068 (italics his).   [75] *Ibid.*, p. 1,082.

threatens Germany through the secret alliance system and, as part of a vicious circle, forces Germany to strengthen her alliance with her one friend, Austria. Antoine is, however, quite skeptical, believing that specialists in foreign policy are always pessimistic, and he is anxious to *"pass finally to serious things"* [76]—that is, to the treatment of Rumelles's ailment.

As Antoine's day progresses, he comes face to face with an extremely important problem—that of euthanasia. When pressed to put a suffering child, who in any case will die within a day, out of its misery, Antoine refuses. But when he later thinks about the objections he gave to his friend Studler, who advised him to perform the act, he concludes that they were feeble. Deeply distressed over the altercation with his friend, since he always hates to be in a situation which cannot be immediately resolved, Antoine falls into a depression. He tries to analyze the problem in detail, though this goes against his usual habits: "Problems which a brief and violent effort at meditation did not suffice, if not to resolve, at least to clarify, always profoundly irritated him." [77] His behavior at the child's bedside now seems to go against his deepest nature, and he has the intuition that in the future he will act differently in a similar situation.

He ruminates on the question of moral law, which he repudiates, and then tries to determine on what grounds he has based his daily actions. It is undeniable that the complete liberty of action he claims for himself has actually been devoted to what others call "the Good," and he cannot find an explanation for his conduct. He senses something deep and strong within himself, rather like a natural law, which governs his behavior. But he has no precise idea of what this natural

[76] *Ibid.*, p. 1,084 (italics mine; I should like to give this phrase the strongest emphasis).
[77] *Ibid.*, p. 1,121.

law is and will not carry his thought any further, will not try
to answer the question which torments him at such moments:
"In the name of what?" [78] He breaks off his train of thought
and goes out to dine, able to think only of his hunger.

The reader has the distinct impression that Antoine will
not go more fully into the "In the name of what?" question
as long as he retains possession of his health, strength, and
natural optimism. He will always be able to break out of an
"embarrassing" situation, when metaphysical or personal
problems invade his consciousness, by wilfully thinking of
something else—whether it be his appetite or his next patient.[79]
The conclusion of *La Consultation* sustains this impression,
for by the end of the day Antoine has recovered from his
bad mood and reaffirms his love of life and his ability to rely
totally upon himself. "He recognized that, even without love,
life alone sufficed for his happiness." [80] Rather egotistically

[78] *Ibid.*, p. 1,126 (italics his). All his life Martin du Gard was
obsessed by the query, "In the name of what?" (*Au nom de quoi*).
There are many echos of this in his unpublished correspondence with
Félix Sartiaux. Sartiaux had argued that *"an independent morality* was
solidly justified, well before 1913." Martin du Gard disagreed, and in a
letter of November 11, 1928, claimed that there is nothing solid, that it
is all very slippery: *"There is no effective morality except when
founded on religious belief,"* and when morality based on religion is
gone, "there is nothing, absolutely *nothing solid,* to put in its place!"
(italics his). He was sure of the importance of this problem, for many
people had written him about the "In the name of what?" passage
when *La Consultation* was first published. Cf., also, an important note
in Gide's *Journal* for March 1, 1927, recording a long conversation on
the subject. Gide was afraid that Martin du Gard had lost his
objectivity and was dominated by his own character, Antoine
Thibault (*Journal, 1889–1939* [Paris: Gallimard, Bibliothèque de la
Pléiade, 1951], pp. 831–832).

[79] By thinking about a patient, Antoine escapes from his despair
over his unrequited love for Gise, whom he had hoped for a time to
marry (*La Consultation, O.C.,* I, 1,095–1,096).

[80] *Ibid.*, p. 1,129.

he summarizes his attributes; he is a man of thirty-two, in perfect physical condition, energetic, intelligent, wealthy: "In sum, everything. Neither weaknesses nor vices. Not a single barrier to his vocation!" [81]

La Consultation is devoted almost entirely to Antoine. However, Mlle de Waize, the old housekeeper, does mention in passing that Jacques has disappeared and is perhaps dead. Only Gise, impelled by her love, believes that Jacques is still alive and constantly expects him to re-appear. Ultimately it is not Gise but Antoine who discovers Jacques's whereabouts. The theme of *La Sorellina*, Part V of *Les Thibault*, is Antoine's successful search for Jacques and their return together to Paris, in order to be present at their father's bedside during his last moments.

La Sorellina opens with another sickroom scene; during the month and a half which separate this volume from *La Consultation*, Oscar Thibault has been steadily declining. His reason is giving way, and guilt feelings about his treatment of Jacques, about the period of the reformatory in particular, are coming to the surface. Oscar's semidelirious remarks about Jacques do not take on their full meaning until the story of his second flight is revealed. In severe pain, with only a short time to live, Oscar is now a completely pathetic figure, who has reverted to singing over and over again a nursery rhyme of his childhood. Antoine, using all the psychological skill he has gained in his medical practice, and by taking the risk of giving away the truth, is able to convince his father for the moment that the remedies are working and that he is on the way to recovery.

At this juncture Antoine, who is beginning to feel the strain of caring for his father, learns through a misaddressed

[81] *Ibid.*, p. 1,130.

letter that Jacques is alive. He traces the letter back to its sender and obtains a copy of a novella, *La Sorellina*, written by Jacques under a pseudonym. Through this ingenious method of indirect presentation of events, Antoine, and thus the reader, learn the details of Jacques's flight, the second of four he is to make.[82] Martin du Gard presents fragments of the text interspersed with Antoine's comments as he identifies figures in the novella as "real" people—himself, other members of the family, friends. Antoine is astonished that Jacques dared to be so cruel in his description of the character who is obviously his father. This vengeful attitude seems especially implacable to Antoine when he thinks of Oscar in his present state. The whole story of Jacques's dual love— for Annetta (Gise, whom he transforms into the hero's sister) and for the Protestant Sybil (Jenny)—is given in a slightly transposed form. Antoine now has enough clues to locate Jacques quickly, and a few days later he takes the train for Lausanne.

The scene of confrontation between the two brothers is powerfully drawn; Jacques, though obstinate and resentful, is susceptible to Antoine's plea and realizes that he has no choice but to give up the life he has built for himself and follow Antoine to Paris. He seems to have found a certain equilibrium at last; he is widely popular in Lausanne and, for his age, remarkably respected.[83] Antoine does not immediately understand that Jacques has become a member of an

---

[82] Even though he used only fragments in his published text, Martin du Gard took great pains with this novella, writing it from start to finish in a style which he imagined not his own, but that of an ardent youth. He was somewhat surprised when Gide told him that he was no good at magic tricks: *"One sees your hand, all the time!"* (R. M. G., *Souvenirs, O.C.,* I, xciii, italics his).

[83] Cf. *La Sorellina* (© Editions Gallimard, 1928), in *O.C.,* I, 1,218– 1,219.

international socialist group, but he does notice his maturity and the authority he has over his friends. This is a totally new image of Jacques, but Antoine accepts it as natural, for "he is a Thibault!" [84] On the train back to Paris, Jacques cannot help but respond to Antoine's affection. Yet at the same time he reacts against his own feeling: "He came to realize how rapidly, though against his will, he had become attached to his brother, to that lifetime friend; and, through his brother, to his entire past! Only yesterday there had been an insurmountable gap. . . . And half a day alone had sufficed." [85]

La Mort du père, following *La Sorellina*, was the last volume to appear before the seven-year gap (March, 1928–November, 1936) in the publication of the Thibault series. *La Mort du père* moves backward in time to the night Antoine left Paris to retrieve Jacques, and it returns to the scene of Oscar Thibault's mental and physical anguish. Though Martin du Gard has been constantly rounding out the portrait of Oscar, presenting more and more of his human qualities,[86] he does not spare him an ounce of suffering. This proud man, certainly the symbol of a social order, becomes almost monumental in his agony. As is usual with Martin du Gard, every physical detail of Oscar's last illness is presented with perfect clinical accuracy. In his review of *La Mort du père*, Paul

[84] *Ibid.*, p. 1,230.

[85] *Ibid.*, pp. 1,249–1,250. This kind of deep character analysis and study of family ties, at which Martin du Gard excelled, is a nineteenth-century element in his work. (See also n. 92 in this chapter.)

[86] When Antoine is pleading with Jacques to persuade him to return to Paris, he tells of how he had gone one day to Oscar's barber, whom he had never patronized just for that reason. He was surprised to learn that Oscar had always talked of his sons, especially of Jacques, and that he had made up a story about Jacques's flight, saying that he was studying abroad and writing home regularly. These and many other details, showing a side of Oscar's nature hitherto unknown, are now given (*ibid.*, pp. 1,208–1,210).

Souday felt that realism had made progress since *Madame Bovary;* Emma Bovary's death is nothing, compared to Oscar's: "I think that Monsieur Roger Martin du Gard has established a record." [87] Robert Kemp agreed that the descriptions are frightening in their precision, but he thought that Martin du Gard's art was of a superior quality, not a "base realism. . . . This work terrifies like a Goya." [88]

The first step is the penetration into Oscar's consciousness of his imminent death. He is transfixed with fear; in the absence of Antoine, the Abbé Vécard, Oscar's confessor, is sent for. Vécard, though the task of assisting *moribundi* is the one he most dreads, faces Oscar's terror with courage, subtlety, and determination, trying to make him pray and reminding him of Christ's suffering. Finally the Abbé is able to calm Oscar, and in his thanks to God is "blended a very human pride, the satisfaction of a lawyer who has won his case. Simultaneously he [becomes] conscious of this and [feels] remorse for it." [89]

The scene then switches to the return of Jacques and Antoine to Paris. With docility Jacques follows his older brother through the necessary procedures of taking breakfast, leaving the station, finding a taxi. In a remarkable passage Martin du Gard describes Jacques's reactions: "All these acts . . . seemed to him to follow one upon the other with a necessity which liberated him from all adhesion." [90] When they arrive at the family home on the Rue de l'Université, Jacques and Antoine find that their father's condition has seriously worsened. It is unclear whether Oscar, crazed with pain, ever recognizes Jacques. The struggle to keep him

[87] "Les Livres," *Le Temps*, April 11, 1928, p. 3.
[88] "Les Livres—*La Mort du père*," *La Liberté*, April 15, 1929, p. 2.
[89] *La Mort du père*, O.C., I, 1,259.
[90] *Ibid.*, p. 1,268.

alive continues; it is a dizzying, exhausting ordeal. Several times he nearly dies, but he somehow manages to survive each crisis with an "abnormal resistance," which only seems to prepare him for further tortures. After many sleepless hours, the people who are caring for Oscar reach a point of total exhaustion, and Antoine, seconded by Jacques, makes the decision to inject a fatal dose of morphine which will end their father's suffering. It is clear that the idea has been in Antoine's mind for some time, for he has the necessary syringe in his pocket. The two brothers arrange to be alone with their father, and the act is performed. The dead man takes on "the mysterious and theatrical aspect of a legendary person." [91]

Oscar's death sets a whole complex of social machinery in motion. Jacques refuses to participate in these activities, and makes plans to leave Paris once again. He first makes a sentimental pilgrimage to the Fontanin home, which he finds deserted, and later pays a solitary visit to his father's grave, after the official mourning party has departed. Antoine would like to dispense with the ritual of prayers, visits, and vigils, but must bow to the old housekeeper, who demands that all the proprieties be observed. When he has a free moment, Antoine goes over his father's papers, and only then does the full image of Oscar Thibault appear. His conservatism, his authoritarianism, his overweening pride, and at the same time a surprising sensitivity, show through in his notes and correspondence. Antoine realizes that there is always more depth to a human existence than one would suppose, and he regrets that he had always been a stranger to his father, that no communication had been possible between them.[92]

[91] *Ibid.*, p. 1,301.

[92] During the memorial service for his father, Antoine meditates upon his lack of comprehension, thinking to himself, "One never attains understanding of a man until after his death. . . . While he is

Oscar's funeral is at Crouy, in the chapel of the reformatory he had founded. There is much pomp and circumstance; colleagues and delegates of various philanthropic societies are present. Martin du Gard portrays a gallery of feeble, decaying old men, who surely symbolize a past generation.[93] One readily sees why leftist critics have been quick to praise this scene; as he looks about the chapel, Antoine remarks to himself:

And it's so true; they are all alike. Interchangeable. To describe one is to mark them all. Shivering, blinking myopic—they are afraid of everything; of thought, of social evolution, of all that poses a challenge to their fortress! . . . They really have the state of mind of people who are under siege, who continually count themselves to be sure that they are all present, behind their ramparts! [94]

While waiting for the train after the funeral, Antoine encounters the Abbé Vécard. A debate ensues which lasts all during the ride to Paris and until the end of the volume. The philosophical niceties of this confrontation between religion

---

still alive, all the things that he can accomplish, and which one ignores, constitute unknowns which falsify one's calculations. Death finally rounds off the contours; it's as if the personage detached himself from his possibilities and isolated himself. . . . One can finally see him from the back, one can make a judgement of the whole" (*ibid.*, p. 1,357). See n. 85 above.

[93] "He [Antoine] looked indulgently over the ranks of old, decrepit, shivering gentlemen, their eyes tearing with the cold, their noses humid, bending their best ear to hear, and punctuating the phrases with signs of approbation. Every one of them was thinking of his own burial, and was envious of these *témoignages de considération* which they were so generously dispensing upon their eminent deceased colleague" (*ibid.*, p. 1,360).

[94] *Ibid.*, pp. 1,360–1,361. See, for example, Georges Altman, "Les Livres: Histoires de familles bourgeoises," *L'Humanité*, April 29, 1929, p. 5.

and atheism are not important in the context of this study. It should be emphasized, however, that the Abbé's side is presented with great fairness. In his *Journal*, André Gide recorded that when Martin du Gard read the manuscript of *La Mort du père* to him, they were both a little disconcerted because the Abbé seemed to triumph. "Roger may well have put more of himself into Antoine than I ever did of myself into Edouard [*The Counterfeiters*]; he [still] allows, despite himself, and by a sort of professional honesty, the Abbé to have the advantage and to dominate the debate from a very high point." [95] Vécard has a genuine esteem for Antoine and cannot believe that he will remain an atheist. Antoine in turn —and he sounds here very much like Martin du Gard himself in his correspondence with Marcel Hébert—emphasizes that his is a case of natural, instinctive unbelief: "My atheism was formed at the same time as my intellect." [96] Vécard is unable to understand how Antoine can hold a purely materialistic doctrine, when his everyday existence as a doctor serving others emphatically denies the truth of such a doctrine. This point troubles Antoine, for he is once again brought up against the incompatibility between his lack of any moral belief, grounded in religious absolutes, and the extreme conscientiousness of his daily life: the question, "In the name of what?"—to which he has never found a satisfactory answer.

The final exchange in this debate is of real importance, both in its own right and because, in closing the volume, it also marks the close of an epoch which ends with the death of Oscar Thibault in December 1913. Antoine does not want to hurt the Abbé, whom he admires, by being too violent in his atheistic pronouncements, and he honestly admits the validity of the Abbé's point that the really difficult moment

[95] P. 879 (note of April 17, 1928).   [96] *O.C.*, I, 1,386.

will be the hour of his own death. As a doctor one of his tasks is to comfort the dying, and he has observed that unbelievers suffer most. He has often wished that he could give them a dose of faith, and has no mystical veneration for "stoicism of the last hour." The writer, one assumes, has in mind the death of Luce in *Jean Barois*. Martin du Gard, insofar as Antoine represents his views (and Gide, who should know, emphasizes that he does), seems to have moved toward a more complex and probably more human attitude toward death. Antoine tells Vécard that he is not ashamed of hoping for the "most consoling certitudes" and that he fears "equally an end without hope and an agony without morphine." [97]

The Abbé Vécard is deeply moved by Antoine's remark, and feels that it is a good sign. He makes a powerful plea for prayer, which Antoine must reject. Rather than cause the Abbé further pain, he remains silent until their parting, thinking to himself that there is an impenetrable barrier between them. The Abbé has the last word: "The Catholic religion, it's something entirely different; believe me, my friend, it is much, much more than you have ever been permitted, up to the present, to catch a glimpse of." [98]

In several senses the Abbé Vécard is right about his interlocutor, the Antoine of December 1913. To be sure, there is one important aspect of human experience which Antoine

[97] *Ibid.*, p. 1,393. Here is another striking example of "internal pressure" in these early volumes. Every indication leads us to believe that Martin du Gard was unaware of its existence when he wrote them. Yet if he had followed his original plan and permitted Antoine to survive the war, continuing a life which would be productive from a worldly standpoint but of necessity philosophically shallow, these words would not take on the prophetic quality they assume in the light of Antoine's own death in *Epilogue*.

[98] *Ibid.*, p. 1,394. (The French reads *entrevoir*.)

has known, and of which the Abbé must be ignorant. This is, of course, heterosexual love. The affair with Rachel has humanized Antoine and made him a less rigid and a more attractive person. From a philosophical viewpoint, Vécard is probably correct. Antoine has not arrived at any adequate formulation of the meaning and purpose of human existence. In an excellent article on *Les Thibault*, Pierre-Henri Simon closes his discussion of the dialogue between "the" free-thinker and "the" priest by pointing out Roger Martin du Gard's "*coquetterie* of impartiality"; he gives the final word to the Abbé. Simon emphasizes the *jusqu'ici*—up to the present moment—in Vécard's assertion. "Should we understand this to mean," Simon asks, "that one day Antoine will see more? *L'Eté 1914* and especially *Epilogue* will bring to [the Abbé's] ominous prophecy a predictable and probably preconceived denial." [99]

Preconceived? Perhaps. In any case, Roger Martin du Gard himself was to pass through a serious crisis and to make a drastic revision in the structure of his novel before he came to write *L'Eté 1914* and *Epilogue*. It may well be that one of the primary reasons for this change, to be discussed in the next chapter, is that the novel as originally planned would not have given Antoine his chance to reply.

[99] "Un Grand Roman de la famille: *Les Thibault*," *Pour la vie*, March 1955, p. 50.

CHAPTER IV

Attainment of Historical Consciousness:
The Break in Les Thibault

In a letter of September 11, 1927, Roger Martin du Gard writes to his friend Félix Sartiaux:

I too am working. To those who tell you that *Les Thibault* is bogged down, you can announce, for 1928, between Easter and November, four consecutive volumes:

Part IV. *La Consultation*
Part V. *La Sorella* [*sic*]
Part VI. *La Mort du père*
Part VII. *L'Appareillage*

Then, eighteen months later, two volumes on the war:

Part VIII. *Le Sinistre.*

And then finally we shall enter into the heart of the matter, for all this is nothing but a "*prologue*." [1]

Nowhere in his published work does Martin du Gard indicate so precisely how far he had progressed with his original plan for *Les Thibault*. It is also apparent in this letter that Martin du Gard has not yet changed his attitude toward the First World War. Just as when he was enthusiastically discussing postwar projects with Jacques Copeau, he views the war

[1] Unpublished; by permission of Mme Félix Sartiaux. (Italicized words are underlined in the original.)

as a "suspension," a "parenthesis." In the novel the war is to be dealt with as briefly as possible, and the "heart of the matter" will surely be the analysis in depth of individual character which Martin du Gard had indicated as his goal in his 1918 correspondence with Pierre Margaritis.[2]

Martin du Gard kept up with his schedule only with Parts IV and V. He was already behind with *La Mort du père*, which did not appear until March 1929, and the manuscript of *L'Appareillage* he later destroyed to make way for *L'Eté 1914*.

The years 1929 and 1930 were primarily devoted to the writing of *L'Appareillage*, which presumably dealt with "getting under way," the initiation of the characters into their new lives after Oscar Thibault's death. It is quite possible that Martin du Gard was already having misgivings about the progress and future development of *Les Thibault*, since he took time out in 1930 to write a novella.[3] *Confidence africaine* is recounted with such extraordinary realism and total objectivity that people refused to believe it entirely a product of Martin du Gard's imagination.[4] The story has been described as a "sort of masterpiece, of an almost absolute perfection."[5] Martin du Gard undoubtedly could have estab-

---

[2] Or perhaps the "serious things," the diagnosis and treatment of individual ailments, which preoccupied Antoine in *La Consultation*—to the detriment of an interest in politics and foreign affairs.

[3] Cf. Denis Boak, *Roger Martin du Gard* (Oxford: Clarendon Press, 1963), p. 126. Boak is the first writer to comment on this, and I believe he is quite justified in asserting that the state of mind which caused Martin du Gard to alter his plan "had its origins in 1930 if not before."

[4] R. M. G., *Souvenirs*, O.C., I, cxxv. *Confidence africaine* (© Editions Gallimard, 1930) is reprinted in *O.C.*, II, 1,105–1,127.

[5] R. L. [René Lalou], "Nouvelles," *Les Nouvelles littéraires*, August 8, 1931, p. 3. The calm tone of this tale of incest so charmed Lalou that he found it difficult to protest against the complete amorality, as far as ordinary social norms are concerned, of the actions described.

lished a reputation in this genre, had not *Confidence afri-caine* served mainly as a respite, a momentary relief from his major task, much as had *La Gonfle*, his second peasant farce (first written in 1922, revised and published in 1928).[6] He returned to *L'Appareillage*, and by the end of 1930 had completed a rough draft, with more than half the volume ready for the printers.

Late in the evening of January 1, 1931, while driving up the long roadway leading to Le Tertre, Roger Martin du Gard and his wife suffered severe injuries in an automobile accident. They were both taken to a hospital, where they remained until the middle of March. During these weeks of immobility, Martin du Gard had the leisure to meditate deeply on his work, and he began to have grave doubts about *L'Appareillage*. He realized that if he remained faithful to the original plan of *Les Thibault*, he would have to produce at least fifteen more volumes.

Certainly I did not feel myself incapable of doing this; I was not at all tired with my subject. . . . But, in musing upon my *Appareillage* with the objectivity which the silence and isolation of the hospital favored, I suddenly had the impression of having given in to complacency, of unconsciously slowing down the pace of my narrative. . . . In stretching out my novel immoderately, I risked not only tiring the reader, but also I might irremediably compromise that to which I attached great value: the unity and the equilibrium of the work.[7]

[6] Reprinted in *O.C.*, *II*, 1,165–1,237.

[7] *Souvenirs*, *O.C.*, *I*, xciv. Jean Schlumberger, however, argues that the long months in the hospital provided Martin du Gard with the leisure to contemplate "the fragility of the human condition. . . . He became afraid. . . . At the idea of all the volumes he would still add to the earlier ones, the convalescent felt overwhelmed; never would he have the force to raise up that mass" (Preface to R. M. G., *Les Thibault*, I [Paris: Imprimerie Nationale, 1960], 7). I believe that this sort of fear was not the real motivation and that Schlumberger is

He first tried a compromise, deleting large sections of *L'Appareillage*, but this rapidly appeared impractical. While enmeshed in these problems, he quite suddenly got the idea of writing a modern drama on the theme of homosexuality, which he composed while convalescing in the Midi during the summer of 1931. The play, *Un Taciturne*, was staged by Louis Jouvet and first performed at his Comédie des Champs-Elysées in October 1931. The critical reception was mixed, the dialogue was praised for its brilliance, as was the cast, which included Jouvet, Pierre Renoir, and Valentine Tessier. There were, however, objections, both on moral and on artistic grounds, to the theme and structure of the play.[8]

According to Martin du Gard's own admission, *Un Taciturne* was a *diversion*,[9] and he had already, more or less consciously, made a decision about *Les Thibault* when he left the hospital: "The only reasonable solution was to abandon the

---

reading literature into life. He may well have been thinking of Jean Barois's accident and have assumed that Martin du Gard's reactions would be the same as those of his fictional creation. It would appear that we can take Martin du Gard at his word, since ten years later he was to begin another gigantic novel, *Le Journal du Colonel de Maumort*. I would agree with Jacques Brenner: "We prefer to think that his architect's instinct warned him, and that it did not deceive him" (*Martin du Gard* [Paris: Gallimard, 1961], p. 68).

[8] Reprinted in *O.C.*, II, 1,259–1,353. Cf. René Lalou, "Le Théâtre," *Les Nouvelles littéraires*, October 31, 1931, p. 10, and Pierre Brisson, "Chronique théâtrale—*Un Taciturne*," *Le Temps*, November 2, 1931, p. 2. Paul Claudel was so furious about the play that, after reading Brisson's review, he wrote to Jouvet suggesting that the contract to produce *L'Annonce faite à Marie* be broken (see *Cahiers Paul Claudel 3* [Paris: Gallimard, 1961], p. 192). Quite naturally Gide was interested in the play, and commented on it frequently in his *Journal*. He thought that Claudel's violent dislike of Martin du Gard was really due to *Jean Barois*, rather than to *Un Taciturne* (*Journal, 1889–1939* [Paris: Gallimard, Bibliothèque de la Pléiade, 1951], pp. 1,095–1,096).

[9] *Souvenirs*, *O.C.*, I, xcv.

ending of *Les Thibault* as originally planned, and to graft *another dénouement* upon the trunk of the six parts already published, endeavoring to make the graft as invisible as possible." [10] From the manuscript of *L'Appareillage* he detached a few brief scenes which were to provide details for *L'Eté 1914*. The rest he threw into the fire.[11] After this striking gesture, which recalls the abandonment in his youth of *Une Vie de saint* and *Marise*, Martin du Gard took almost three years to recover his equilibrium and settle down once again to *Les Thibault*. By February 1932 his new plan at least was completed, as is indicated by a note in Gide's *Journal*.[12]

Before he began the actual composition of the new Part VII, *L'Eté 1914*, Martin du Gard allowed himself another interlude, and in the spring of 1932 wrote *Vieille France*. This work could be termed a long novella or a short novel. (It covers eighty-six pages in the Pléiade edition; among the shorter volumes of *Les Thibault*, *Le Cahier gris* takes up ninety-three pages and *La Consultation* eighty-three.) Created in a sort of euphoria, *Vieille France* was completed in two and one-half months, in a single *élan*, contrary to Martin du Gard's usual methods. It remained one of his favorite works, the only one among his books which he would consent to republish without making any changes.[13] *Vieille France*

[10] *Ibid.*, p. xcvi (italics his).

[11] Since a prospectus in earlier volumes of *Les Thibault* had announced its impending publication, the destruction of *L'Appareillage* was known or guessed at long before the publication of *Souvenirs*, which gives the full details. See René Lalou, *Roger Martin du Gard* (Paris: Gallimard, 1937), pp. 16–17.

[12] Pp. 1,112–1,113, note of February 9, 1932: "Immense joy to know that Roger is finally liberated from his *Thibault*—or at least resolved to reduce to two the number of volumes which remain to write." Gide goes on to comment favorably on the new plan.

[13] See Jean Schlumberger, "*Vieille France* et l'art," *N.N.R.F.*, December 1958, p. 1,068.

is an extremely powerful and controversial work, and at the
time of its writing Martin du Gard was as close to a Marxist
position as he was ever to come.

In addition, Martin du Gard had serious financial difficulties, which had to be dealt with before he could concentrate
upon the delicate and arduous task of grafting he had set
himself. With the suspension of the publication of *Les Thibault*, his funds were rapidly running out, and for a moment
he thought he would have to put together and publish a
number of short stories, the plans for which he had among
the "baggage" of his great quantities of notes. His friend
and publisher Gaston Gallimard, however, generously came
to his aid and offered him a regular monthly payment for an
indeterminate length of time, so that he would be free to
complete his great novel. Temporarily abandoning Le Tertre,
which was very expensive to maintain, Martin du Gard retired with his wife to the South of France, where he regained
his courage and set to work in earnest:

> But I did not really recover my peace of mind until the end of
> 1933 (in the little Mediterranean port of Cassis where we had
> taken refuge), when I finally had in front of me, spread out on
> the table of my hotel room, all the preparatory *fiches* for *L'Eté
> 1914* and the *Epilogue*. A new plan had been grafted onto the old
> trunk. I had only to follow it, and to compose my four final
> volumes.[14]

In his *Souvenirs* Roger Martin du Gard merely notes
briefly that the three volumes of *L'Eté 1914* appeared in
November 1936, and *Epilogue* in January 1940. Since Martin
du Gard's death in 1958 and the publication of excerpts from
his correspondence, we know that the completion of *Les*

[14] *Souvenirs*, *O.C.*, I, xcvii. For an account of Martin du Gard's
laborious and isolated existence during this period see Carlo Rim,
Mémoires d'une vieille vague (Paris: Gallimard, 1961), pp. 42–44.

Thibault was not quite so simple, that his troubles did not end with the completion of the preliminary *fiches*, that he had grave misgivings about the whole project, misgivings which continued until shortly before the publication of *L'Eté 1914*. In October 1933, for example, when he should have been—according to his *Souvenirs*—making an enthusiastic beginning, he writes:

> I am cruelly entangled. This ending of *Les Thibault* is definitely becoming an exquisite torment, a trap imprudently held open in the past, and which has closed down upon me. I do not know yet from what point I am going to pick this all up. The enthusiasm is no longer there. . . .
>
> What I really need is to find once again that good devil which inspired me when I was writing the scenes of the Dreyfus Affair in *Jean Barois*. And this would be the same as running after one's youth!
>
> How much more simple it would be to live without submitting oneself to that secret imperative which forces us to be faithful to ourselves, or at least to seem to be so! [15]

Martin du Gard's doubts are due to a new orientation in *Les Thibault*, one which almost seems to have been imposed upon him against his will: a focus on historical events and ideological conflicts. In these areas he felt himself incompetent; he did not have at his fingertips the kind of documentation that he had amassed for the treatment of the Dreyfus Affair in *Jean Barois*. He had written to Pierre Margaritis that *Jean Barois* was the result of three years of continous writing and of ten years of daily note-taking, of carefully cutting out articles and filing them in special folders.[16]

[15] Letter to Jean Schlumberger, quoted in his "Roger Martin du Gard," *Livres de France*, January 1960, p. 11.

[16] R. M. G., "Consultation littéraire: Lettres à Pierre Margaritis," *N.N.R.F.*, December 1958, p. 1,126 (letter of February 6, 1918).

Lacking such preparation for writing in detail about the summer of 1914, he was forced to seek outside assistance. He submitted the manuscript of *L'Été 1914* to an expert, Marcel Lallemand. Lallemand criticized it quite severely for historical inaccuracies, in particular for an inadequate discussion of international socialism on the eve of the First World War, and for an implausible presentation of the positions taken by the socialist characters when confronted with the danger of war. Several of Martin du Gard's letters to Lallemand were published in the memorial edition of the *N.N.R.F.*, and they show that at moments Martin du Gard was close to despair. He wrote in August 1935: "You bring me the support of a competence which I do not have, alas! and the lack of which I have often felt, to the point of real distress, to the point of asking myself if I have the right to persevere in this insane wager. . . ." [17] He had a strong sense of being constantly on dangerous ground:

[17] R. M. G., "Lettres à un ami," *N.N.R.F.*, December 1958, p. 1,137 (letter of August 29, 1935). The French reads "folle gageure." In another letter he spoke of his "folle entreprise" (*ibid.*, p. 1,140). It is very curious that many years before they could have known of this correspondence, a number of critics were using the same terms as Martin du Gard in describing *L'Été 1914*. Some, such as C.-E. Magny, argued that he failed in his *gageure*, others, such as François de Roux, that he carried it off. André Thérive speaks of Martin du Gard's new *gageure*, and he is not certain whether Martin du Gard has really won it. The didactic tone in *L'Été 1914* bothers Thérive, and only Martin du Gard's "immense talent," he thinks, prevents the novel from becoming a second-rate humanitarian apologia ("Les Livres," *Le Temps*, January 7, 1937, p. 3). Pierre Loewel finds the historical parts of the novel a failure. *L'Été 1914* "violently unbalances the rest of *Les Thibault*." Yet when Martin du Gard describes a troop retreat, his pages "approach perfection." This is because "once liberated from his insane task [*folle tâche*], once he returns to his Thibaults, the talent of the author regains its plenitude" ("La Vie littéraire," *L'Ordre*, December 21, 1936, p. 2).

I have never, nor so painfully, felt my limits as much as I have for the three years that I have been working on the completion of *Les Thibault*. And if I am so impatient to be done with it all and to be able to deal with subjects more purely psychological, it is not, I think, out of cowardice, but because the wise policy, at my age, is to cultivate *one's own* field and to take from it the largest possible harvest, rather than constantly confronting one's own limitations in always trying to surpass them.[18]

During another period of discouragement, as the self-imposed deadline for submitting the manuscript of *L'Eté 1914* to the patient and generous Gaston Gallimard drew near, Martin du Gard wrote:

What impresses me so strongly is that all your criticisms bear exactly upon those points in which I am incompetent, where I had thought that I had camouflaged my incompetence as well as possible. So I don't see any escape. I am treating a subject of which I understand nothing, of which I shall never understand anything, unless I were to relive a second incarnation in the skin of a revolutionary. *There is no repairing the situation. . . .* My work is vain: a failure from the origin, from the beginning.[19]

There is good evidence that Martin du Gard did not give up his effort to repair the situation and that he went beyond his researches in libraries, his extensive study of contemporary newspapers, his anxious questions penned off to Marcel Lallemand, and actually frequented gatherings of young Socialist workers, coming away with a favorable impression.[20]

----

[18] "Lettres à un ami," p. 1,138 (italics his). The sense of determinism in these passages is quite striking. Martin du Gard wants all along to create psychologically oriented works, but is prevented from doing so by factors which one would assume to be external and beyond his control.

[19] *Ibid.*, p. 1,142, letter of May 16, 1936 (italics his).

[20] R. M. G., "Lettres à l'architecte," *Cahiers du Sud*, January 1959, p. 344 (letter of February 28, 1940, to F. M., whom I have definitely

It must also be emphasized that Martin du Gard never doubted his literary ability. "It seems to me that, up to the present, none of them," he writes of Lallemand's criticisms, "go against my aims as a novelist, against my characters." [21] It was his lack of technical historical competence which so upset him. The difficulty of his "insane wager" lay in his effort to integrate his characters into history: "No one will ever know the trouble to which I have gone to weave together all these threads—French political life, European political life, and the personal lives of my characters." [22]

Somehow Martin du Gard completed *L'Eté 1914*, getting it into a form which he felt suitable for publication. He must have been at least partially satisfied that with the aid of Marcel Lallemand he had been able to attribute plausible political attitudes to the various characters. In 1937 he won the Nobel Prize for *L'Eté 1914*.

At this juncture, several questions must be considered. How successful was Martin du Gard in pulling together *Les Thibault*? How much of the grafting process shows through? Martin du Gard, admittedly, had to discard or pass over lightly a number of characters whom he had introduced in earlier volumes with the intention of treating them in detail later on. How damaging is this to the unity of *Les Thibault* as a whole?

On the other hand, what is our evaluation of *L'Eté 1914* and *Epilogue* as separate volumes? For the moment, suffice it

---

identified as Florent Margaritis, the son of Martin du Gard's friend Pierre Margaritis, to whom *Les Thibault* is dedicated). Martin du Gard here indicates his preference for the young socialists he has met over F. M.'s colleagues at the Ecole des Beaux-Arts.

[21] "Lettres à un ami," p. 1,137 (letter of August 29, 1935).
[22] *Ibid.*, p. 1,140 (letter of January 18, 1936).

to say that critics have been sharply divided; writers with a leftist political orientation have tended to be favorable to *L'Eté 1914*, rightest commentators to be more negative. Howard C. Rice's remark, made in 1941, appears valid today: "These final volumes belong as much to history as to literature, and much of the praise or blame bestowed upon them has inevitably been based on the critics' political prepossessions." [23] A preliminary conclusion which emerges from a study of the critical writing is that it is necessary to make a choice between the first six and the last two parts of *Les Thibault*. The difference is so great, the change in conception so profound, that the critics have felt compelled to favor one group of volumes or the other. That a cleavage in the novel exists no one denies, even those who emphasize the "preparations" in the earlier volumes—such as the appearance of the diplomat Rumelles—for the treatment of the First World War.

In the remainder of this chapter a theoretical position which is as far as possible from an aesthetic judgement will be developed. It can be demonstrated, with a fair degree of certainty, that the attainment of historical consciousness [24]

---

[23] *Roger Martin du Gard and the World of the Thibaults—A Biographical and Critical Estimate* (New York: Viking Press, 1941), p. 20.

[24] The term "historical consciousness" was, to my knowledge, first used with a meaning approximating the one I attribute to it by Pierre-Henri Simon in his *L'Esprit et l'histoire—Essai sur la conscience historique dans la littérature du XXe siècle* (Paris: Armand Colin, 1954). See especially pp. 17–18, where Simon points out that the concept "l'être-dans-l'histoire" has tended to become the consciousness of the twentieth century, and that historical events have speeded up this "conversion of the spirit to time." In a period of tranquility, men naturally repose "in the illusion of escape from the ravages of time and care less about their own history." Men can have a permanent, solid conception of the universe, and can be humanists, classicists, like the

literally forced Roger Martin du Gard to make the change
in the novel. Thus the reader does not necessarily have to
make up his mind. The two segments of the novel are equally
valid given their context, and the element of choice enters
only if one feels that one must decide about the artistic validity of integrating history and ideology into the novel. This
writer's personal view is that such an integration is within
the bounds of art, but this must remain a subjective opinion.
An objective statement about the inevitability of the break in
Les Thibault can be made, however, and in the process new
insights into the subtle and complex relationships between
history and literature will come to light. In fact, one could
argue that, paradoxically, the real reasons why critics find
Martin du Gard's novels such a reliable source for the summer of 1914 is because he himself is a very interesting source
for the between-the-wars period.[25]

Régis Michaud made a shrewd guess when he wrote in
1938: "The pressure of political and social events around

---

narrator of Thomas Mann's *Doctor Faustus,* who feels so out of place
in his epoch and longs for such stability. Those who still possess it can
be proud "of a continuity of the human, can scrutinize the past to find
rules and examples, can await with serenity a future which will not
dissipate their acquired wealth." Cf. Jean-Paul Sartre's statement in
Situations, II (Paris: Gallimard, 1948), 242, that about 1930 "the
majority of Frenchmen discovered with stupor their historicity."
Sartre comments on the earlier optimism, which disappeared as the
term *entre-deux-guerres* became common, and continues: "Our life as
individuals, which had seemed to depend on our efforts, on our virtues
and our faults, on our good luck and our bad, on the good or evil
wishes of a very small number of persons; now [our life] seemed to
be governed, even in its smallest details, by obscure and collective
forces, and the most private circumstances reflected the state of the
entire world. Quite suddenly and uncomfortably we felt ourselves
situated [*situés*]" (italics his).

[25] See the discussion of the novel's claim to suprahistoricity in
Chapter I.

1930 very likely had something to do with the new turn of his [Martin du Gard's] novels." [26] In Chapter III, Martin du Gard's attitude toward the First World War during and immediately after the conflict was discussed. By 1930 he could no longer view it as a suspension, a parenthesis, for the European situation had become too ominous. The facts are widely known and need not be repeated here. It was becoming ever more apparent that the return to peace and stability which Martin du Gard had hoped for so strongly was not going to be realized, that the First World War was not the war to end all wars, but rather an introduction to further conflict.

One could describe this change in Martin du Gard as a complex dialectical process. The thesis would be the original plan of *Les Thibault,* and, concurrently, Martin du Gard's fundamental predisposition against any sort of political commitment. The antithesis would be of a dual nature—both the internal pressure existing in the earlier volumes (which has been noted on several occasions, the most striking example being the debate between Antoine Thibault and the Abbé Vécard) and the pressure exerted by external events. The synthesis would then become Martin du Gard's attainment of historical consciousness and its dual result—the conclusion of *Les Thibault* as he ultimately decided it, and his own political and social involvement.

In later years Martin du Gard seems to have forgotten the hope he had expressed in his correspondence with Pierre Margaritis of writing a novel of purely psychological analysis, his optimism of the 1920's, when he outlined *Les Thibault* as far ahead as 1935, and his impatience in 1927 to be done with the volumes on the war period and to get to the "heart of the matter." In a letter of March 5, 1954, to an American

[26] "Roger Martin du Gard," *Books Abroad,* Spring 1938, p. 150.

scholar who had defended the change of plan in *Les Thi-bault*,[27] Martin du Gard sounds a good deal like the Thomas Mann of 1924, the Mann of the Preface to *The Magic Mountain*. He does not admit that he once thought otherwise, that it took the pressure of historical events at the end of the 1920's to bring him to an awareness of the necessity to alter the structure of a novel series which thus far had not gone beyond December 1913. Martin du Gard asserts, referring to criticism by Mme C.-E. Magny, who has written one of the most interesting studies of *Les Thibault*, in which she is quite unfavorable toward the later volumes:

There is truth in what she says when she points out a certain change of tone in *Les Thibault*, beginning with *L'Eté 1914*. My excuse is that this change in tone reflects a historical truth. The intrusion of the 1914 war upon European society brutally shook up all values, created a new and dramatic climate, in which political events cast individual destinies into the shadows. To the extent that *Les Thibault* has a documentary interest and constitutes the history of a particular epoch, the later volumes express very faithfully the disorder brought about by the war.[28]

[27] The article in question is Thomas White Hall's "A Note on the So-Called 'Change in Technique' in *Les Thibault* of Roger Martin du Gard," *French Review*, December 1953, pp. 108–113.

[28] Quoted, with permission of Thomas White Hall, from an appendix to his "Roger Martin du Gard's Philosophy of Life as Viewed Through His Treatment of the Theme of Love" (unpublished Ph.D. dissertation, University of Maryland, 1958). Mme Magny's chapter on *Les Thibault* is in her *Histoire du roman français depuis 1918*, I (Paris: Editions du Seuil, 1950), 302–350. Cf. in particular p. 311, on the "feeble continuity" between the first six parts and *L'Eté 1914*. Her preference is for the earlier volumes; the work is "sliced into two parts" (p. 312) and in her opinion even Martin du Gard's "considerable skill" cannot control the "perpetual oscillation" between international events and individual destinies (p. 316).

By examining a number of documents, including unpublished correspondence and review articles, we can reconstruct
the process, in our view dialectical, which brought about
Martin du Gard's new estimate of the significance of the
First World War and the role it would have to play in his
novel. It is striking that, when they could not possibly have
had the slightest idea of what the original plan for the later
volumes was, the critics were growing aware of a need to
change *Les Thibault*. As early as 1922, when only the first
two parts had appeared, Benjamin Crémieux made the criticism that the novel is not dated; the reader does not know
whether the action takes place before or after the war.
"A cyclical novel of this sort cannot be valid today unless it
has the war (I mean by this: 'private life' during or since the
war) as a basis." [29] With his usual perceptivity, Paul Souday
of *Le Temps* remarked in his review of *La Belle Saison* (1923)
that in *Les Thibault* Martin du Gard had up to the present
seemed more interested in persons than in ideas. Souday won-
dered if "a very philosophical conclusion" would be reserved
for the reader.[30]

In 1960, Louis Martin-Chauffier authorized the publication
of a letter which Martin du Gard had sent him in December
1926. It is surprising to discover that Martin du Gard was
already entertaining serious doubts about the progress and
future of *Les Thibault:*

For weeks on end, the difficulty of my task appeared *insurmountable* to me. Observe that at the point of development at
which my characters now find themselves, it is absolutely
necessary that I go deeper; otherwise my enterprise is nul. I have

---

[29] "*Les Thibault, I—Le Cahier gris,* par Roger Martin du Gard,"
N.R.F., June 1, 1922, p. 755.
[30] "Les Livres," *Le Temps,* November 22, 1923, p. 3.

gone beyond the point at which an author usually closes his exhibition and presents new puppets. In my case, I must keep them on the scene, and penetrate ever further into their psychology: it's a question of life or death. . . . I must dig deeper. I have a terrible fear that I won't be able to do it, and, for the first time in my life, I am not finding joy in my work.[31]

One of the ways to reach for new depth in his characters would be for Martin du Gard to bring them face to face with history, and I think that in the years 1926 to 1931 he was coming more and more to this realization. The method he had described in his 1918 letters to Pierre Margaritis no longer seemed valid. Martin du Gard may even have sensed this himself in reading over later volumes (*La Consultation, La Sorellina, La Mort du père*). In any case, the critic Henri Bidou thought he discerned an increasing level of tension in *La Consultation* and *La Sorellina* in 1928, before *La Mort du père* appeared, and eight years before the publication of *L'Eté 1914*.[32]

By 1930 Martin du Gard must have been becoming ever more aware of the irremediable break created by the 1914 war and of his own more or less conscious preparation for it as his novel series progressed. He was witnessing "the complete disintegration of the whole of pre-1914 Europe. To illustrate this is one of the main aims of *L'Eté 1914* and *Epilogue*." [33] Thus the new orientation in the narrative. Whether this change in orientation was an error—aesthetic, psychological or otherwise—is a question which must ultimately be answered subjectively.

What should be emphasized is the degree to which Martin du Gard was forced by historical developments to make his

---

[31] "Lettre inédite," *Livres de France*, January 1960, p. 8 (italics his).
[32] "Parmi les livres," *La Revue de Paris*, September 1, 1928, p. 207.
[33] Boak, *Roger Martin du Gard*, p. 129.

decision. J.-B. Severac reviewed *La Consultation* and *La Sorellina*, and pointed out that these two volumes carry the
action up to the eve of the war. Severac asks, "Is it to be in this
great event that the conflicts which he has chronicled will
find their resolution? This is probable." [34] In reviewing the
same volumes for *L'Opinion*, André Thérive reminded his
readers that these volumes take us up to November 1913.
"The odds are that the war will change or kill several of the
characters, and that in any case a new century will open for
this family as was the case for Europe." [35] In another review,
Thérive added that he believed he could already distinguish,
in *La Consultation* and *La Sorellina*, which trace Antoine's
maturation process, "the history of a *generation*, which is
pursued with constancy through a hundred episodes, in appearance disconnected, which life takes upon itself to assem-
ble, to unify." [36] It may well be that in the earlier volumes of
Les Thibault, the historical period Martin du Gard was analyzing permitted him to employ a psychological method and
still attempt a treatment *en roman somme* of what he thought
significant in the epoch under consideration. Now a historical
method becomes necessary, if he is to maintain the level of his
endeavor, if he is to remain faithful to that secret interior
imperative of which he had complained in his October 1933
letter to Jean Schlumberger.

I would argue that historical change in the twentieth century both forced Martin du Gard, as a conscientious novelist,
to alter the tone of *Les Thibault* and provided him with new

---

[34] "*Les Thibault* IVᵐᵉ et Vᵐᵉ Parties," *Le Populaire*, June 27, 1928,
p. 4.
[35] "Littérature—La suite des *Thibault*," *L'Opinion*, June 23, 1928,
p. 9.
[36] "*Les Thibault*, par Roger Martin du Gard: (IV) *La Consultation*,
(V) *La Sorellina*," N.R.F., July 1, 1928, p. 126 (italics mine).

material which made it possible for his work to attain a new grandeur and relevance. Benjamin Crémieux, in his review of *La Mort du père*, is quite certain that with Oscar Thibault's death the first part of the Thibault cycle has drawn to a close. Yet the other characters are "in the prime of life and the work itself is in a state of rapid expansion. One senses in it a *latent grandeur*." [37] Crémieux is impatient to see the final results and to be able to measure this potential greatness. He wonders whether *Les Thibault* will end powerfully, but only realistically,[38] or whether the novel will conclude by giving us "the sentiment of destiny." For *Les Thibault* to become a truly great novel, Crémieux feels, the reader must be able to identify with the leading characters, to find in them "the image of our destiny, real or possible." [39] I suggest that for this identification to continue, in the minds of readers experiencing the Europe of the 1930's, the expansion of *Les Thibault* to encompass a world vision was absolutely necessary and inevitable. We have seen how critics were calling for such a change when they could not have known what Martin du Gard's original intentions were. Even if his accident had not provided Martin du Gard with the leisure to meditate on the desirability of continuing on his course and publishing *L'Appareillage*, it seems quite certain that he would eventually have come to the decision to revise his plan for *Les Thibault*.

[37] "*La Mort du père*, par Roger Martin du Gard," *N.R.F.*, July 1, 1929, p. 261 (italics mine).

[38] Realism in the sense of nineteenth-century bourgeois naturalist realism.

[39] *Ibid.*, p. 262. (This does not, of course, imply that Crémieux would be entirely satisfied with *L'Eté 1914*. To my knowledge, he never reviewed the work, perhaps because the increasing pressure of his duties at the Quai d'Orsay, where he served as a high functionary, prevented him from devoting attention to literary criticism.) Cf. the discussion of identification in Chapter I.

Martin du Gard's doubts and hesitations, which can be traced back as far as 1926, his need for *diversion*, witnessed by the writing of *Confidence africaine*, and the evolution of the European situation in the late 1920's—all support the contention that he could not escape the attainment of historical consciousness.

Martin du Gard, who admitted his bourgeois heritage and struggled against it all his life, while realizing that he could never overcome it,[40] was not sure that he would be able to deal effectively with the changing political and social situation. In June 1931, he told Félix Sartiaux: "The future seems to me to be laden with catastrophic events. Our fifth decade will without a doubt permit us to witness the beginnings of a vast European social disorder. What will remain then of our few books? How will we adapt ourselves, with our cumbersome baggage, to that new order, of which we shall undoubtedly experience only the initial disorder?"[41]

Martin du Gard had to come to terms with the facts that individual destinies had been submerged by historical actuality, and that, to all appearances, this state of affairs, which

[40] Cf. R. M. G., "Lettres à un ami," p. 1,152, letter of July 8, 1937: "I think you are completely correct in emphasizing how many of my qualities are due to my bourgeois origins. One cannot change his skin, and it's the beginning of wisdom to accept oneself as a given, and to move ahead from there. All my life I have *struggled against*, and at the same time, *made my peace with*, these elements" (italics his). Pierre-Henri Simon states in more universal terms the problem facing Martin du Gard (*L'Esprit et l'histoire*, p. 23): Western man in the early years of the twentieth century "lost the experience and the sense of history." He possesses no general vision. The bourgeois of this epoch knows about history; "he does not feel himself *in* history. It took, to reawaken him, the tocsin and the cannon of August 1914" (italics mine).

[41] Unpublished letter of June 22, 1931; by permission of Mme F. Sartiaux.

he had once believed to be a momentary and tragic deviation, had become permanent.

In *L'Eté 1914* all the major characters cease to be private persons, because their creator has understood that "le temps du privé est fini." [42] With *L'Eté 1914* the personal tragedies of the earlier volumes of *Les Thibault* are overwhelmed by the tragedy of an entire society, "which will finish by engulfing even those who seemed to us to be the least tragic, such as Daniel de Fontanin. . . . Tragedy is no longer for those who seem *predestined* for it, like Jacques and Jenny [and Jean Barois], not even for those who seem most able to refuse it, to escape from its grasp, like Antoine. It is exterior, in the world." [43] It is only now that, to use Clément Borgal's term,

---

[42] Paul Nizan, "Roger Martin du Gard: *Eté 1914*," *N.R.F.*, January 1, 1937, p. 96. Nizan does not believe that great novels of the future can be novels of "private life": "Since 1914, every life is public. . . . Private adventures, which are no longer anything but evasions, seem of a rather low quality. . . . No one escapes the world any more; private life has ceased to be possible, as has the private thought which measures the world by a single man."

[43] Pierre Daix, *Réflexions sur la méthode de Roger Martin du Gard* (Paris: Les éditeurs français réunis, 1957), pp. 18–19. Both Daix and Nizan (see n. 42 above) believe that Martin du Gard succeeds artistically in portraying this transition. It is most significant that Gaëtan Picon, who asserts very strongly that the earlier volumes are superior to *L'Eté 1914*, comes to almost exactly the same conclusions concerning Martin du Gard's aims: In *L'Eté 1914* there is "the apparition of a new world which his technique cannot translate [into art], because his spirit really refuses to accept it. The history of a few individuals possessing in themselves the law of their development and situated in a society whose relative stability makes témoignage possible, gives way to History—whose becoming, whose uncertainty, prevents the total and closed perspective of tradition. Then it is the end for inventories, destinies, analyses; now begins an obscure movement, of which one can give only an immediate image" ("Roger Martin du Gard," *Paragone*, December 1958, p. 82; Picon's capitalization).

time becomes "concretised": "What was, up to this moment, only life, becomes suddenly transformed into destiny." [44]

[44] "A la Recherche du temps," *N.N.R.F.*, December 1958, p. 1,093. It is of course a valid critical stance to argue that life is the only proper concern for the novelist, that when he gets involved with destiny he becomes a polemicist, a historian, or something else.

CHAPTER V

The Conclusion of Les Thibault

Roger Martin du Gard was the first major French writer of his generation to begin a *roman-fleuve* (the first volumes of Jules Romain's *Les Hommes de bonne volonté* did not appear until 1932, ten years after the publication of *Le Cahier gris*). The success of the early volumes of *Les Thibault* must have served as an encouragement to other writers in the 1930's, who made the genre a very popular one indeed. However, there is great disparity of aim and method between these writers and Martin du Gard.[1]

The contrast between *Les Thibault* and *Les Hauts Ponts* (1932–1935) is striking. The action in Jacques de Lacretelle's four-volume novel series takes place almost entirely in the

---

[1] Marcel Proust died in 1922, the same year that *Le Cahier gris* was published. See Chapter II for a discussion of the relationships between his great novel and the Dreyfus Affair. The same conclusions appear valid for Proust's briefer treatment of the First World War in the last two volumes of his novel. The important passage in which Proust discusses the function of the novelist rules out both the Dreyfus Affair and the First World War as legitimate concerns for the artist. Proust's *optique* remains the same; the reader sees the war only from the point of view of the upper segment of society. The immense struggle going on around them does not affect the *invertis*, who play such an important role in Proust's novel, in their busy search for pleasure. See especially Vol. XIV of *A La Recherche du temps perdu, Le Temps retrouvé*, I (Paris: Gallimard, 1927), 42, 61, 91, 97, 170–171.

Vendée, in a conservative and aristocratic milieu profoundly disassociated from historical change and the external world. The novel is not precisely dated, and there are apparent inconsistencies between historical dates, when given, and ages of the different characters. It can be estimated that the action covers the period from 1872 to 1921. The novel is not without interest as a psychological document and as an acute and unsparing analysis of provincial life, particularly of the overwhelming desire to own property and to maintain family continuity and status. In one of the novel's rare references to an actual historical event, Jean de la Fontange, a major character in the earlier volumes, goes on a May day in 1873 to visit Les Hauts Ponts, the chateau belonging to his neighbor Alexandre Darembert. He says he is coming with an important piece of political news; the Duc de Broglie has become Prime Minister after the ousting of Thiers from the presidency. Fontange knows that this development will be welcomed as a hopeful sign by the many royalists in the area. In reality, however, he is using this item of news as a convenient *prétexte* to spend some time with his neighbor's wife Sabine.[2] The reader has the distinct impression that any other detail of current interest would have served Fontange's amorous purposes equally well. This is the extent to which the external world impinges upon the closed existences of Lacretelle's characters.

Both in size and scope Georges Duhamel's ten-volume *La Chronique des Pasquier* (1933–1945) merits comparison with *Les Thibault*.[3] In the Preface to the first volume the narrator, Laurent Pasquier, asserts that the long work he plans will be

---

[2] Jacques de Lacretelle, *Les Hauts Ponts*, I: *Sabine* (Paris; Gallimard, 1932), 77–79.

[3] For the *rapport* between Martin du Gard and Duhamel, see especially R. M. G., *Souvenirs*, *O.C.*, I, lxxiv–lxxxv.

no more than personal *mémoires* and will have "no historical character and even no historical interest if the thoughts, works, and adventures of a simple citizen lost in the crowd are really lacking in historical interest." [4] Though the Pasquier family is a tightly knit clan, and though the narrator almost always turns his attention toward his family, he does remark in the second volume that the Pasquier world is not "so closed that one never sensed there the splendors, the influences, the uproar of the universe." [5]

Discussions of historical events do appear in the work from time to time, despite the *anti-politique* [6] attitude of the father, Raymond Pasquier. The narrator recalls conversations on such topics as colonialism, strikes, the death of Bismark, but the details blend in with family affairs in a confusing sort of "surimpression." [7] In determining whether Duhamel's novel is of any relevance to our conerns, the acid test would be what happens when the characters are confronted with the First World War. In Volume VIII, *Le Combat contre les ombres,* the action is carried down to the summer of 1914. Laurent Pasquier, who was born in 1881, the same year as Antoine Thibault and Roger Martin du Gard, is now an important young scientist. During the summer of 1914 he is involved in a series of personal crises related to both his career and his emotional life. The significant fact is that these crises are resolved before the outbreak of war, that they are totally removed from any historical context. Laurent Pasquier has already resigned from his research position and made the decision to marry; he is quite surprised when his

[4] Georges Duhamel, *La Chronique des Pasquier,* I: *Le Notaire du Havre* (Paris: Mercure de France, 1933), 32.

[5] II: *Le Jardin des bêtes sauvages* (Paris: Mercure de France, 1934), p. 61.

[6] *Ibid.*   [7] *Ibid.,* p. 62.

fiancée tells him that they must hurry with their plans, for war is threatening. "War? What war? Ah, yes, I think, it seems to me that I've heard people talking about a war. Why a war?"[8] Only now as various members of the Pasquier family prepare to go off to the armies, does the war become an issue to be dealt with.

The narrative skips over the war years entirely and resumes in 1921, in Volume IX, *Suzanne et les jeunes hommes*. Duhamel is now concentrating on an entirely new set of problems centering on the personal life and theatrical career of Suzanne Pasquier, the youngest member of the family. It is only through a casual reference early in the volume that the reader becomes aware that the war has ended: one of Suzanne's fellow actors was wounded in 1917 and now has a stiff right hand.[9] The director of her company, Eric Vidame, who seems in part to be modeled after Jacques Copeau, lives in a closed world and is interested only in "actors, authors, and the public."[10] Even though there are gaps in his little troupe, even though several of the survivors suffer from war wounds, the war is a forbidden topic in Vidame's presence. For him it is merely a shadow to be disregarded, since his real world is the theatre.[11] For Duhamel the significant world is obviously that of the Pasquier family, and he must have felt that it was not within his province as a novelist to integrate that world, more than superficially, with historical actuality. Thus in his *roman-fleuve* Duhamel passes over the interlude of the war and makes a fresh beginning. This markedly

---

[8] VIII: *Le Combat contre les ombres* (Paris: Mercure de France, 1940), 286. Cf. p. 278 for further reference to Laurent's complete ignorance.

[9] IX: *Suzanne et les jeunes hommes* (Paris: Mercure de France, 1941), 10.

[10] *Ibid.*, p. 25.   [11] *Ibid.*, p. 26.

resembles Roger Martin du Gard's original intention, before he came to the decision to alter the plan of *Les Thibault*.[12]

The twenty-seven volumes of Jules Romains's *Les Hommes de bonne volonté* (1932–1946) have attained a wide popularity. Romains is admittedly attempting an expansion and full realization of ideas he had expressed earlier in his *La Vie unanime*.[13] One critic has suggested that Romains's gigantic novel is a deliberate challenge to *Les Thibault*.[14] Be that as it may, the two works are so fundamentally different that there are few grounds for comparison between them, despite the large amount of attention they both devote to the First World War.

There are two major areas of difference. The first is methodological; Romains integrates real historical figures into his novel, places them in contact with fictional characters, even places himself inside their consciousness and imagines what their thoughts would be on a given occasion. A large troop of historical personages finds its way into Romains's complex landscape: Caillaux, Jaurès, Kaiser Wilhelm, Joffre, and many others—even Romains himself.[15] Such an integration irretriev-

---

[12] It seems significant that most critics believe that the later volumes of Duhamel's work decline in quality. C.-E. Magny, for example, feels that there is a weakening in the "creative spontaneity" of the work; none of the Pasquier children is as powerfully drawn as their father (*Histoire du roman français depuis 1918*, I [Paris: Editions du Seuil, 1950], 307).

[13] Jules Romains, *Les Hommes de bonne volonté*, I: *Le Six Octobre* (Paris: Flammarion, 1932), v (Preface).

[14] Dorothy Bussy, "Roger Martin du Gard," *New Statesman and Nation*, December 4, 1937, p. 917. Mme Bussy is perhaps overly harsh on Romains when she suggests that Martin du Gard is an artist "and not the most brilliant, and most brilliantly advertised, of super journalists."

[15] IV: *Eros de Paris* (Paris: Flammarion, 1932), 255-256. Perhaps the best example of intermingling is the rather frequent appearance of

ably damages the historical realism of a work, though it does not necessarily detract from its artistic validity. Martin du Gard was careful to avoid this method, as is witnessed by his discreet handling of the Dreyfus Affair in *Jean Barois*. In *Les Thibault* he remains faithful to the same principles of nonintrusion.

The second difference is more a matter of attention and intention. The summer of 1914 does not play a prominent role in Romains's novel. The Sarajevo assassination is mentioned on page 248 of Volume XIV, *Le Drapeau noir*, and the remaining fifty pages deal with the preparations of all Europe for the conflict. Romains then moves directly to the war itself, which he treats in *Prélude à Verdun* and *Verdun*, the two volumes widely considered to be the best in the series, which contain a number of great battle scenes described with real artistry. There is another jump—from April 1916 to the

---

Jaurès in the earlier volumes. Cf. the long interview between Jaurès and the imaginary character Gurau (III: *Les Amours enfantines* [Paris: Flammarion, 1932], 284–300). Among other topics, Jaurès speaks to Gurau of his fear of the danger of war; he believes that revolution is inevitable, but that war is not. Jaurès admits that there could be somewhere a man who, like himself, hopes for the revolution, "but with a more somber desire, convinced . . . that from a general war the revolution will spring, but completely indifferent as to whether it emerges more or less soiled, more or less bloody" (*ibid.*, p. 299). This mythical figure is of course Lenin. Romains closes his next volume by giving the thoughts he imagines for Jaurès on the occasion of his great pacifist speech of December 1908—a solicitude, a paternalistic feeling, for the masses who expect so much from him: "If I can only remain with them! If only I can be *still here!*" (IV, 264, italics Romains's). In the context of future events these words are overly prophetic; any novelist faces this danger, given his *post facto* knowledge which his characters cannot have. There are many other examples of this foreshadowing, even a "prediction" of the cruelties of the Hitler epoch, including the persecution of the Jews (XV: *Prélude à Verdun* [Paris: Flammarion, 1938], 184).

spring of 1919—and then the novel continues for eleven more volumes. The major characters, Jallez and Jerphanion, survive the war, as does the diabolical Quinette. Jerphanion goes back to teaching and tries to understand and to adapt himself to the postwar situation.[16] Jallez reports on the decadence, poverty, and social disintegration of Vienna for an American newspaper. Quinette gets involved in further intrigues.

Roger Martin du Gard also attempts an integration of history into his novel. But it is always history as viewed through the consciousness of his fictional characters. And not one of his heroes survives the war. *L'Eté 1914* deals with a six-week period, from June 28 to August 10, 1914 (actually only three weeks, since there are breaks in the narrative). In the Pléiade edition, it takes up 751 pages, whereas the first six parts of *Les Thibault* cover only 813 pages. It is not surprising that *L'Eté 1914* has been criticized for "inflation," though the change is not quite so drastic as these figures indicate. In the preceding volumes the action is concentrated into brief periods, with intervals in the narrative of up to five years elapsing between volumes. Mme Magny has termed Martin du Gard's method the technique of *noeuds d'événements,* and feels that it gives a "compact character," a "density," to the earlier volumes.[17] The inflation in *L'Eté 1914* comes from the addition of ideological discussion and historical events to the *noeuds d'événements.*

In *L'Eté 1914,* which opens on a warm summer's day in Geneva, the change in tone is not immediately apparent.

---

[16] True, Jerphanion is deeply changed by his war experience, and in the midst of the horror of Verdun, he wonders if he will ever be able to adjust to postwar life (XVI: *Verdun* [Paris: Flammarion, 1938], 208).

[17] *Histoire du roman français depuis 1918,* p. 310.

Attention is focused upon individuals, particularly upon a familiar individual—Jacques. Martin du Gard sets the scene and slowly fills in detail, much as he does in *La Belle Saison*. Jacques is having his portrait painted by an English friend, Paterson, one of a group of impoverished young revolutionaries living in Switzerland.[18] Better off than many of his fellows, Jacques makes an adequate living by contributing to newspapers and reviews and shares in the interminable conversations and excited planning for the future which take place in the *Local*. The recognized leader of the group is Meynestrel, *le Pilote*, a character who gave his creator a great deal of trouble,[19] and who in the final version of the novel has many Leninist qualities. His nickname refers both to his leadership qualities and to his career as a pioneer in aviation. Other characters are introduced, including Alfreda, who lives with Meynestrel, and whose silent and devoted presence is an absolute necessity for him,[20] and Mithoerg, the bespectacled Austrian apostle of violence. In these early pages Martin du Gard adds a homely and realistic detail which is typical of his constant effort to pull together levels in his novel. Along with questions of ideology—of atheism, anticlericalism, internationalism—a troubling thought keeps gnawing at Jacques's consciousness: He cannot remember whether or not he put out the alcohol lamp in his hotel room. Meanwhile at the

[18] *O.C.*, II, 12. The portrait will reappear as the only souvenir Jenny has of Jacques. Cf. *Epilogue*, *O.C.*, *II*, 834.

[19] R. M. G., "Lettres à un ami," *N.N.R.F.*, December 1958, pp. 1,139, 1,141–1,143. A good portion of this correspondence deals with Meynestrel and how to make him a believable personality, while at the same time attributing to him a plausible political attitude.

[20] Meynestrel's total reliance upon Alfreda is an important theme in the novel and will acquire a particular significance as a catalytic factor uniting the fictional and historical planes. Cf. especially *O.C.*, II, 22, 66, 70, 451.

Local other revolutionaries, who represent all the countries of Europe and even Asia Minor, are busy arguing over their usual topics: violent action versus philosophical action (ideological preparation), progressivism versus the need to "push" evolution forward, the dangers of war, weaknesses and differences in the socialist movements of the various countries.

Despite his deep affection for his friends and his recognition that they, like him, are *purs*, Jacques is frequently oppressed by a feeling of solitude and a sense of his difference from the others. Jacques's individualism and idealism, which are closely linked to his bourgeois heritage and education, are emphasized constantly by Martin du Gard. In speaking of the nation, Jacques stresses the difficulty of rejecting one's national heritage, the cultural and linguistic roots which are deep in a man; one can "expatriate oneself, but one cannot *se dépatrier*." [21] Though he has been without religious belief for a long time, he is almost always annoyed by the anticlericalism of the others. Frequently he defends values, forms of living, which his comrades condemn as "bourgeois," though he manages to retain their respect and confidence. He is ever challenging the notion that hatred and destruction are inevitable and necessary, and the concomitant disdain that many of his friends feel for patient, humanist, progressivist leaders like Jaurès. [22] For the Austrian Mithoerg (and Mey-

[21] *Ibid.*, p. 19.

[22] For Meynestrel he remains "incorrigible little Jacques" (*ibid.*, p. 77). However, Jacques is conscious of the motives leading him into revolutionary activity. The acceptance of violence is not only for reasons of efficient action: "The truth is that we cling to violence for much less avowable motives, much more personal ones: because we all have, in the bottom of our hearts, some revenge to take, some rancor to satisfy" (*ibid.*, p. 73). Jean Barois never arrives at this realization, though Luce suggests the personal motivation behind his immediate support of the Dreyfusists. Cf. *Jean Barois*, O.C., I, 369.

nestrel basically shares his view) the goal of revolution justifies any sort of action: "The aim is to liberate man. Despite
himself, if necessary!" [23] Jacques takes strong exception to
this attitude, since it is a menace to the "spiritual domain,"
and causes individual values to suffer. Martin du Gard's fellow
novelist Jacques de Lacretelle suggests that there is a perhaps
unconscious "bel éloge à la bourgeoisie" in the portrait of
Jacques; one could say that Jacques, with his "tenacity, fidelity, capacity for self-denial . . . uses weapons which he
owes to his origins, in struggling against those origins." [24]

The argument almost goes beyond the point of friendly
interchange when Mithoerg accuses Jacques of being merely
a rationalist dilettante and a false revolutionary, one who is
capable of heroic action: "But what is an individual act?
Nothing! A true revolutionary must accept the fact that he is
not a hero. He must accept the fact that he is *just any one* lost
in the community." [25] The importance of this passage should
be emphasized, since it relates to the manner and significance
of Jacques's death. Just at this moment, Martin du Gard
neatly breaks off the debate, for the date is June 28, 1914, and

[23] *O.C.,* II, 75.

[24] "Critique des livres: *Les Thibault,* VII, *L'Eté 1914,* par Roger
Martin du Gard," *L'Ami du peuple,* December 26, 1936, p. 4. However, a Marxist writer feels that Jacques does rise above his bourgeois
origins in his final and fatal attempt to save the peace (Antun
Polanscak, "Roger Martin du Gard et *Les Thibault,*" *Studia Romanica et Anglica-Zagrabiensia,* December 1960, p. 119). I would
tend to disagree, or at least to clarify Polanscak by pointing out that
Jacques's action and, more important, his conception of it, remain
solitary. He never becomes a true hero of socialist realism.

[25] *Ibid.,* p. 83 (italics mine). Mithoerg himself, after war is declared,
goes back to Austria to proclaim himself a deserter: "So that they
will execute me, in front of everyone!" (*ibid.,* p. 677). The reader
never learns whether Mithoerg remains faithful to his definition of
the true revolutionary, which sounds very much like a remark one of
Louis Aragon's Communist heroes would make.

the shouts of newsboys announcing a political assassination are heard.

Following a two-week break in the narrative, Jacques returns from a trip to Vienna with the first news of the dangerous situation there. A long, undoubtedly too long, *exposé historique*[26] is given to the assembled group, in order to persuade them of the threat of a Europe-wide conflict. The others are gradually convinced of the seriousness of the threat, and the decision is made to alert pacifist forces throughout Europe. Superficially, Meynestrel goes along with these plans, though from the beginning he is of the opinion that war is inevitable, that the European proletariat is inadequately organized, that a general strike is an impossibility. In private he tells Alfreda—who is already reacting negatively to his cold, almost inhuman dedication to the revolutionary cause and is turning her attention toward the Englishman Paterson—that there is no hope, that the present course of action is to behave "comme si" a pacifist campaign would have an effect.[27]

Once again, for the last time in the volume, there is a gap in the narrative. Henceforth, as the international crisis deepens, personal and historical events will become more and more compressed and follow headlong, one after the other. When the story resumes, the scene is a hot and deserted Paris on Sunday, the nineteenth of July. Antoine Thibault has adopted the surname Oscar-Thibault, has completely remodeled his

[26] *O.C.*, II, 88ff. This exposé has been criticized for its inordinate length and for its lack of relevance to the novelistic form.

[27] *Ibid.*, p. 105. Alfreda is coming to believe that nothing counts for Meynestrel except the revolution, and for the first time she thinks of him as "*something else* than a man" rather than as "*more and better* than a man" (*ibid.*, p. 106, italics his). This is the first indication that the airplane accident which gave *le Pilote* a limp also emasculated him.

father's residence, has set up a laboratory and now employs three research workers. He is so preoccupied with his ambitious projects that he has little time for Anne de Battaincourt, his new mistress. (The affair between Antoine and Anne is treated in brief, scattered scenes, which have often been praised for psychological finesse by critics who do not like the historical aspects of the novel.) [28] Antoine is oblivious to any dangers on the international scene. Jacques, in Paris on a mission of liaison and observation, visits Antoine for the first time since their father's death. The elder brother is incredulous when Jacques speaks of the menace he sees hanging over Europe. "Scientific discipline had given him the habit of thinking that in the social world, as in that of organic life, everything is a problem; that, in every domain, the search for truth demands application, study, and competence. Thus he considered politics as a field of activity foreign to his own." [29]

Despite his scepticism, the thought suddenly crosses Antoine's mind that the previous winter a *gendarme* had come to change his *livret de mobilisation.* At the time he had not even bothered to look at it; now he cannot remember where he put it.[30] For an instant he is affected by Jacques's fiery words and feels the "anguish of a presentiment." [31] But this quickly

[28] See especially *ibid.,* pp. 215–228, the scene of the drive into the country and dinner in an expensive restaurant, and pp. 276–282, the scene with Simon de Battaincourt during which Antoine makes the final decision to break with Anne.

[29] *Ibid.,* p. 128.   [30] *Ibid.,* p. 129. Cf. above, p. 58.

[31] *Ibid.* Martin du Gard explains that Jacques's words touched a "secret point" in Antoine, who has the vague sense of being at the mercy of a collective madness *"possibly of a cosmic order, which was in the air"* (italics mine). Here and in two other long passages (pp. 480, 570), there is an implicit fatalism which is rather difficult to evaluate, since it seems out of keeping in a careful, objective study of the causes of the war. A concern with causation is undeniably pres-

passes, and in an elder-brotherly fashion he vigorously takes Jacques to task. A long argument on the themes of war and revolution ensues—more pages of ideological discussion.

Antoine seems very candid at this time, and at first is totally opposed to Jacques's position. Jacques in turn is forced by his brother's prodding to take a more revolutionary stance than he had in Geneva.[32] To support his contention about the threat of war, Jacques refers to a front-page article in *Le Matin* for July 19, entitled, "If War Were to Break Out," which, he argues, was not placed there by chance. (Many other examples of this sort of careful documentation by Martin du Gard could be given, and conservative critics are in error when they attack him for basing his account solely on *L'Humanité*.) [33] Antoine will not allow himself to be con-

---

ent in *L'Eté 1914;* one critic even suggests that a historian in the thirtieth century could write a good thesis on the causes of the war merely by using *L'Eté 1914* (André Thérive, "Les Livres," *Le Temps,* January 7, 1937), p. 3. Such a study might conclude that the war could have been avoided. Cf. Denis Boak, *Roger Martin du Gard* (Oxford: Clarendon Press, 1963), p. 139: "A large part of the novel is basically concerned with a *demonstration* that the First World War, and all the misery caused by it, were avoidable" (italics his). Yet the fatalism in the passages mentioned above makes this interpretation difficult to support. If there is a message in the novel, it is probably a warning about future conflicts. There is evidence to support this view, including Martin du Gard's own pronouncements in his Nobel Prize speech and elsewhere. Perhaps Léon-Pierre Quint has best defined Martin du Gard's aim, when he suggests that Martin du Gard is the sole author to have "truly *démystifié* the war" ("Roger Martin du Gard, le constructeur," *Monde nouveau,* July 1956, p. 45). To "demystify" by a painstaking search for the deep significance of events is not the same as posing alternatives.

[32] Jacques now refuses to accept reformist progressivism and thinks to himself that Mithoerg would be pleased if he could hear him (*O.C.,* II, 163).

[33] *Ibid.,* p. 142. All sorts of documents, speeches, official pronouncements are quoted. A few examples of newspapers are *L'Action*

vinced, claiming that his life is clearly planned, his tasks definite, and that "taking Europe's pulse" is not one of them.

This debate is cut off by a surprising interruption, which is again indicative of Martin du Gard's effort to fuse ideology and the individual dramas of his characters. Jenny de Fontanin arrives with the news that her aging libertine father is in a coma after a suicide attempt. Thus she and Jacques meet for the first time since his flight—itself mysteriously connected with his love for her—at the end of *La Belle Saison*. The critic Jacques Madaule has suggested that there is a symbolic intention here; Jacques and Jenny find each other on the same day "as her father, the deplorable Jérôme de Fontanin, fired a bullet into his head, as though he wished to perish at the same moment as the old world." [34] While Antoine puts on his "professional mask," Jacques and Jenny (who is more upset by the sudden appearance of Jacques than by her father's condition) remain in a state of total disarray. From

-----

française (cited on pp. 248–249), *Figaro, Le Matin, L'Echo de Paris, L'Humanité*, Clemenceau's *L'Homme libre* (all cited on pp. 291–292), *La Bataille syndicaliste, Vorwärts, Vienna Arbeiterzeitung, Leipziger Volkzeitung* (pp. 328–329), *Paris-Midi* (pp. 463–464). Closely related to this question is another criticism often made by conservative nationalist commentators. Because of his search for impartiality, because of his attempt at a just apportionment of war guilt, Martin du Gard is accused of playing the game of German propaganda. Cf. especially Henri Massis, "Les Idées et les faits—Lectures—Du Prix Nobel et d'un écrivain pacifiste," *La Revue universelle*, February 1, 1938, p. 355 and *passim*. Martin du Gard does, in a general sense, "envelop the two groups of belligerents in the same condemnation." However, a careful reading of the text of *L'Eté 1914* shows a definite shading of blame toward Germany's side. (Cf. the unfavorable treatment of the German socialist characters, *L'Eté 1914*, pp. 54–55.) There is also the important incident of the Stolbach documents, completely fabricated by Martin du Gard, which casts a good deal of blame on the Austrian and German General Staffs.

[34] *Reconnaissances*, III (Paris: Desclée de Brouwer, 1946), 325.

now on the brief and pathetic interlude of the love affair which springs from this chance meeting will be closely bound up with the coming of the war.

Before returning to Geneva on Monday, July 20, Jacques runs a number of errands in connection with his liaison duties, and happens into the famous Café du Croissant. Here he observes Jaurès from a distance, and the "stimulating vision" of a somber and distracted, though ever oratorical Jaurès gives Jacques new courage.[35] This is typical of Martin du Gard's method of presenting real historical figures with the utmost plausibility.

In Geneva the milieu is one of intense discussion and feverish planning for a general strike. Jacques is quickly sent by Meynestrel to Belgium, where in a rather melodramatic detective sequence he receives documents from a Russian fellow socialist. (Jacques manages to visit or contact every major European country—surely this is part of Martin du Gard's endeavor to bring history closer to the reader through identification.) From Belgium he goes once more to Paris, arriving there on July 23. Tension is beginning to mount, though most newspapers are still concentrating on the Caillaux affair. With the announcement of the Austrian ultimatum the following day, Martin du Gard's canvas becomes ever more vast, as he tries to capture the shifting mood of Paris—and through the Parisian microcosm and the activities of his international socialist characters, the mood of all Europe—in the dramatic days that follow. He presents the reader with a mass of detail: quotations from speeches and newspapers, descriptions of rallies and manifestations, information gleaned by Jacques and other socialists, and much more. But always at the center of the novel are the glosses on events provided by the main

[35] *O.C.*, II, 206.

characters, through their discussions of and reactions to historical developments—identification again. This method is especially visible, perhaps overly visible and therefore not successful, in the discussions which are held in Antoine's offices, between him and his co-workers and any guests who happen to be present.

The first of these debates takes place on Saturday, July 25, 1914. Jacques joins the group, and a vehement argument quite naturally ensues. In an attempt at diversity and possibly objectivity, Martin du Gard has given each of Antoine's assistants—Studler, Jousselin, and Roy—different attitudes toward the war.[36] Martin du Gard makes Manuel Roy a spokesman for the position of Charles Maurras and the Action Française, and while Roy as a person is treated with sympathy, it is clear that Martin du Gard cannot control his intense dislike of bellicose nationalism, and the other characters demolish Roy's arguments without difficulty.[37]

Antoine no longer disregards his brother's foreboding prophecies; the general atmosphere and the information he has gained while treating his patient, the diplomat Rumelles, now confirm them. In private Antoine tells Jacques that he has found his military papers, and that he is assigned to Compiègne on the first day of mobilization.

Martin du Gard next switches back to the level of concern

---

[36] Cf. Boak, *Roger Martin du Gard*, p. 149. Boak feels, and I think with justification, that this scene is "rather contrived."

[37] No one can deny Martin du Gard's partiality here. Massis is perfectly correct when he notes that Martin du Gard has his nationalists "scream out *la Marseillaise*," while his socialists "sing *l'Internationale*" ("Du Prix Nobel et d'un écrivain pacifiste," *La Revue universelle*, February 1, 1938, p. 356). Cf. Martin du Gard's favorable description of the great socialist manifestation at Brussels with "a column of young patriots waving flags and screaming." He describes the behavior of the patriotic crowd as the "stampeding of a herd" (*L'Eté 1914*, *O.C.*, II, 554).

for individual characters and deals with the love affair between Jacques and Jenny, which is furthered by their meeting
on the *quai* of the Gare de l'Est, where they go to see Daniel
de Fontanin off for his regiment. This scene of adieux has
been praised for its "pure objectivity." It is carried off almost
entirely by a description of movements, with no hint of the
emotion felt by Jacques and Daniel, except as expressed by
their movements.[38] Jacques is at first determined to leave
without confronting Jenny, but in an excellent example of the
"fortuitous detail" [39] often employed by Martin du Gard, his
decision to return and search for her is brought about by a
baggageman's demanding the cart on which he has been sitting. Otherwise he would have succeeded in collecting his
thoughts and hurried back to join his fellow socialists at the
offices of *L'Humanité*, "surrendering once again to the feverish rhythm of his life." [40] He finds Jenny and traps her, and
for eight days, until the afternoon of August 2, she becomes
an intimate part of his existence. She follows him like a
shadow as he frantically moves about Paris making contact
with the ever declining pacifist forces. When they part after
their first evening together, the thought of war suddenly
returns to Jacques's consciousness, and with it a wave of
mortal fear. He is more than ever determined to continue his
pacifist activity: "For this love, which had involved his entire
life, he had more than ever the need of a new world, a world
of justice and purity." [41]

In the course of his activities on July 27, Jacques receives

[38] Brian Pocknell, "The Nature and the Limits of Realism in the
Works of Roger Martin du Gard," unpublished Master's thesis, University of Manchester, 1959, p. 174.

[39] *Ibid.*, pp 174–175.   [40] *O.C.*, II. 311.

[41] *Ibid.*, p. 325. Here is yet another example of Martin du Gard's
effort to integrate the political and individual levels in his novel.

an urgent message from Meynestrel which orders him to Berlin on a secret mission. This leads to the adventurous episode of the Stolbach documents, which has all the elements of a *roman-policier* and which has been severely criticized, for it is Martin du Gard's only major departure from the historical record.[42] We cannot resolve the question of whether this departure lies within the novelist's province, or whether it is unjustified because of the strict historicity of the rest of *L'Eté 1914.* This is another question which can only be answered subjectively. We shall suggest later some reasons why Martin du Gard felt this step to be necessary.

Jacques leaves Jenny, despite their growing intimacy, and travels to Berlin. There he is handed a packet of documents, stolen from an officer on the Austrian General Staff, Colonel Stolbach. He transports the documents to Brussels and hands them over to Meynestrel. The Geneva socialist group is attending a great rally, and *le Pilote* has been shouting, "Guerre à la guerre" with the rest, though he firmly believes that nothing will prevent the outbreak of war and that war is even

[42] Cf. Boak, *Roger Martin du Gard,* p. 140: "Since this episode is purely invented, it seriously weakens Martin du Gard's claim to historical accuracy, and renders him vulnerable to the charge of fabrication for propaganda purposes." To be sure, Martin du Gard never publicly claimed historical accuracy; this claim is rather the implied result of one possible definition of the historical novel. On Martin du Gard's accuracy, cf. Harry W. Osborne, "A Critical Analysis of *Les Thibault* by Roger Martin du Gard," unpublished Ph.D. dissertation, University of Wisconsin, 1949, pp. 84–86 and Appendix A. Osborne has made a careful comparison of the novelistic and historical accounts, using Sidney B. Fay's and Harry Elmer Barnes's texts as reference, and concludes that there are only three points of error. The first two are minor matters which could well be the result of inadequate information available to the characters. The third is of course the affair of the Stolbach documents; here, Osborne writes, the novelist "takes precedence over the historian" (p. 86).

necessary to create a really revolutionary situation. In the documents he finds irrefutable proof of complicity between the Austrian and German General Staffs. The documents are thus of incalculable importance and could serve as a powerful weapon in the struggle against war. Rather than give them immediately to one of the socialist leaders, Liebknecht for example, Meynestrel puts them away, thinking to himself, "Were there only one chance in a hundred of being able to prevent the war, the risk must not be taken!" [43] He makes this decision just before Alfreda determines to leave him and go off to England with Paterson. Jacques Madaule thinks that one of her reasons for abandoning Meynestrel may be his "inhuman attitude" toward the war, which she has already sensed, and which has offended her.[44] Given Martin du Gard's careful timing of episodes, this view seems justified. While Alfreda could not have known of the significance of the

[43] *O.C.*, II, 435.

[44] *Reconnaissances*, p. 324. At the same time there is a touch of violence and madness in her passionate determination to leave with Paterson, which seems to indicate that Martin du Gard had a more complex double intention here, in order to link up her parting even more closely with the coming of the war. When Jacques sees Alfreda and Paterson in the crowd during the great demonstration, Martin du Gard uses words which could almost describe the victory of the spirit of war: "She seemed to be celebrating her own triumph, her liberation, the victory of instinct" (*O.C.*, II, 453). Cf. Pierre-Henri Simon, *Histoire de la littérature française au xxᵉ siècle*, II (Paris: Armand Colin, 1957), 40–41. Simon sees the *romanesque* aspect of *L'Eté 1914*, "patterning in a double and subtle counterpoint the sensual and terminating love of Antoine and Anne de Battaincourt, and the instinctive passion of Alfreda and Paterson which throws Meynestrel to suicide." I would add that the contrast between these two affairs and the "pure" love of Jacques and Jenny is also striking, and I would emphasize how intimately all three affairs are tied to historical developments.

papers nor of Meynestrel's action, it would suffice for her to think him capable of such a gesture.

Meynestrel calmly lies to Jacques, telling him that his trip was not worth the trouble and danger, and Jacques, disappointed, goes off to join the gigantic pacifist demonstration. Extracts from the speeches of the leaders—Vandervelde for Belgium, Hasse (Social Democratic Deputy) for Germany, and Jaurès for France—are given. This is a moment of extraordinary enthusiasm, of intoxicated certainty that the pacific will of the people will triumph. One is reminded of Romains's portrayal of Jaurès at the tribune, and there is an ironic, quite striking parallel between Martin du Gard's description of this prewar scene and Romains's treatment of the first Armistice Day celebrations, November 11, 1919.[45] The enthusiasm soon fades, as discouraging news arrives from all quarters. During the train trip back to Paris, Jacques notices that the factories are already guarded; he learns with astonishment that the vehement pacifist Gustave Hervé, editor of *La Guerre sociale*, has turned *patriotard* and is calling for proletarian participation in the coming war.

At the same time, Antoine, who has to go directly to the Quai d'Orsay to treat Rumelles, since the diplomat is now too busy to leave his post, gets a detailed report from this "inside" source. Antoine feels that Rumelles is so exhausted that he is divulging all he knows. Rumelles's general attitude is one of helplessness and hopelessness; none of the governments can back down now, and war is absolutely inevitable. He tells Antoine that for some days the staff of the Quai d'Orsay has had a sense of powerlessness, "the impression that the hour of politics, of diplomacy, has passed." In each country

[45] Jules Romains, *Les Hommes de bonne volonté*, XVII: *Vorge contre Quinette* (Paris: Flammarion, 1939), 238–243.

the military leaders are now speaking; "they are the stronger: they speak in the name of national security; and all the civil powers capitulate before them." [46]

Even had he heard this realistic appraisal, Jacques would not have been deterred from his pacifist crusade; with Jenny faithfully and doggedly following him, he multiplies his efforts, moving about a Paris in which warlike signs are multiplying, and makes a speech in the working-class quarter of Montrouge. By Friday morning, July 31, most of the socialists he speaks with have a discouraged and defeatist air. The leaders have not called for a general strike, have not issued a single *mot d'ordre*, and though Jacques will struggle to delude himself for yet another day, it is already clear that the workers, disoriented, will obey a government order of mobilization. Jacques finds Antoine nervous and tired after a night spent sorting papers: "The turmoil around him was severely weakening the bases upon which he had so precisely constructed his life: science, reason. He was suddenly discovering the impotence of the mind and, confronted with so many unleashed instincts, the uselessness of the virtues which had always sustained his laborious existence: moderation, *le bon sens*, wisdom and experience, the desire for justice." [47]

Antoine's luncheon guests are naturally obsessed with the question of war, and another heated political discussion takes place. Jacques is about to make a strong revolutionary pacifist pronouncement, when he notices with surprise and emotion a *désarroi* in his usually superbly confident and supposedly invincible elder brother, and he detects a "strange prayer" in

[46] *O.C.*, II, 475. For an excellent historical account of this process in France, see Jere Clemens King, *Generals and Politicians* (Berkeley: University of California Press, 1951), ch. ii, "Five Months of 'Military Dictatorship' August–December 1914."

[47] *O.C.*, II, 516.

Antoine's glance—a plea not to betray the full extent of his beliefs before Antoine's friends. Jacques changes his tack momentarily, though a bit later he states his conviction that no amount of potential social progress can justify a war: "Anything, rather than the abdication of reason, of justice, before blood and brute force! Anything rather than that horror and absurdity! Anything, anything, rather than war!" [48] Jacques, definitely serving here as a spokesman for Roger Martin du Gard, voices exactly the views held by his creator at the time of the writing of *L'Eté 1914*.[49] As Jacques prepares to leave, Antoine calls him back, and they converse alone. He asks Jacques what he will do in the event of mobilization. Jacques replies that he will of course refuse to be called up, and Antoine challenges this as an "isolated act of insubordination," which can have no value and cannot even help the cause of peace. Antoine admits that such intransigence would demand a rare strength of character; all his sympathy and pity would go out to a man capable of such action. "But I would still term him a useless dreamer. . . . And *I would declare him wrong!*" [50] Even though there is no common ground between the two brothers, even though Jacques finally leaves without Antoine's making a gesture to detain him, Martin du Gard himself holds Antoine's opinion of the futility of insubordination. The contradiction inherent in his agreement with both

[48] *Ibid.*, p. 525. The French reads: "*Tout, tout, plûtot que la guerre!*"
[49] Cf. R. M. G., "Lettres à un ami," *N.N.R.F.*, December 1958, p. 1,150, letter of September 9, 1936: "Am hard like iron for neutrality. Principle: *tout, plutôt que la guerre! Tout!* . . . Even fascism in Spain! And don't push me, for I would say: yes . . . and 'even fascism in France!'" Before 1939, Martin du Gard was to change his mind and overcome the deeply ingrained pacifism so prevalent in the French mentality of the 1930's. (Or at least he came to realize that his pacifism was no longer relevant.)
[50] *O.C.*, II, 538 (italics his).

Jacques and Antoine provides an excellent example of the "fruitful doubling" which Martin du Gard had envisioned back in 1920, while outlining his plan for *Les Thibault.*

On Friday evening, July 31, Martin du Gard has his protagonists Jacques and Jenny dine at the Café du Croissant, and thus observe as casual spectators the assassination of Jaurès. In this scene, of such great symbolic significance in representing the final dashing of pacifist hopes (even though it is quite conceivable that Jaurès, had he lived, would have come over to the nationalist camp), Martin du Gard maintains strict plausibility. It is through the eyes of Jacques and Jenny, who have good reason to be in a socialist café, that the reader participates in this tragic episode. The death, in turn, is closely linked with the rapid progress toward the consummation of Jacques's and Jenny's love.[51]

The following morning, after reading the demands for a *Union sacrée* in all the newspapers, Jacques tries to fight off his despair over the war which all see coming and refuses to accept a fatalistic concept of events. Despite the night spent with Jenny, he feels "himself terribly alone. Alone, because faithful and pure. Alone, but also as if *protected* by this pathetic isolation." However great his distress, he knows that he is "right, that he defend[s] the truth." [52] He is still unsure about what he will do if mobilization is decreed; the idea of retreating to a neutral country to live peacefully and "gagner sa croûte" repels him as an act of cowardice.

[51] In the taxi returning to her home, where he will henceforth stay to lessen the risk of arrest, "in spite of his fatigue, he felt a sort of paradoxical exaltation, a more violent taste for living than ever" (*ibid.*, p. 556).

[52] *Ibid.*, p. 562 (italics mine). Cf. above, pp. 126–127 and nn. 24, 25. As in the Genevan conversations at the beginning of the novel, Jacques shows himself to be a very particular sort of socialist. The influence of his bourgeois heritage upon him is apparent. His death, too, will be a solitary action, in my view a nineteenth-century action.

When the announcement does come, on the afternoon of August 1, Jacques feels a moment of relief because the situation is at least clear. Then anger and mortification take over: "He was not so revolted or discouraged as he was confounded and humiliated: humiliated by the atrophy of the popular will, by the incurable mediocrity of man, by the impotence of reason!" [53] If he wishes to escape to Switzerland, using the false papers he possesses, he must leave before the evening of August 2. After that date foreigners will not be granted exit permits. While Jacques is struggling to decide whether or not to escape, the idea is already beginning to form in his mind that what he must do is translate his beliefs into action, action which will demonstrate his faith in the internationalist ideal. He does resolve to go to Switzerland, no matter what happens, and to take Jenny with him.

He first visits his brother, and in the old Thibault residence the last in the series of long discussions on the international crisis takes place. With passivity and stoicism, Antoine accepts the mobilization, the disruption of his cherished projects, of his ordered existence. Dr. Philip, Antoine's *patron*, who is also present, makes extensive comments on the situation, remarks which have often been quoted, and which have been taken to represent Martin du Gard's position.[54] Philip feels that with July 1914, "something is finishing, of which we were: and

[53] *Ibid.*, p. 581. Again Jacques sounds much more like a disappointed bourgeois liberal than a socialist; one is reminded of Martin du Gard's own correspondence with Marcel Hébert.
[54] Cf. the discussion in Chapter I of the famous passage on the three great crises in Philip's existence. Martin du Gard's lifetime aim has presumably been to elucidate these crises. Perhaps the other best-known passage, which has been seen to contain the essence of the novel, is where Philip draws the parallel with Oedipus, who also had his warnings (*L'Eté 1914, O.C.*, II, 595–596). See also Georges Poupet, "La Vie littéraire: Oedipe aussi était averti: A propos de *L'Eté 1914*," *Le Jour*, December 7, 1936, p. 2.

something is beginning in which we, the old, shall not participate." [55] He asks Jacques when he is departing for the front,
and Antoine answers, stuttering as he does only in rare moments of intense emotion, "My brother, with him it's an—
another thing." [56] Antoine finds Jacques's attitude completely
unjustified, though Philip believes in the legitimacy of every
mystique. He defends Jacques in a passage which suggests
that Martin du Gard, to the extent that Philip represents the
author's views, was of two minds on the question, and did not
side completely with Antoine: "Would humanity progress
without a *mystique?* Reread history, Thibault. . . . At the base
of all the great social modifications, some sort of religious
aspiration toward the absurd has always been needed. Intelligence leads only to inaction. It is faith which gives man the
élan he must have to act, and the stubbornness which he must
have to persevere." [57]

Once more Jacques and Jenny go out into a Paris actively
preparing for war. They find the offices of *L'Humanité* deserted, and the few young socialists remaining at the Café du
Progrès are caught up by the collective madness, are patrioti-
cally resolved to accept the call to mobilization.[58] No one
even mentions the general strike. Jacques, whose suicidal tendencies frequently appeared in the earlier volumes of *Les
Thibault*, thinks to himself: "Better to die than to accept that
which I disapprove with all my heart. Better to die than this
repudiation [of the internationalist ideal]!" [59] The following
morning, after bidding adieu to Antoine and thus making up

[55] *O.C.*, II, 596.   [56] *Ibid.*, p. 597.   [57] *Ibid.*, p. 598.
[58] One says that he hates war. "But I am French. The country is
under attack. I am needed; I shall go! I shall go, *la mort dans l'âme*"
(*ibid.*, p. 606). One is reminded of the novel *La Mort dans l'âme*, by
Jean-Paul Sartre, which can be profitably compared with *L'Été 1914*.
In 1914 only a socialist, rather than a whole nation, could go to war
"with death in his soul."
[59] *Ibid.*, p. 619.

the bitter argument which took place when he disclosed his
love for Jenny, Jacques searches the crowd of *mobilisés* for
one kindred soul. Everywhere he sees the same resigned courage, and not one sign of the blazing anger he feels. "And it
seemed to him that, at this moment, all the liberty that remained in the world had no refuge but in him." He has a sense
of power and pride in his rebellion, and resentment even flares
up briefly against Jenny, "for existing, for waiting for him,
for tearing him from the solitude surrounding him." [60] He
cannot believe that there is nothing left for him to do, not a
single gesture he can make. A chance remark by the old an-
archist Mourlan provides him with a sudden insight into a
course of action which is still open to him. Mourlan suggests
that "some small unknown quantity would perhaps suffice, a
brusque recovery of consciousness, for it all to change, all of a
sudden." Jacques, caught by the idea, forces Mourlan to
clarify his thought, and Mourlan exclaims, "If, suddenly, between the two armies, a flash of consciousness tore away this
density of lies!" [61] The soldiers, in a moment of lucidity, might
realize their true situation and turn against the leaders who
have put them where they are.

While Jacques is preparing to leave for Geneva, an idea is
slowly forming in his mind: "He knew by what tangible act,
by what solitary and decisive act, he could finally, after so
many days of inactivity, of sterile anxiety, *struggle for his
faith,* and provide an obstacle to the war! An act which, without a doubt, would involve a total sacrifice." [62] Jacques calmly
accepts the necessity of his contemplated act because of his
"mystical certainty" that this is the "only and supreme way

---

[60] *Ibid.,* p. 638.   [61] *Ibid.,* p. 645.

[62] *Ibid.,* p. 659 (italics mine). Again the comparison with Sartre's
La Mort dans l'âme is striking. The key to the difference between
Jacques's death and that of Mathieu in *La Mort dans l'âme* lies, I
believe, in the phrase "struggle for his faith."

to awaken the consciousness of the masses, to change brutally the course of events, and to bring to a halt the forces in coalition against the people, against fraternity and justice." [63] When Jenny tells him that she has been too cruel to her mother, that she must return to her and make amends, and that she will join him in Switzerland as soon as possible, "his overwhelmed and incredulous expression reflect[s] nothing of his first, vivid thought, which [comes] to him despite himself: 'My mission . . . Now I am free!' " [64] Though he does feel genuine disappointment and pain, he is so intoxicated with the thought of his own heroism and isolation that for the most part he is relieved, since everything is now simplified and he can leave alone.

Back in Geneva on the morning of August 3, Jacques locates Meynestrel, who has undergone a drastic transformation. No longer is he the brilliant leader, *le Pilote*, who organized and presided over discussions at the *Local*. He is a broken man, unkempt, dirty, with a touch of madness in his eye; Jacques had prevented him from committing suicide when he first learned of Alfreda's desertion, but he cannot overcome his grief. Still he does not blame her: "If there is a single notion which I no longer have today, *after all that*—it is definitely that of responsibility!" [65] Jacques tries to pull him out of his lethargy and outlines to him (and thus to the

---

[63] *Ibid.* Even Jacques, in his more lucid moments, as he makes the arrangements for his supreme gesture, loses this "mystical certainty" and realizes that the only effect of his action will be his choosing a last escape, an evasion through death which is in keeping with his deepest nature and with the course of his life.

[64] *Ibid.*, p. 672.

[65] *Ibid.*, p. 679 (italics R. M. G.'s). One assumes that Meynestrel is referring both to personal and international events. Antoine makes a similar remark in *Epilogue* when meditating on the case of a soldier who feigns illness to avoid being returned to the front lines (*O.C.*, II, 957).

reader for the first time) the plan which he has formulated. His proposal is to fly over the front lines in an airplane and scatter bilingual manifestoes calling for the soldiers to throw down their arms and fraternize.[66] To make the risk totally his own, Jacques wants Meynestrel to teach him how to fly, but *le Pilote* is caught up by Jacques's enthusiasm and determines to organize the flight himself. He is perfectly aware that this would be a suicide flight and that the dropping of leaflets would have no immediate effect: "Later on, perhaps: after months of suffering and massacre!" he thinks to himself; "but everything which could demoralize, could sow the seeds of revolt, would be good." [67]

Jacques is sent off to Basel to prepare the manifesto and to arrange for its translation and printing. Martin du Gard gives

[66] Thus badly stated, Jacques's project seems even more insane than it appears in the novel. He points out to Meynestrel that each poor soldier who left his home a few days previously with his rifle barrel garnished with flowers and singing national anthems is now only "a *pauvre type* face to face with reality" (*O.C.*, II, p. 681). This *pauvre type* is shocked, hungry, and suffering, and might be reached by an appeal to revolt. Although Martin du Gard intended to have Jacques die in his original 1920 plan for *Les Thibault*, the inspiration for the actual flight over the lines came from the death of the Italian anti-Fascist poet Lauro de Bosis over Rome in 1931.

[67] *O.C.*, II, 683. Meynestrel is portrayed by Martin du Gard as willing to go along with the plan and as seeing some utility in it. Before Jacques leaves him, he says with real warmth: "You have rendered me a fine service. . . . I would inevitably have finished up by an insane gesture. This one, at least, will have some utility" (*ibid.*, p. 686). There is no indication in the text that he purposely crashes the plane, as a number of critics have implied. Cf. Magny, *Histoire du roman français depuis 1918*, p. 317. Mme Magny speaks of Meynestrel's "death instincts" and hints that the crash was deliberate. Brian Pocknell feels that it is Meynestrel who is "responsible for the failure of Jacques's plan to drop leaflets, and indirectly, for his death" ("Realism in the Works of Martin du Gard," p. 144). Cf. below, n. 72.

long fragments of this document in the text of *L'Eté 1914;* it is an impassioned appeal to the soldiers of both sides, emphasizing that they have been duped, contaminated by shameful propaganda, sent off to massacre each other, that they are the pawns of the ruling classes. While Jacques is writing, he is in a dreamlike condition, close to delirium, feverish and exalted —a state of mind which seems intended to parallel closely the madness of all Europe. Whenever possible he remains alone, oblivious of the miserable quarters his fellow socialists have found for him. Sometimes he rambles about the splendid city of Basel, which is concisely and powerfully described by Martin du Gard.[68] Jacques's thoughts are incoherent and follow no logical pattern; he constantly deludes himself with visions of a new era of equality and justice among men.

The idea of death is of course omnipresent, particularly of a voluntary death, which he imagines as a total giving, such as he had been incapable of before—even to Jenny, even to the revolutionary ideal. At the same time he is proud, for he imagines himself the master of his destiny; he believes that, having made a deliberate choice in the manner of his dying, he will perform at last one useful act which will somehow compensate for the uselessness of his life: "a death which will be both an act of faith and his last protest as a rebel, his last revolt against the absurdity of the world—a calculated enterprise, which will bear his imprint, which will be laden with the precise significance which he had wanted to give it." [69] For one or two brief moments he is fully cognizant of what he is doing, and he admits to himself what he has

[68] Martin du Gard visited Basel, as well as many other cities, in order to be absolutely precise in his documentation. See André Mantaigne, "Une Récompense et un homme," *La Lumière*, October 29, 1937, p. 6.

[69] *O.C.*, II, 710. The way in which Jacques does meet his death provides an ironic contrast with these words. Only Antoine will have this privilege of choosing the manner of his death.

doubtless realized all along but has wilfully kept from his consciousness: "I am acting as I am only out of despair. I am acting as I am only to flee myself. . . . I won't stop the war. . . . I won't save anyone except myself. . . . But I shall save myself in fulfilling myself! . . . To be right, against them all! And to escape into death." [70]

Word comes from Meynestrel that the flight will take place at dawn on the morning of August 10, and that the rendez-vous will be made on a plateau near Basel. In a wagon carrying him out of the city, Jacques dozes off and has a long, feverish dream in which he is judged by M. Faîsme, the head of the reformatory at which he had been incarcerated, who had so often humiliated him. Thus his whole childhood, his whole life, are closely bound up with his present action, as the rigid determinism of the following important passage indicates:

By what routes, what detours had the child of yesterday been led by destiny to this present evening? A series of chances? No. Definitely no! . . . All his actions are linked together. This he feels, this he has always vaguely felt. His existence has been merely a long and spasmodic submission to a mysterious orientation, to a fatal *enchaînement*. And now it is the end, the apotheosis. . . . He has gone beyond fear. . . . This deliberate death is really the completion of this life. It is the condition of this last gesture of fidelity to oneself . . . of fidelity to the instinct of rebellion. . . . Since his childhood he had said: "No!" He never had any other way of affirming himself. Not "No" to life. "No" to the world! Well, here is his final refusal, his final "No!" to that which men have made of life.[71]

---

[70] *Ibid.*, p. 706. Cf. p. 715, the other occasion when he realizes the absurdity of his supposed heroic and meaningful sacrifice.

[71] *Ibid.*, p. 717. This notion of death as conscious affirmation can be compared to the final thoughts and death of Mathieu Delarue in Sartre's *La Mort dans l'âme* (Paris: Gallimard, 1949), pp. 192–193.

At dawn Jacques and his friends hear the cannon in Alsace and at the same moment the distant sound of an airplane. The scene switches quickly to the airplane, and there is a brilliant description of the sensation of flying. What happened when the aircraft landed to pick up Jacques, to refuel, and to take aboard the leaflets is discovered by the reader through Jacques's semihallucinatory flashback. Somehow he had climbed into the plane, and someone had strapped him in and put a helmet on his head. He recalls that Meynestrel had been working with the engine and had asked for a mechanic, but that the mechanic had already left with the wagon.

After a few moments of intense intoxication, of a sense of extraordinary freedom, Jacques notices that Meynestrel seems to be trying to manipulate some part of the engine, which shortly afterward stalls. The plane crashes, before a single leaflet can be dropped. I mention these details to make it perfectly clear that it is mechanical failure which brings down the plane—an uncontrollable outside force, not Meynestrel's suicidal impulses nor a malevolent burst of machine-gun fire, as some critics have imagined.[72]

Meynestrel is incinerated in the crash. Jacques's agony—an uncommunicable agony, for he is too badly wounded to speak—lasts a whole day. The retreating French soldiers find him, take him for a spy, and carry him off with them on a stretcher. Martin du Gard thus has the opportunity to portray, with an "atrocious realism," [73] the disorder, exhaustion, heat, stench, misery of the defeat, in passages which have

[72] See *ibid.*, pp. 729–731. Cf. above, n. 67, and Germaine Sneyers, "Revue littéraire—*L'Eté 1914*, par Roger Martin du Gard," *La Revue générale*, January 15, 1937, p. 117: "Shot down by the French." See also Louis Jalabert, "Romans et nouvelles," *Etudes*, January 5, 1937, p. 135: "A burst of machine-gun fire brought down the plane."

[73] Pierre-Henri Simon, "Un Grand Roman de la famille," *Pour la Vie*, March 1955, p. 53.

been highly praised, even by critics who are opposed to Martin du Gard's integration of history on the *gros plan* into his novel.[74] Finally, as the German advance continues and becomes more threatening, Jacques is abandoned. The simple soldier Marjoulat, who has never even killed an animal before, puts a fatal bullet through Jacques's head, then flees, crying out an insult, "Fumier!"—because, as Albert Camus has pointed out, he detests what he has just done.[75]

Pierre-Henri Simon ponders the significance of Jacques's death: "A derisory or a grandiose gesture? An absurd and useless sacrifice, or one which is heroic and charged with spiritual seed? It is for the reader to decide." [76] Many readers have decided; many, including Albert Camus, have found in Jacques's death only futility and a hopeless pessimism.[77]

[74] Cf. Boak, *Roger Martin du Gard*, p. 157, on the "tour de force" of the account of Jacques's death. Pierre Loewel, who is quite negative about the historical material in *L'Eté 1914*, feels that this scene has a "remarkable power" ("La Vie littéraire," *L'Ordre*, December 21, 1936, p. 2).

[75] Albert Camus, Preface, *O.C.*, I, xx.

[76] "Un Grand Roman de la famille," p. 53. The French reads "sémences spirituelles." Simon believes that Martin du Gard prefers the second interpretation. Simon is definitely wrong as far as Martin du Gard's personal view is concerned, though I would argue that he is justified in drawing a positive message out of the work, even if this was not Martin du Gard's intention. Henri Bidou's perceptive conclusions on this question are most helpful. He points out that we are not told what Jacques thought during his death agony. "Possibly he said to himself that this sacrifice of the precursors, as obscure as it was, and it had to be obscure to retain its virtue, was not useless. This blood apparently shed in vain, this martyr without witness and without glory, finished off with an ignoble insult, is this not precisely the death of the apostle?—*with the condition that one believes in the apostolate*" ("Le Mouvement littéraire," *Revue de Paris*, January 15, 1937, p. 446). Because Martin du Gard did not believe does not necessarily mean that the reader cannot.

[77] Camus speaks in his Preface, *O.C.*, I, xx, of a certain type of being

Since Martin du Gard's own death in 1958 and the subsequent publication of his letters to Marcel Lallemand, we know that he shared the pessimistic view held both by his character Antoine Thibault and his friend Albert Camus. Martin du Gard wrote in 1945 of the letters he frequently received from idealistic young people and of his reactions to their childish affirmations:

"Ah, if you only knew what Jacques represents for me! I feel myself to be his equal! He is my brother!" To such persons, I always feel like replying, "Too bad for you!" They think, in complete naïveté, that they will give me pleasure. They are persuaded that, because I depicted the character with tenderness, Jacques enjoys my particular predilection, that he is, in my eyes, a model. . . . Those good folk have read me wrong. I would really astonish them if I confessed to them that I pass upon Jacques about the same judgement as does Antoine, who profoundly loves his brother, but who declares, I think, somewhere, that all in all, Jacques lived and died like an imbecile.[78]

In the same letter Martin du Gard very firmly states his opinion on a closely related question, which has been ex-

---

who does not have enough patience for action; only the pure act suffices for him. The terrorist stands "at the summit of this human family," and Jacques is one of the first examples in French literature. "He dies alone; his example itself is useless. . . . Those who, like Jacques, want to change life in order to change themselves, leave life intact and finally remain what they are, that is the moving yet sterile witnesses of all that which, in man, refuses and will always refuse to live."

[78] "Lettres à un ami," *N.N.R.F.*, December 1958, p. 1,145. The passage from *Epilogue* which Martin du Gard probably had in mind is that in which Antoine describes Jacques's death as an "inept end" (*O.C.*, II, 769). There is also a passage in which Antoine meditates on Jacques's nature and concludes that he probably would never have been more than an "elderly adolescent," had he survived (*ibid.*, p. 931).

tensively discussed in the critical literature [79]—whether he preferred Jacques or Antoine. A conception of *Les Thibault* based on Jacques fails, Martin du Gard claims, to discern that the younger brother "with all his heart, his generosity, his intelligence, with all his personal charm, is, on the intellectual and moral planes, a 'false intellect' [*esprit faux*]—irredeemably false; and, on the plane of his life, an 'impulsive' [*velléitaire*] with no consistency." [80]

Is it still legitimate, then, to take the opposing stance, to argue that Jacques's action was a "magnificent gesture"? [81] Can one agree with Paul Nizan, who views Jacques's death as glorious and inspiring, as holding the key to the future?

Nothing is dead as far as the reasons which made him live are concerned. . . . It would be possible to see only the weakness of man, because we know, as Martin du Gard knows, what were the answers of history to the questions that Thibault was asking himself before being killed on a stretcher by a *gendarme* maddened with fear. But we see only his grandeur.[82]

Can one even consider an argument like that of Jean Grosjean, who sees Jacques as a saint, hero, and martyr, and Antoine as a despicable character, nothing but "stinking energy and false

---

[79] Cf. especially Camus, Preface, *O.C.*, I, xviii–xix, xxi–xxv; Jacques Brenner, *Martin du Gard* (Paris: Gallimard, 1961), pp. 85–89; André Maurois, *Etudes littéraires*, II (Paris: S. F. E. L. T., n.d.), 201–202.

[80] "Lettres à un ami," pp. 1,145–1,146.

[81] Jean Larnac, *La Littérature française d'aujourd'hui* (Paris: Editions sociales, 1948), p. 85.

[82] "Roger Martin du Gard: *Eté 1914*," *N.R.F.*, January 1, 1937, p. 99. A Marxist writer like Pierre Daix also finds hope in Jacques's death. Cf. Régis Michaud's remark that "Jacques Thibault was right in doing what he did, although it was useless. Martin du Gard did not say all this, but it is all there in his books" ("Roger Martin du Gard," *Books Abroad*, Spring 1938, p. 151).

*bon sens"? *[83] Can one agree with Claude Roy, who claims
that each reader, in choosing between Jacques and Antoine,
has the right to his own preference? [84]

Under ordinary circumstances, one might well state emphatically that Martin du Gard must be taken at his word. To
do anything else would be to engage in the purest speculation,
the sort of wrenching and twisting at which critics excel
when they dissect works of literature and find theories that
their authors had not, consciously at least, placed in them. In
this case, however, the issue is not so clear. Martin du Gard
himself has written, in thanking Jean Schlumberger for his
praise of *Epilogue*, "I am very happy to think that this book
brings something new to Antoine, for I have always had the
impression, throughout the course of the *Thibault*, that I have
sacrificed him to Jacques, despite myself." [85]

Pierre Daix points out that in *L'Eté 1914* Antoine was
totally sincere in his belief that Jacques was a fanatic and that
later, in *Epilogue*, he changed his mind and felt that Jacques's
thoughts were uneasy, roving, never fixed. There is a kind of
"higher objectivity" which emerges from a reading of the
entire novel, a series of successive illuminations which ultimately give a more rounded view of Jacques and Antoine
and quite probably bring them closer together than Martin
du Gard had consciously intended.[86] Daix's idea could be

[83] "Un Grand Hagiographe," *N.N.R.F.*, December 1958, p. 1,115.
His remarks on Jacques are on pp. 1,108, 1,111, 1,113. The critics
Roger Giron, André Rousseaux, and Camille Cé all argue that Jacques
is Martin du Gard's preferred character.

[84] "Roger Martin du Gard ou le Massif Central," *Libération*, February 28, 1956, p. 2.

[85] Quoted in Jean Schlumberger's Preface to R. M. G., *Les Thibault*, I (Paris: Imprimerie Nationale, 1960), 10.

[86] *Réflexions sur la méthode de Roger Martin du Gard* (Paris: Les
éditeurs français réunis, 1957), p. 67.

developed further, since Antoine could not have known, as the reader does, how strong an imprint Jacques's bourgeois heritage had left on his attitudes. In their debates Antoine saw Jacques as a violent and uncompromising revolutionary; he had no inkling that Jacques was beset by inner doubts, that Jacques's faith in the man of tomorrow was intermittent at best. The younger brother's pity and love for mankind were infinite, but he was not certain that man was perfectible:

He remained sceptical as to the moral possibilities of man. And, in the secret of his being, there was this pathetic refusal: He did not believe, he really could not believe, in the infallibility of this dogma—the spiritual progress of humanity. To correct, reorganize, perfect the condition of man by a total change of institutions, yes, certainly! But to hope that this new social order would also renew *man*, in automatically creating a fundamentally better species of humanity—he could never arrive at that point. And, each time that he became conscious of this fundamental doubt, so profoundly anchored in him, it was with a poignant sentiment of remorse, of shame, of despair.[87]

Furthermore, though Martin du Gard in his letter to Marcel Lallemand refers to the passages in *Epilogue* where Antoine expresses his belief that Jacques's death was absurd and futile, he does not mention certain other passages. The Antoine of 1918 finds himself infinitely distant from the patriotism of a Mme de Fontanin and much more receptive to the internationalism of Jenny, who has wholeheartedly adopted Jacques's ideas. He thinks, "How much better I would understand him now than before!" [88] Moreover, though Antoine used to find Jacques's disgust with money silly, he now realizes, "It was

---

[87] *L'Eté 1914*, *O.C.*, II, 164 (italics his). When Jacques gives Jenny her first lesson in socialist thought, he echoes the same doubts (*ibid.*, p. 372).

[88] *Epilogue* (© Editions Gallimard, 1940), in *O.C.*, II, 848.

he who was right. How much better we would understand each other today!" [89]

It would seem that the questions of the meaning and significance of Jacques's death and of the author's partiality to Jacques or Antoine must remain open; any answers have been and must be subjective, based primarily upon the reader's ideological presuppositions. Perhaps, however, the problem of Jacques's death can be examined with greater objectivity from a more literary point of view, by considering the position of *L'Eté 1914* in a certain literary evolution. [90] The examination will cast some light on a problem touched upon already, that of Martin du Gard's deliberate deviation from the historical record by his fabrication of the Stolbach documents, in a work which otherwise is so accurate.

With real insight Clément Borgal has suggested that in *L'Eté 1914* Martin du Gard is making events submit to his characters. [91] The Stolbach incident involves the international socialist movement centered in Switzerland and the highest political and military personalities in the Austro-Hungarian and German empires. It is clearly implied in the novel that if

[89] *Ibid.*, p. 820. Antoine adds that he was becoming poisoned by his wealth: "Without the war, I would have been lost." He thinks that he probably would have taken the credit for the first discoveries which his assistants would have made in his laboratories, had the war not intervened. His new determination to change his pattern of living, to sell the Thibault house, and so on, after the war is one of the themes of *Epiloque*. The shadow of bitter irony is cast over the decision, since it can be no more than an intention. Cf. *ibid.*, p. 786.

[90] For the relationship between Martin du Gard and his acknowledged master, Tolstoi, see Martha O'Nan, "The Influence of Tolstoi upon Roger Martin du Gard," *Kentucky Foreign Language Quarterly*, Spring 1957, pp. 7–14.

[91] *Roger Martin du Gard* (Paris: Presses Universitaires, 1957), p. 117.

the documents had been handed over to the proper persons, the effect would have been immeasurable, and that the documents thus provided a last chance to stop the headlong course of the European nations toward war. Why was this incident added to the account of the true events of the summer of 1914? Borgal answers that the addition was made because Jacques Thibault plays a role in the theft of the documents, and that his participation in these events is on a level far beyond that of Stendhal's Fabrice del Dongo's participation in the events of Waterloo.[92] Borgal's point could be further amplified, since not only Jacques, but also three other important characters (the Meynestrel-Alfreda-Paterson triangle) are involved, and Martin du Gard carefully relates the destruction of the documents to Meynestrel's own personal difficulties.[93]

In making events submit to his characters, Martin du Gard is not only moving beyond Stendhal's presentation of Fabrice at Waterloo; he has also taken a giant step beyond the "temporary paralleling" of individual and historical destiny we found in Flaubert's *L'Education sentimentale* and his own earlier *Jean Barois*. Through his use of the Stolbach documents, through his choice of socialist characters who would naturally be deeply involved in the international situation, Martin du Gard has maintained, during a narrative covering

[92] *Ibid.*, p. 118.

[93] It must be emphasized that Meynestrel does not burn the documents, thus negating any possibility of their future utilization, until after Alfreda has left him. At this point the balance between personal and historical problems seems to be tipped toward the personal, and Martin du Gard could be seen as presenting a perhaps naive, though widely held, view of historical causation. One thinks of rumors that major historical decisions are made by the world's leaders because of a moment's *mauvaise humeur*, because of desire for a woman, and so forth.

a full six weeks, a paralleling, an almost inextricable intertwining of individual and historical destiny. This reaches its culmination in the symbolic gesture of the suicide flight, which can be seen as the ultimate confrontation of the privileged hero with the realities of twentieth-century history, as the last nineteenth-century act in a major work of French literature, and as the last possible of such acts. No longer will a character in literature be free to work out his destiny, as was Jean Barois, through the multiple determinants of his heredity and environment. In these transitions must lie the suprahistoricity which so many critics have sensed in *Les Thibault* but never formulated clearly. Thus Martin du Gard's art both reflects and dramatically deepens our perceptions concerning our history. Only now does the full significance of Clément Borgal's brilliant conclusion become apparent. During the few exalted moments in the airplane, Jacques is moving, or imagines that he is moving, "on the same dimension as the world whose fate is being played out at the same time as his own":

Alone in his airplane (*le Pilote* at this moment being only a chauffeur, a "utility") *he has the sensation of holding in balance a universe which is in full madness*, of being the strongest, at the price of a little luck.
Perfect accord of rhythms, doubtless ephemeral. But after his death, all is consummated. There is room only for an epilogue.[94]

The insult shouted by the terrified soldier, though it marks the end of *L'Eté 1914*, was not to be the final word in Martin du Gard's great novel, and almost immediately after the publication of *L'Eté 1914* he began work on a concluding volume, to be entitled simply *Epilogue*. He had installed himself in his small apartment in Nice and was deep in his manuscript when

[94] Borgal, *Martin du Gard*, p. 118 (italics mine).

notification came, on November 10, 1937, that he had been awarded the Nobel Prize for *L'Eté 1914*. His reaction to the news was somewhat surprising; he fled from his home and retired for a few days to a small village, using a false name, to escape reporters. Rumors even spread that he had been assassinated.[95] Surreptitiously he boarded the train to Sweden to receive the award, though once he arrived, he cast off his usual reserve and permitted a number of interviews.[96] At the ceremony he made an important and revealing speech of acknowledgement, which caused his name to be removed from the "club des timides" (to which he had been appointed by the Swedish newspaper *Dagens Nyheter*, along with King Leopold, Greta Garbo, and Charles Lindbergh).[97]

After a trip through Germany and Austria, which deeply affected him and left him more than ever apprehensive for the future,[98] he returned to Le Tertre and resumed work on *Epilogue*. The volume was completed by March 1939, and soon thereafter Martin du Gard and his wife set off on a long cruise and a holiday in Martinique, where they were trapped by the disruption of boat services at the outbreak of the Second World War. They managed to return to France by a

[95] Cf. Malcolm Cowley, "Nobel Prize Novel," *New Republic*, December 29, 1937, p. 232. His family covered for him so well that *Time* reported that "he was traveling when the Nobel Prize was announced, and for several days his family, not knowing how to locate him, doubted that he knew he had won it" ("Prizewinner," November 29, 1937, p. 69).

[96] Reported in France by Elsa Thulin, "Roger Martin du Gard à Stockholm," *Les Nouvelles littéraires*, December 18, 1937, p. 1.

[97] S. de C., "La Distribution des Prix Nobel 1937," *L'Illustration*, December 18, 1937, p. 460. The speech will be discussed in Chapter VI.

[98] Martin du Gard gives his somber reactions to Berlin in a letter to Charles du Bos of January 17, 1938, reprinted in *Cahiers Charles du Bos*, May 1959, p. 45.

roundabout route, via Puerto Rico and New York, and arrived in time for the appearance of *Epilogue* in January 1940. (Publication had been delayed by the onset of the war.) Thus, as Denis Boak points out, the critics who find purposely ironic references in *Epilogue* to the Second World War are manifestly in error.[99]

Superficially, *Epilogue* is a return to the concentration on individuals and the analysis in depth of individual character which mark the earlier volumes of *Les Thibault*. The narrative begins on May 3, 1918—this four-year gap between volumes is by no means unusual. The focus is now almost entirely on one person—Antoine, the surviving member of the Thibault family. There is no more close contact with the external historical world. That ended with Jacques's death. Yet the Antoine of *Epilogue* will not have the opportunity to adapt himself to a new civilian life in postwar France, to marry and perpetuate the Thibault name. All he will be granted is an opportunity to find some replies to the Abbé Vécard, his interlocutor in *La Mort du père*. Antoine is given by the author but one week of life after the Armistice of November 11, 1918.

Epilogue is truly an epilogue; it serves (apart from any philosophical message) to tie together loose ends of novelistic intrigue left over from *L'Eté 1914*. It is not, or is only in a very limited sense, an open-ended volume; as R. Robidoux has stated, it is not a volume of "temps retrouvé," in the manner of Proust, but one of "temps accompli, bouclé, terminé." [100] The principal theme of *Epilogue* is surely death; the volume begins and ends with death, and its shadow is

---

[99] *Roger Martin du Gard*, p. 164.

[100] Réjean Robidoux, *Roger Martin du Gard et la religion* (Paris: Aubier, 1964), p. 310.

omnipresent throughout. The images of those already dead are constantly recalled to mind.[101]

Epilogue is divided into two distinct sections joined by a series of letters. The first part follows the narrative form of the rest of *Les Thibault*, whereas the final part comprises the journal Antoine keeps from July 1918 until his death. When he learns by telegram of the death of the old housekeeper Mlle de Waize, Antoine is in the South of France in a clinic for victims of gas warfare. He has been partially immobilized since being gassed in November 1917, a misfortune which takes place off stage, before the narrative of *Epilogue* begins. Although his voice is feeble and hollow and speaking is an effort for him, he has retained a professional interest in his own condition and in the treatment of the other patients, while keeping a very complete clinical journal of the history of his malady. He has also gained the friendship and respect of several of the doctors. Despite long hours of suffering and frequent relapses, many vestiges of the old, superbly confident Antoine remain. He is totally convinced that by a rigorous and patient effort he will be able to rehabilitate himself and take up his active role in society once again: "With tenacity, there are very few impossible things! . . . Up to the present, everything which I have willed energetically I have done. Why should I not succeed this time, too? . . . I want to recover. I shall recover." [102]

From the very beginning of the volume, Antoine and the other characters discuss current developments, Antoine al-

[101] In particular, Oscar, Jacques, and Rachel. Daniel intends to commit suicide as soon as his mother dies, and her death, too, will not be very far in the future. Antoine, with his perceptive doctor's eye, notices immediately that Mme de Fontanin has the "complexion of a cardiac case" (*Epilogue*, *O.C.*, II, 852).

[102] *Ibid.*, p. 790.

ways from a strongly pacifist and Wilsonian point of view. A good example of these discussions is the commentary on the German attacks in Flanders in the spring of 1918. One man remarks that the enemy offensive seems to be halted, and Antoine adds that their advance must have cost dearly in human lives. Another doctor estimates that the English lost 200,000 men in one month on the Yser, and Dr. Bardot, Antoine's personal physician and friend, exclaims: "If those figures were known by Allied public opinion!" But this is wartime, Bardot continues, and the realities of the situation must be kept hidden; no one is sure today what public opinion really is, though he is convinced that not one French soldier in twenty feels strongly enough about Alsace and Lorraine to consent to one more month of war to regain the lost provinces. Yet the whole world believes that Clemenceau and Poincaré are "the authentic spokesmen of general French opinion. . . . The war has created an unprecedented atmosphere of official lies!" [103] Employing the same technique as in *L'Eté 1914*, Martin du Gard interrupts this tirade by bringing the chief doctor, Professor Sègre, onto the scene. Similar commentary breaks constantly into the narrative of *Epilogue*, and has been sharply criticized by some writers.[104] History, therefore, is very much present in the volume, though always

[103] *Ibid.*, p. 765. One sees readily why the work was bitterly criticized as being antinational, especially because of the date of publication. There were those who felt it should have been banned by the censorship. For example, see Robert Kemp, "La Vie intellectuelle —D'*Epilogue* considéré comme un prologue," *La Revue universelle*, March 1, 1940, pp. 365–370.

[104] Cf. Boak, *Roger Martin du Gard*, p. 166: "Where Martin du Gard's own comments are introduced [in the dialogue of characters, especially Antoine, since Martin du Gard never injects the first person into his novels], when he allows Antoine to indulge in speculation about the League of Nations, the impact of the volume is weakened, much as similar preoccupations had detracted from *L'Eté 1914*."

seen from a distance; the violent and intimate contact of characters with historical events ended with *L'Eté 1914* .

Antoine determines to take a leave and go to Paris for Mlle de Waize's funeral. When Gise comes out of the chapel to meet him, she does not recognize him for an instant—another sharp, yet indirect, indication of how dramatically Antoine has changed.[105] They return to the Thibault home, the first visit for Antoine since the summer of 1914. He is deeply moved by the experience, and finds himself thinking that he is more *chez père* than *chez moi*. Antoine's relationship with his father is one of the important themes of *Epilogue*; Oscar Thibault's ghost "could almost be said to haunt the book." [106] In a pile of old mail Antoine discovers a package containing the amber necklace which had belonged to his mistress of *La Belle Saison*, Rachel, who he later learns died in Africa in 1916. His meditations on the affair with Rachel form another important theme in *Epilogue*. It was "a sorry adventure, but that sorry adventure is, despite all, the best that there is in my sorry life." [107]

---

[105] *O.C.*, II, 776. This effective and realistic technique is twice repeated during the account of Antoine's visit to Paris, and each time Antoine endures a moment of anguish. See p. 802, the encounter with the waiter at Maxim's, and p. 860, the meeting with Nicole, a Fontanin cousin.

[106] Boak, *Roger Martin du Gard*, p. 173. See *Epilogue*, *O.C.*, II, 813–814, 851, 921, 954–955, for Antoine's meditations on his father. As his own death draws near, he feels that he has been too severe toward Oscar, and in a striking passage he looks back on his father's agony and recalls the childhood nursery song his father kept repeating on his deathbed. He wants to hurry with the writing of a projected analysis of Oscar's character, so that Jean-Paul will have a fairer image of him (*ibid.*, p. 979). He never writes it.

[107] *Epilogue*, *O.C.*, II, 997. On Rachel, see *ibid.*, pp. 788, 794, 907, 916–917, 930, 967, 974, and 1,005. For earlier references to the amber necklace, which symbolizes the exotic and mysterious Rachel, cf. *La Belle Saison*, *O.C.*, I, 893, 997, 1,050.

The evening of the funeral Antoine dines with his old friend the diplomat Rumelles, and thus Martin du Gard is able to bring much "inside track" political commentary into his narrative. Rumelles has an exhausted and nervous appearance, and is completely frank and cynical in his *private* estimate of the current political and military situation. (I emphasize the word "private" because Rumelles's precautions against being overheard are what make his remarks plausible and not merely the result of Martin du Gard's *post facto* superior knowledge of then-secret governmental intrigues.) [108] Rumelles admires Clemenceau and is highly scornful of Wilson, whom he feels to be a vague dreamer, an idealistic professor, who has to be humored for the moment so that the Allies can extract from America as much desperately needed material and men as possible. Much of the news is propaganda, he admits; but this propaganda is just as necessary as the "resupply of provisions and munitions." A government cannot direct events, but it can direct opinion: "Our principal duty is the *arranged* transmission of facts." [109] The nation's faith in ultimate victory, in its leaders, and in the justice of the Allied cause must be maintained at all costs.[110]

The following day Antoine pays a visit to the old Thibault summer residence at Maisons-Laffitte. It has been converted into a military hospital, directed by Mme de Fontanin. The

[108] Any historical study of political leaders of the period makes Rumelles's cynical realism appear highly believable. For an account of some of the shady dealings of Clemenceau himself, see Geoffrey Bruun, *Clemenceau* (Cambridge: Harvard University Press, 1943), pp. 113–114, 126, 128, 130–131.

[109] *O.C.*, II, 810 (italics his).

[110] Rumelles gives several examples of these deceptions, including his belief in the necessity of hiding the fact that Allied bombardments of Stuttgart cost more innocent victims than all the shells that "Bertha" could launch on Paris.

nearby Fontanin home has become a "bizarre phalanstery," [111] at which reside Daniel, who has had a leg amputated in the war, Gise, Jenny, and Jean-Paul, her illegitimate son born of her brief union with Jacques.

In following scenes Martin du Gard ties up the destinies of the various secondary characters. Daniel has greatly changed and appears distracted, passive, negligent. Through a number of small details and through erroneous guesses made by the other characters, the reader gradually comes to suspect that Daniel has, like Meynestrel, been emasculated. This is later verified in a letter to Antoine, in which Daniel also announces his intention to commit suicide as soon as his mother has passed away. With what might be seen as exaggerated cruelty,[112] Martin du Gard reserves this punishment for the dynamic and sensual Daniel, who resembles in so many ways that other suicide, his father Jérôme. Gise has found her role as dedicated nursemaid to Jean-Paul, in whom the presence of her beloved Jacques survives, and Jenny, somewhat less reserved and awkward after giving birth to her son, functions smoothly as hospital worker, widow, and mother. At several points Martin du Gard indicates, and even has Jenny admit to herself, that her present situation is about the best possible for her, that she could never have been happy with Jacques for any length of time.[113] Mme de Fontanin has become violently patriotic and anti-German; she enjoys the sense of usefulness

---

[111] *Ibid.*, p. 792. One can readily imagine how terribly shocked Oscar Thibault would have been by these developments, in particular by the complete reunion of the remnants of the two families, the Thibaults and the vilified Protestant Fontanins.

[112] Cf. Léon S. Roudiez, "The Function of Irony in Roger Martin du Gard," *Romanic Review*, December 1957, pp. 275–276. Roudiez argues that Martin du Gard has a sadomasochistic attitude toward his characters.

[113] *O.C.*, II, 839. Antoine claims here that their love could never have been anything but a "misunderstanding." Mme de Fontanin thinks that

and power she gains from her task of organizing the hospital.

Before returning to his clinic, Antoine is determined to pay a call on his old *patron,* Dr. Philip. The scene of this *consultation,* the central episode in *Epilogue,* is one of the most remarkable in all Martin du Gard's work. We have already commented on Philip's observation in Volume IV, *La Consultation,* that the graver the hour, the more one deludes oneself, even if one is a doctor.[114] Also, as Antoine enters and as he leaves, Philip makes the same little moist sounds with his lips that he made at the bedside of the doomed Héquet child.[115]

He immediately begins to question Antoine, seriously, professionally, and this troubles Antoine, since it is the first time he himself has been the recipient of such attention. Martin du Gard is provided with a convenient opportunity to have Antoine tell how he was gassed, which involves an ironic coincidence. If Antoine had not been previously wounded, the slight amount of gas he had inhaled would not have affected him so seriously. With an air of enigmatic concentration, Philip takes out his watch and measures Antoine's pulse. Antoine remembers the advice Philip had given him many years ago—that this is an infallible means of reassuring the patient and of giving the doctor a moment of calm in which he can make his diagnosis. Philip continues with a careful examination and concludes by telling Antoine with an air of great sincerity and perfect optimism that his case is annoying, nothing more.

Over dinner Philip changes the subject, and the discussion

---

they would have made each other suffer greatly (pp. 858–859). Jenny's own ambivalence toward Jacques is noted on p. 880.

[114] See above, p. 85.

[115] The references are to *Epilogue,* O.C., II, 884, 902, and to *La Consultation,* O.C., I, 1,070.

centers once more on the war and the political future of
Europe—another interruption in the narrative. As Antoine
prepares to leave, he turns suddenly to ask a final question of
Philip, his *patron*, his close collaborator for so many years,
and detects in Philip's look an involuntary admission of immense pity. For the first time, in one brutal instant, Antoine
becomes conscious of the fact that he is fatally stricken. His
first thought is to leave as quickly as possible to be alone with
his terror.

A strange nocturnal scene follows: a solitary Antoine
moving slowly across a blacked-out Paris during an air raid.
Martin du Gard is attempting something which is perhaps
impossible; he is trying to get inside the consciousness of a
man who is doomed and knows it. Denis Boak has pointed out
that the death scene of Oscar Thibault is one of the most
effective ever written, but that the horror of Oscar's last
illness and death was essentially "external"; he was unaware
of his condition until his last days. Antoine, on the other
hand, is a doctor, is fully aware of his imminent death for several months. Thus Martin du Gard is here writing of a character's facing death "from the inside." [116] He is presenting a
character who is an atheist, who has no hope for an afterlife,
who will neither be converted, like Jean Barois, nor pacified
by a priest, like Oscar Thibault.

At first Antoine feels an extreme lassitude; he is completely
indifferent to his surroundings, totally obsessed with his new
knowledge. With lucid objectivity he goes back over the
history of his case and now realizes that each relapse has been
more severe and each recovery briefer. One thought calms
him: As a doctor, he has always the recourse of taking his
own life to avoid undue suffering. Thus the subject of euthanasia, which had been one of the rare problems capable of

[116] Boak, *Roger Martin du Gard*, p. 168.

forcing the young and vigorous Antoine of prewar days to meditate, now returns to him. He takes immediate steps to procure the necessary drugs.

At this point the narrative is broken off, and Martin du Gard inserts a series of letters, in which further loose ends are tied up. Antoine, already back at his clinic, informs Jenny of his impending fate and tries to explain to her the effect of this revelation on him, the foreignness which the external world has taken on in the face of the overwhelming reality that he has only between two months and a year to live. With the extraordinary powers of adaptation of human nature, and of his nature in particular, he has after several weeks arrived at a sort of anesthetized indifference. Now he is exercising his will, dedicating himself to a remaking of contacts with the world surrounding him, to a "progressive reintegration into life." [117]

His first concern is for Jenny, especially for her child Jean-Paul, who comes to represent the future and all An-

[117] *O.C.*, II, 912. Antoine writes in his journal that he must not consider only his own insignificant and miserable fate: "*One must not be blinded by the individual*" (*ibid.*, p. 920; italics R. M. G.'s). This is an echo of a remark by Luce in *Jean Barois*, when he faces a potentially fatal operation: "*Let us not be blinded by the individual*" (*O.C.*, I, 553, italics R. M. G.'s). Cf. Boak, *Roger Martin du Gard*, pp. 169–170. Boak has criticized Martin du Gard for implausibility, contending that the shock of Antoine's realization should have left him totally preoccupied with his own fate, incapable of regaining contact with the outside world, and that it thus seems strange for him to develop such a keen interest in politics. Martin du Gard does indicate that this readaptation is a difficult struggle for Antoine, and that it is never more than partial. Also, as a doctor, Antoine has the "security" of knowing that he can choose the moment to end his life. He is reserving this choice for later: "When one has been passionately enamoured of life, one does not detach himself from it easily" (*O.C.*, II, 913). This process of adaptation seems psychologically valid to me, though verification would go beyond the bounds of this study, perhaps utilizing studies of behavior in concentration camps.

toine's unrealized aspirations. Antoine later admits that his
real reason for keeping a journal is to leave a record for
Jean-Paul, who is now a bright and promising lad of three,
with his father's streak of temper and stubbornness. He hopes
that at a later date Jean-Paul will be curious enough to read
the journal in order to learn about his uncle.

Starting from this more limited familial concern, Antoine
begins to develop broader interests, to read the newspapers
again. One could quite accurately compare the conclusion of
Epilogue—both the contents of correspondence and of the
journal Antoine keeps in the last months of his life—to a
curve rising from the low point of indifference and despair
which follows his realization that he is doomed. The peak
would come in the months from July to September 1918,
when in his journal he comments on the war and the problems
and possibilities of the coming peace. This high point is also
marked by his effort—spasmodic, intermingled with notations
on his worsening condition and on other personal matters—
to construct a philosophy of life, to determine the meaning of
existence or lack thereof. These philosophical passages seem
to represent a more or less successful attempt to find a reply
to the Abbé Vécard, and at the same time they are a statement
of Martin du Gard's own beliefs. There are indeed few works
which reveal the image of their author as perfectly as does
Epilogue. Then in October and November 1918, the curve
drops sharply; the notations are more scattered and briefer, as
Antoine's total attention inevitably turns inward with the
approach of death.

Antoine's private journal begins on July 2, 1918, and contains some medical detail, though it is separate from the technical journal he has kept since he was gassed, which his friend
Dr. Bardot has promised to publish. (Here is another reason
for him to hang on to life as long as possible: to write a com-

plete account of his malady, which will have a utilitarian purpose, aiding his fellow doctors in the treatment of similar cases and in further research.) He is haunted by the need to survive in some form, by the terror of total disappearance. Among the first preoccupations which are reflected in the journal is his desire to "organize" his death, to arrange for the disposition of his laboratory, and to make provisions for Jean-Paul's future. The concern for Jean-Paul leads to a proposal to marry Jenny as a matter of pure form, in order to give Jean-Paul legal status and the Thibault name. Despite his pleas, Jenny refuses, claiming complete responsibility for her acts and arguing that the stigma of an irregular birth will be an additional force pushing Jean-Paul into the rebellious course his father would have wanted him to follow. Antoine gives up: "The time when it was impossible for me to accept the slightest defeat has long passed." [118] The Thibault name will thus be extinguished with Antoine's death, and the *Thibault* cycle brought to a close with much less difficulty than if Martin du Gard had pursued his original plan.[119]

Extensive commentary on the current military and political situation is also included in Antoine's journal. There is much enthusiastic praise for Woodrow Wilson's speeches and

[118] *O.C.*, II, 943.

[119] Here is another reason, one related to the novel's structure, for the break in *Les Thibault* and the change in plan. Even though the war was a major crisis in the original outline and Jacques was to die, Antoine was to survive and marry Jenny (thus legitimizing Jean-Paul and also having a girl child by Jenny). It would have been very difficult to break the novel off cleanly. With the new version, the narrowing down of attention to Antoine alone, to the last member of the central generation, the novel can logically be closed. Antoine can dedicate his journal to Jean-Paul, with all the ironies this implies. But there is no artistic necessity to trace out Jean-Paul's destiny; he will not bear the name of Thibault.

programs. The French and English leaders are "petits affair-istes" who remain the instruments of "those imperialist tradi-tions which they pretend to condemn in the adversary." Antoine is certain that a League of Nations, the self-determi-nation of peoples, the suppression of warlike regimes, a gen-eral disarmament, and other Wilsonian ideas mark out the route which Europe must take. And when he has a good day, he remarks, "I think I owe this as much to Wilson as to the in-jection!" [120] He stresses that he is not a utopian, that his scepticism resists when Wilson speaks of purifying the world, though he does accept Wilson's belief that the world can be made safe for the peace-loving nations, that some sort of rational organization and planning is feasible. If Europe does not accept Wilson's reasonable peace, there will be new mas-sacres, though he is quite certain that Wilson will prevail.[121]

Toward September he, his fellow patients, and many of the doctors become highly indignant at what they feel is an Allied plot to turn the projected League of Nations into a coalition against the Central Powers, and Antoine's hope is that Wilson is too alert, too wise to "fall into that imperialist trap!" [122] During October, as his condition worsens, Antoine's political comments become fewer and briefer, and he retreats more and more from the world of life and combat. By the second of November he is completely bedridden. There is a cursory notation on November 10, but significantly enough no men-tion of the Armistice nor of any other world developments in the week which is left to him or, rather, which he allows himself.

[120] *O.C.*, II, 926.
[121] *Ibid.*, pp. 931–932.
[122] *Ibid.*, p. 979. Cf. p. 922, where Antoine further severely criticizes Clemenceau as an imperialist.

Antoine's journal has been described as a document of "crucifying lucidity," [123] and the term certainly applies to the important element of metaphysical speculation it contains. The earlier volumes show clearly that Antoine does not have a "head for philosophy," and he now admits this with perfect frankness, perhaps even being too hard on himself.[124] Only his suffering and his knowledge of his impending death (combined, of course, with the important fact that he is writing for someone, Jean-Paul) push him to scribble down hasty notes during nights of insomnia, to go back and worry again the question, "In the name of what?" This doctor, who frequently describes himself as an *homme moyen*, without real culture, comes to believe that health and happiness act as blinders, that sickness makes one finally lucid: "(The best conditions, to understand oneself and to understand man, would be *to have been sick*, and to regain one's health.) I have a great desire to write: 'The man who has always been in good health is inevitably an imbecile.' " [125]

One is reminded of Baudelaire's conception of the artist as an "eternal convalescent," [126] and of the "delicate child of life," Thomas Mann's Hans Castorp, who is a very ordinary young man indeed, who would surely have remained so and experienced little, had not illness and its accompanying fever condemned him to a long sojourn on the Magic Mountain.

Antoine tells Jean-Paul that while he was practicing medi-

---

[123] Pierre-Henri Simon, "Un Grand Roman de la famille," *Pour la Vie*, March 1955, p. 54.

[124] Cf. *Epilogue*, O.C., II, 963. Antoine rereads a philosophical *exposé* he has written and decides that his weaknesses are all too visible; he tells Jean-Paul that at school philosophy was the only examination he failed and had to repeat.

[125] *Ibid.*, p. 989 (italics his).

[126] See Charles Baudelaire, *L'Art romantique* (Paris: Louis Conard, 1925), pp. 59–60.

cine, he never knew anxiety. The reader, with his "higher objectivity," knows that this is an exaggeration; for in rare moments, such as at the death of the Héquet child or during his debate with the Abbé Vécard, he had been forced to question the simple philosophical structure on which he had based his life. It is true, nevertheless, that Antoine did not have to search far to attain an equilibrium; a few principles, suited to his nature and to his experience as a doctor, satisfied him entirely: "In sum; an elementary philosophy of a man of action, based on the cult of energy, exercise of will, etc." [127] Only after his first wound did he begin to doubt his previous modes of thinking and acting. And now of course in his journal he goes much further in his questioning.

The results of his inquiries are certainly not optimistic. "In the name of nothing" [128] is the only answer he can find to the question, "In the name of what?"—even when he substitutes for it the queries: "What is the significance of life?" "With what does it all rhyme?" This answer is difficult to accept, "because of the eighteen centuries of Christianity so deeply ingrained in us. But the more one reflects, the more one has looked around oneself, and into oneself, the more one is penetrated by this evident truth: 'It rhymes with nothing at all.' Millions of beings are formed on the terrestrial crust, swarm there an instant, then decompose and disappear, ceding their places to other millions, who, tomorrow, will disintegrate in their turn. Their brief apparition does not 'rhyme' with anything. Life has no sense. And nothing has any importance, unless it be to struggle for the smallest possible quantity of unhappiness during the course of this ephemeral sojourn." [129]

[127] *Epilogue, O.C.,* II, 947.
[128] *Ibid.,* p. 964.
[129] *Ibid.,* p. 988.

Martin du Gard told his friend Félix Sartiaux, in a letter of October 6, 1943, of his conviction that man has no preordained or meaningful destiny in this world or in any other. A less absurd universe would be more comfortable. "But I still prefer my disappointments [in the face of this reality] to the false consolations of metaphysical hocus-pocus. I think that I have very completely expressed my viewpoint on page 322 of *Epilogue*. (In writing, I did not even realize to what point I was resuming there *my* 'conclusion'. . . .)" [130]

The passage to which Martin du Gard refers begins with Antoine's recounting a memory. He recalls the hospital nursery he had often passed during the course of his duties; the children would be on all fours, playing with blocks. Some were incurable; some were crippled; others were convalescing. Some were retarded, others very intelligent:

> In sum, a microcosm. . . . Humanity seen through the large end of the opera glass. Many were content with stirring haphazardly the blocks which they found in front of them, with turning and re-turning them on their several faces. Others, more intelligent, sorted out the colors, lined up the blocks, composed geometrical designs. Some, more venturesome, amused themselves by constructing little shaky edifices. Once in a while, a studious, tenacious, inventive, ambitious spirit would give himself a difficult task, and would succeed, after ten vain attempts, in building a bridge, an obelisk, a high pyramid. At the end of the recreation period, everything collapsed. Nothing remained on the linoleum but a mass of scattered blocks, all ready for tomorrow's recreation. This is on the whole an image which resembles life fairly closely. Each of us, *without any other aim but to play* (whatever noble pretext one may attribute to oneself), assembles, according to his caprice, according to his capacities, the elements which existence furnishes him, the multi-

[130] Unpublished; by permission of Mme Félix Sartiaux. (Italicized words are underlined in the original.)

colored blocks which he finds around himself at birth. The most gifted attempt to make of their lives a complicated construction, a veritable work of art. One must try to be among this group, so that the recreation can be as amusing as possible. . . .

Each according to his means. Each with the elements which chance has supplied him. And does it really matter whether one is more or less successful with one's obelisk or one's pyramid? [131]

By September 1918, Antoine's own means are rather limited. But he makes full utilization of them. As his death approaches, he remains faithful to his atheistic principles and refuses entry to a priest, who hopes to receive his deathbed confession and to perform the last rites. Rather than endure the horrible agony of slow suffocation, he gives himself, on November 18, 1918, the long-reserved fatal dose of morphine, just when edema sets in in his legs—that is, at the last possible moment that he will be free to make this gesture. This can be seen as a supreme act of will, the anticipation of death by choosing the moment of death. The final notation in the journal is "Jean-Paul."

Given the date of publication of *Epilogue*—1940—and the multiple ironies in a work whose protagonist is an ardent Wilsonian who dedicates his journal to a boy who will be twenty-five in 1940,[132] one is not surprised that a thoughtful reviewer like Edmond Jaloux finds himself "profoundly demoralized" after reading the volume.[133] Germaine Sneyers, writing in March 1940, finds *Epilogue* a book totally without hope: "Like his hero who is a doctor and who judged his own case

[131] *O.C.*, II, 988–989 (italics his). A correlation has been made with the Pléiade edition.

[132] Cf. *ibid.*, p. 980: "Jean-Paul, I ask myself what your ideas on the war will be, later on, in 1940, when you will be twenty-five. You will without a doubt live in a reconstructed, pacified, Europe."

[133] "L'Esprit des livres—*Les Thibault: Epilogue* par Roger Martin du Gard," *Les Nouvelles littéraires*, April 20, 1940, p. 3.

with lucidity, while impotent to cure it, Roger Martin du Gard makes a terrible diagnosis of his epoch, but without offering any remedy." [134] Mme Sneyers reminds us that of the Thibaults, only a bastard will survive; the family wealth is gone; the work, in her opinion, ends with a failure on every level. *"It is up to the reader to reconstruct.* This is not an easy task." [135]

"Up to the reader to reconstruct"—no one can doubt the bleakness of Martin du Gard's pessimism, his refusal to accept any of the consoling absolutes offered by the world's religions.[136] Yet he makes, despite all, an irrational wager on man, on the continuity of the human adventure—the Pascalian *pari* turned in upon itself. Antoine keeps a medical record of his illness so that others may benefit from the study of his case. He keeps his journal for Jean-Paul. Thus Robert Kanters is, I believe, justified when he writes in a remarkable review of *Epilogue*—dated February 1940, but not published until

[134] *Romanciers d'entre deux guerres* (Paris: Desclée de Brouwer, 1941), p. 269.

[135] *Ibid.*, p. 270. Jacques Madaule thanks Martin du Gard for so much "lucid cruelty." A novelist is not a "vendor of illusions. Certain truths must be faced, and they are bitter. *But it is up to us to see that the life and death of a man regain a meaning*" ("Roger Martin du Gard: *Les Thibault Epilogue*," *Esprit*, November 1940, p. 55; italics mine).

[136] Jean Paulhan, who knew Martin du Gard well through the *N.R.F.*, writes that his personal conclusion was one of "despair without recourse . . . an absolute pessimism" ("Roger Martin du Gard," *N.N.R.F.*, October 1958, p. 579). Roger Ikor makes an interesting distinction, suggesting that as an individual Antoine is victorious "and merits the triumphal death he conquers. *Les Thibault* is an optimistic work, in the exact measure that optimism and victory are permitted man by natural laws." Ikor points out that Martin du Gard's optimism only goes as far as "man confronted with himself; . . . his metaphysical pessimism remains absolute" ("L'Humanité des Thibault," *Europe*, June 1946, p. 45).

September of that tragic year—that the appearance of this work "in these first months of war takes on the value . . . of an act, of an act of optimism." Kanters notes that Jean-Paul in 1940 is confronted with the fact of war, whether he is in Switzerland like his father or at the front like his uncle. "In any case he also must make a deep and solemn act of faith in human progress; so can we with our Thibault friends face the present war, and judge this war, and judge the peace, and have the same confidence, beyond the war and the peace, in the destiny of man." [137]

[137] Robert Kanters, "Simple Adieu aux Thibault," *Cahiers du Sud*, September 1940, p. 435.

CHAPTER VI

The Dilemma of Political Involvement

Robert Kanters is not the only critic who sees Martin du Gard's work as having the value of an act. *L'Eté 1914* is, for Jacques Madaule, "an act in the most vigorous sense of the term, a call to all men of good will, before, as on the tenth of August, 1914, it is once again too late." [1] Albert Camus feels that it is legitimate to view *Les Thibault* as the first of the *romans engagés*,[2] and the conservative critics who attacked Martin du Gard so bitterly were certainly conscious of the qualities of *engagement* his novels contain. It was perfectly obvious, even before Martin du Gard aired his political views to anyone but personal correspondents, that he was an "esprit de gauche." [3] When he received the Grand Prix Littéraire de la Ville de Paris, in October 1937, some of the journalists covering the event were highly surprised and asked themselves if "the Municipal Council had not completely passed over to the Popular Front." [4] After a period of condemnation in the Soviet Union, Martin du Gard's work was totally rehabilitated in 1956, significantly enough the year of the

[1] "Chronique," *La Vie intellectuelle*, January 10, 1937, p. 314.

[2] Preface, *O.C.*, I, xvii.

[3] Georges Altman, "Les Livres: Histoires de familles bourgeoises," *L'Humanité*, April 29, 1929, p. 5.

[4] André Mantaigne, "Une Récompense et un homme," *La Lumière*, October 29, 1937, p. 6.

Twentieth Party Congress. Mme Galperina wrote in the Moscow *Cahiers de la littérature étrangère* praising his work highly: "We would like to say to Martin du Gard that his works help us to live." [5] The Russians also put out in 1958 a thorough Martin du Gard bibliography, the best available source for materials published before his death.[6]

Nevertheless, a piece of literature is not a manifesto, a petition, an electoral program, even when it is deeply concerned with historical events and ideologies. It is to some degree removed from the political and social environment surrounding its creation. Literature can be seen as sublimation, as a substitute for more direct action, and Martin du Gard believed that the artist should limit himself to what could be termed the "second degree act" of literary production. He wrote to Jean Paulhan in May 1930, at the time of the publication of *Confidence africaine*, "You ask of me, with a flattering persistence, some little thing for your review. *I was going to reply to you,* yet once again, that everything I have to say passes automatically into my *Thibault*, when I got the idea of pulling out for you a few sheets from an old diary." [7] The passage "everything I have to say passes automatically into my *Thibault*" has often been misinterpreted by critics, who pull the statement slightly out of context and take it at

[5] Cited in Alain Prévost, " 'Vos Oeuvres nous aident à vivre,' écrit-on à Moscou à propos de Roger Martin du Gard," *Libération*, January 14, 1957, p. 2. Martin du Gard wryly told an interviewer in 1957 that the Russians were preparing an edition of 250,000 volumes of *Les Thibault*, for which he would receive "not one kopeck" (cited in Gene J. Barberet, "A Remembered Talk with Roger Martin du Gard," *Books Abroad*, Autumn 1958, p. 379).

[6] The work is A. V. Paevskoi and N. M. Eischiskina, *Roger Martin du Gard* (Moscow: Publishing House of the All-Union Book Press, 1958).

[7] Cited as a prefatory note to R. M. G., *Confidence africaine*, O.C., II, 1,107 (italics mine).

face value. It is incontrovertible that Martin du Gard had much to say that he could not, in spite of all his efforts, fit into *Les Thibault*, nor into any of his other plays and novels.

Many literary critics and scholars have not bothered with an examination of Martin du Gard's involvement with political and social actuality, and this omission is surely justifiable, given the nature of their concerns. However, when such writers go so far as to assert that Martin du Gard never wrote an article, or signed a petition, or granted an interview, it seems clear that they are carrying their neglect of this aspect of his life too far. In an important fragment of his *Journal*, dated May 20, 1945, Martin du Gard himself furthered such misconceptions. He complains of constant requests from friends and readers that he publish some kind of *témoignage*.

God keep me from it! This long horror which we are living through . . . has not yet moved into the past. It is thus in the domain of *reportages;* and the confused and contradictory thoughts which it can evoke are a matter for journalists only. For the others, the period of maturation has not even begun: we are still at the stage of interior interrogation—and of silence. To be sure, at my age the risk of disappearing, before having taken the step back which is necessary to formulate some sort of historical judgement, is great. But the risk of saying stupidities is worse; and, between the two, I have chosen.

. . . Those among the writers—and I am thinking of the best— who believe that they must descend into the arena and deal with current events, most frequently only do a bad job. It is striking to observe that they never manage to escape banality: what they say one finds—and sometimes the same day—elsewhere; these ideas, which seemed personal to them, are in the air; they are spontaneously being born everywhere at once; writers never manage to give these ideas a more adequate rendering. (And still more! . . . These writers of natural talent, who have always had such a sure taste, who have always been so scrupulous with the choice of terms, do not hesitate, when they are speaking of politics, to employ the politician's vocabulary of hollow formulas. . . .) I am not accusing them, for I know that through their duty, in order to "serve," they abandon their work, and in general that which means the most to them. One can only respect this difficult sacrifice. But one has the right to deplore its existence; these writers are allowing themselves to be blinded by an apparent "immediate duty"; and in order to hatch utilitarian articles of which nothing will remain, they neglect their true duty, which, it seems, would be to pursue their work as writers.[8]

"No one was less *engagé* than he," writes Louis Martin-Chauffier, and "no one complained more of no matter what *engagement* on the part of his friends, going so far as to confuse a *prise de parti*, on a particular occasion, with a *parti pris*." [9] It would appear from Martin du Gard's own words that the critics who argue that he always remained aloof from historical actuality are correct, that Jean Rostand, the only writer to take the extreme reverse position, is completely in error when he asserts: "His pity, his appetite for justice made him see in every accused person an innocent, in every offended cause a cause to defend. *Never did he refuse the prestige of his name to a humanistic-sounding protest.*" [10] One would assume that Pierre Brodin knew what he was talking about when he claimed that Martin du Gard "had always abstained from participating, from close range or from a distance, in a polemic." [11] A writer as astute as Clément Borgal

[8] Published in R. M. G., *Souvenirs, O.C.,* I, cxxv–cxxvi.

[9] "L'Homme qui fuyait la renommée," *Livres de France,* January 1960, pp. 4–5.

[10] Jean Rostand, "En Toute Cause offensée il voyait une cause à défendre," *Le Figaro littéraire,* August 30, 1958, p. 8 (italics mine).

[11] *Les Ecrivains français de l'entre-deux-guerres* (Montreal: Editions Bernard Valiquette, 1942), p. 191. This error is repeated in Brodin's *Présences contemporaines,* II: *Littérature* (Paris: Editions Debresse, 1955), 267.

states that Martin du Gard always stood aloof from any public manifestation,[12] that despite all pleas, including a published request by Georges Duhamel in 1952, he did not give in and make known his views on current problems.[13] Borgal also states that Martin du Gard never wrote for any periodical— no critical notes, no articles, no short stories—"no publication[s], outside of his books." Borgal does admit one exception, the 1919 article in the *N.R.F.* on Jacques Copeau and his Théâtre du Vieux-Colombier.[14] The error in Borgal's interesting and valuable pioneering work on Martin du Gard is not very surprising; the surprise comes when one discovers the actual depth of Martin du Gard's public commitment.

One first begins to suspect that there is some truth in Jean Rostand's claim when one has delved deeply enough into the literature on Martin du Gard to realize that different writers remember a different article or statement as the sole exception to his general rule. At the same time, a study of the available materials shows that Rostand is greatly exaggerating when he says that Martin du Gard never refused the prestige of

[12] *Roger Martin du Gard* (Paris: Editions universitaires, 1957), p. 13.

[13] *Ibid.*, p. 22. The reference is to Georges Duhamel, "Explorations et expériences (Souvenirs)," *La Revue de Paris*, December 1952, p. 6. Duhamel notes that Martin du Gard's disciplined work habits have kept him from commenting in the press; otherwise Duhamel would have known "the sentiment of [his] friend on the great problems of the hour . . . which hold us spellbound and darken our skies."

[14] *Roger Martin du Gard*, p. 24. Borgal repeats the error in two other articles, and distinguished critics like Gaëtan Picon and René Lalou also make it. It is curious that, though the book itself does not make this mistake, the advertising flyer of Jacques Brenner's *Martin du Gard* (Paris: Gallimard, 1961), reflects the common view. After the usual praise of Martin du Gard's virtues, the flyer states, "It is known that Martin du Gard never agreed to give an interview, even at the time of the Nobel Prize, and that he always refused to let himself be photographed for newspapers."

his name for a humane cause. In November 1958, Francis Jourdain published two letters dating from 1933, which Martin du Gard had sent him. An effort was being made to form a committee of "personalities" to aid writers who were exiles from Nazi Germany. The committee already included such members as Romain Rolland, Henri Barbusse, and Charles Vildrac, and a copy of its manifesto was sent to Martin du Gard. His reply stressed his interest in the activities of the group, his lifelong stand against anti-Semitism, and, at the same time, his repugnance for violent manifestoes which might end by hurting the victims they were supposed to protect.

Words mean little, you will say. This is quite possible. But I am a writer, and for me words count. Perhaps this is the proof that I am not a man of action. In any case, I am too much in the habit of weighing my terms to be able to sign, with full approval, professions of faith whose generous tendencies I support, but whose tenor I do not approve.[15]

Jourdain replied, politely but severely criticizing Martin du Gard's abstention, and Martin du Gard wrote a second time, attempting to defend his position and noting that in recent years hardly a week passed without a request for his signature on a protest or manifesto. For many of his friends (Gide especially) the signing of such documents was a generous formality. Up to the present he had resisted such pressures.

(*I did sign three or four times* on particular occasions, which generally I now regret.) Such commitments, solicited with insistence . . . , wrung from me through friendship, prove nothing at all. And the time is close, if it has not already arrived, when these public manifestoes, of a sonorous and vain humanitarian-

[15] Francis Jourdain, "Sur Deux Lettres de Roger Martin du Gard," *Les Lettres nouvelles*, November 1958, p. 500.

ism, will have completely lost their already limited effectiveness. At bottom, they are much less manifestations of humanity than of *politique*. I do not want to *faire la politique*. I do not want to put my little finger into *la politique*.

Still, he adds, we live in an epoch when the future is especially unpredictable: "What I am writing to you here, who knows if tomorrow I shall not deny it? Who knows if tomorrow I shall not myself also be pushed into abandoning my pen in order to combat and act according to my convictions? Who knows if, then, we shall not find ourselves side by side?" [16]

At the time, however, Martin du Gard refused to sign the manifesto, and in November 1934, he was still undecided. He wrote to Marcel Lallemand that for several months he had been "oscillating between the desire to block up [his] ears and the temptation to enter more into the dance."

For the moment, I am the man who turns his back. I repeat to myself that I have passed thirty years and more in struggling against all dogmatic beliefs and getting rid of every passionate conviction in myself; that life "as a spectator" is without a doubt my real lot. That taking sides is a necessity of *action*, but not at all of *thought*, nor of *art*. (On the contrary?) That one must admire those who struggle, those who construct; but not forget that we are of another "climate." . . .

Flux and reflux. Soon perhaps I shall be saying with Mauriac: "Whether we will or no, we all today have a temporal mission." [17]

There is a sense, in both of these passages, of the pressure of contemporary events on Martin du Gard's artistic and personal ideals. It is our contention that the same forces which were working upon Martin du Gard, driving him to enter

[16] *Ibid.*, p. 501. This letter alone would be adequate to refute those who claim that Martin du Gard never joined in a polemic.

[17] R. M. G., "Lettres à un ami," *N.N.R.F.*, December 1958, p. 1,146 (italics his).

the political arena more and more actively, were also influential in leading to the change in plan in *Les Thibault*. This is the other side of the coin of the dialectical process analyzed in Chapter IV. The fact that entering into political life went against Martin du Gard's most basic predispositions, as did the integration of history and ideology into his novels, makes a study of his life and work especially exciting for the historian. The case of Roger Martin du Gard illustrates with a remarkable clarity the complex relationships between historical developments and literary production. If our hypotheses are valid, the peak period of political involvement for Roger Martin du Gard should come in the 1930's, when he was reaching his decision to destroy *L'Appareillage* and was writing *L'Eté 1914* and *Epilogue*, and when, we have argued, he attained full historical consciousness.

The most significant biographical details which point up Martin du Gard's atheism, pacifist humanitarianism, and generally leftist attitude have already been mentioned. Likewise, the analysis of his major literary works has shown that his political-ideological commitments are not only present but quite clearly visible and widely recognized by critics. Should any doubt remain, his posthumously published "Projets de Préface pour *Jean Barois*" (*N.R.F.*, December 1959) are definite proof that he was conscious of the severe attack on religious faith in his earlier work.

In the light of what is now known from these "Projets de Préface," it is interesting to find support in an unpublished letter for Gide's shrewd estimation that Paul Claudel's intense dislike of Martin du Gard was based upon *Jean Barois* rather than the later and more blatant play, *Un Taciturne*. On June 2, 1914, Martin du Gard wrote Marcel Hébert that he had been informed of a heated discussion which had recently taken place at the *N.R.F.* offices: Claudel had violently protested the publication of an article by Martin du Gard in the May issue of the *N.R.F.* Martin du Gard had reviewed a book by Hébert on the Joan of Arc myth, and his remarks on the Catholic Church were aggressively antagonistic.[18] Claudel wrote to Jacques Riviére of the *N.R.F.*, "One more note like that of M. du Gard and I shall definitely quit your review." [19]

In order to analyze more effectively the data which deal particularly with Martin du Gard's public involvement, a division will be made into two major categories: religious and socio-political. Religion will be discussed first, as in general it appears to have been a secondary concern for Martin du Gard. In his mature years he seems to have succeeded in "exorcizing" religious problems, and therefore to have felt himself less obliged to immerse himself in actuality under pressure of these questions. He no longer needed to proclaim his atheism publicly; the didactic tone of *L'Une de nous*, of parts of *Jean Barois*, and of the article on the Joan of Arc myth was no longer necessary. Of course in reality he only pushed into the background problems which were to torment him all his life: Albert Camus has written, "Like every true

[18] R. M. G., "Notes sur *Jeanne d'Arc a-t-elle abjuré?*, par Marcel Hébert," *N.R.F.*, May 1, 1914, pp. 891–893. Martin du Gard takes this opportunity to speak his mind on what he considers to be the development of a myth. "In effect, the *representation* of Joan is evolving in a clearly perceptible manner, under our eyes, in the popular mind: it is being progressively idealized. And it is no less curious to follow the parallel movement which this evolution imposes upon the official interpretations of the Church" (p. 891; italics his). Martin du Gard reviews the facts of Joan's death and notes that up until the turn of the century no one had complained of her abjuration. Now, however, "little by little the official historians of the Church are getting upset; being unable to deny the facts, they denature them, they lessen their significance. They quibble infinitely" (p. 892).

[19] Quoted in Martin du Gard's unpublished letter of June 2, 1914, to Marcel Hébert.

artist, Martin du Gard can never finish with his obsessions once and for all." [20]

Because of its lack of objectivity, its greater resemblance to a polemical tract than any of Martin du Gard's other works, *L'Une de nous* merits brief comment at this time. The work, published in 1910, could be seen as a final and public statement of his break with Catholicism, which, as is known from the Hébert correspondence, he had made in 1901. Later he regretted his bitterness and never authorized republication of the novella.[21] The attack on religion is toned down in *Jean Barois*, and the effort at impartiality is even greater in *Les Thibault*.

L'Une de nous opens with a biblical citation (oddly, the source is incorrect; the passage is from verse 4 of Psalm 32 and not from Psalm 31) which sets the tone: "For day and night thy hand was heavy upon me." *L'Une de nous* is the account of the monumental sufferings of a young woman, Marise, married to a syphilitic cousin. Precise medical descriptions are included, of the kind found in Martin du Gard's later work, and Germain Mussey, the blond-bearded doctor in the story, is a prefiguration of Antoine Thibault. Marise, who has a feeble-minded child, is pregnant again; her husband becomes partly paralyzed and also feeble-minded.

Marise, who has always acted in good faith, has moments of violent protest and contemplates suicide. She cannot believe

[20] Preface, *O.C.*, I, xvii.

[21] When a request was made to republish *L'Une de nous* in a limited deluxe edition, Martin du Gard refused, claiming that he did not like the work: "A poor sketch, hardly worth the effort of bibliophiles, I tell you!" He was upset because he had written it with an "intense emotion," and compared it to an "old photograph when one would like to destroy the negative!" (unpublished letter of November 8, 1927, to Félix Sartiaux).

that God would abuse her so much, and prayer brings no relief. Her arguments about religion with the simple-minded Sister Angelina are reminiscent of debates on a much more advanced level in Martin du Gard's later works. Marise sees as "monstrous counsel" [22] the nun's advice that one must love one's trials, for the nun has experienced nothing comparable to her own miseries. Finally Marise passes beyond rebellion into a sort of gray world of steady, moderate unhappiness, taking care of her two "children," her husband and her son. The concluding words of the story are "Come along, my children, put away your toys; it's time for beddy-bye." [23] Then, with obvious irony, Martin du Gard adds as a postscript a sentence from the evening prayer: "We thank you, O Lord, for all the blessings which every day your goodness heaps upon us."

In 1913 *Jean Barois* was published, followed in 1914 by the anticlerical article in the *N.R.F.* Marcel Hébert died in 1916, and Martin du Gard wrote a memorial tribute, which was not published until 1921, though he valued it enough to include it in his *Oeuvres complètes. In Memoriam* is primarily devoted to an appraisal of Martin du Gard's old teacher, to whom he was so attached, though there are a number of indications of his own antireligious sentiments.[24] He is also indignant over the spying and intrigues which he believes Hébert's fellow

[22] (Paris: Grasset, 1910), p. 93.
[23] *Ibid.*, pp. 101–102.
[24] *O.C.*, I, 561–576. Cf. especially p. 564, "By nature, I had no sentiment of piety" Because Hébert's enemies had accused him of leading people away from Catholicism, Martin du Gard emphasizes that he, of all Hébert's pupils, had been "the one whose religious sense was the least developed. He admitted it with chagrin" (p. 569). They spoke frankly, and when Martin du Gard told Hébert of his loss of faith, he offered his young charge, as a last resort, "the compromise of symbolism" (*ibid.*). We recall, of course, the Abbé Schertz's similar offer to Jean Barois.

abbés used against him at the time of his expulsion from the clergy.[25] When the modernist Albert Houtin prepared a biography of Hébert in 1925, Martin du Gard consented to the inclusion of *In Memoriam* and of two hitherto unpublished letters which further emphasize his rejection of religion.[26] In 1927 alone, Martin du Gard wrote two articles, though much against his will and only at the request of friends.[27] One was a memorial note on Albert Houtin, who had died in the interim,[28] the other a comment on the moral influence of Alfred Loisy. Loisy was the most famous of the modernists, the intellectual leader of the movement which had included the generous and dedicated, but not very philosophically adept, Marcel Hébert. Martin du Gard begins by stressing that those who requested a statement from him have probably confused Jean Barois with his creator. There is nothing autobiographical in that novel, and because of his complete lack of religious sensibility, the modernist crisis would not have interested him at all, had not his mentor Marcel Hébert been "one of the noblest victims of the drama." [29] However, in a brief note added as an afterthought, Martin du Gard does not appear to be so withdrawn from the issues raised by modernism. He is worried about the young postwar generation, and wonders if it can understand what modernism had

[25] *Ibid.*, pp. 571–572.

[26] Cited in Albert Houtin, *Un Prêtre symboliste, Marcel Hébert* (Paris: F. Rieder, 1925), pp. 138–139, 188–189.

[27] After agreeing to write the second article, he stated definitely that it would be the last; from then on his friends would receive a "non possumus" to such requests (unpublished letter of May 12, 1927, to Félix Sartiaux).

[28] R. M. G., "Mon Souvenir de M. Houtin," *Chronique des idées,* October 1927, pp. 148–150.

[29] "Influence morale de Loisy (Lettre à M. Paul-Louis Couchoud)," *La Chronique des idées,* July 1927, pp. 49–50. The article also appeared in *L'Europe,* April 15, 1927, pp. 561–562.

meant "to intellects with a different formation from theirs":

I see them, in large numbers, huddling under the tutelage of the church. They seem, for the most part, to feel a *malaise*, a sort of agoraphobia: Terrified by the flattening of all the dikes around them, stumbling with vertigo before these empty spaces, bewildered by insecurity, they are deliberately seeking prohibitions. What can the liberating work of a Loisy represent in their eyes? The tenacity with which their elders had set about to break down the props, which, precisely, are so painfully lacking to them today, must appear outrageous, incomprehensible, to them. Besides, objections of a historical order do not affect them: their faith has foundations which exegesis does not know how to reach. Bitter lesson of facts! Will these religious aspirations, and this pitiful need to believe, *which one notices even in the look of dogs,* remain so tenacious that the labor of critical intellects will continue to have no effect on the majority of consciences? [30]

After 1927, twenty-four years of silence on these questions. Martin du Gard's views had been made eminently clear, and his concerns were elsewhere; only an event which affected him very deeply could force him to speak out again on religion. The death of André Gide early in 1951 was such an occurrence. Robert Mallet, in his fascinating book *Une Mort ambiguë*, describes the scene of Gide's funeral. Near the coffin was a man in religious garb, and the ever aggressive Paul Léautaud asked, "Who's that in disguise?" [31] The individual in question turned out to be a Protestant pastor, and as the coffin was placed in the grave, he stepped up and read from the Scriptures. Mallet, surprised, looked around; every-

---

[30] *Ibid.* (italics mine). One also observes in this passage a reflection of the general crumbling of values in these years and of the doubts that were beginning to assail Martin du Gard.

[31] (Paris: Gallimard, 1955), p. 141.

body had a nervous air, and Martin du Gard looked really indignant.[32] After the ceremony, Martin du Gard, deeply moved, made a solemn public protest in the name of Gide's friends.[33] A serious debate ensued, primarily between Martin du Gard and Gide's nephew, Dominique Drouin; in his book Robert Mallet writes at length of his recollections of it. Mallet's personal view is that the debate was somewhat superficial, and that Gide wanted to leave his posthumous dispositions a mystery, that this was in keeping with his elusive nature. Gide's real intentions remain an open question, one for Gidian specialists to resolve. What should be noted here is that quite quickly Martin du Gard put together a volume of *Notes sur André Gide*, which was published in the spring of 1951. In these *Notes*, Martin du Gard takes pains to point out that Gide had often expressed his wish for a simple, civil burial, and that he had remained loyal to his agnostic principles, opposed to all churches, until the end.[34] Martin du Gard

[32] *Ibid.*, pp. 142–143.

[33] *Ibid.*, p. 145.

[34] The most important passages on this question in the *Notes* are *O.C.*, II, 1,401, note of July 2, 1932, and pp. 1,422–1,423, a note of May 1949. In the first, Martin du Gard says that Gide told him that he did not want any religious ceremony after his death. He wished it to be *"strictly civil and private."* In the second, Martin du Gard quotes Gide as speaking out against all churches; they must be "dethroned! Their ruses must be unmasked!" When Gide was in a clinic and in pain, Martin du Gard suggested that at such a moment a belief in an immortal soul would be a real consolation. Gide replied that the hypothesis of an eternal life was unacceptable to him *"instinctively, and intellectually"* (all italics R. M. G.'s). Gide's own journal provides considerable justification for Martin du Gard's assertions. In a note of May 27, 1949, Gide describes his life in the clinic as a sort of purgatory brightened by the regular visits of his "incomparable friend," Martin du Gard. "I do not know if ever in the past I have so enjoyed the deep benefit of friendship. . . . No! Religion does not do any better, nor so naturally!" (*Journal, 1942–1949* [Paris: Gallimard, 1950], p. 315).

concludes his notes on Gide with a sentence which surely reflects his own innermost preoccupations: "We must be deeply grateful to him for having known how to die so *well*." [35]
The matter did not rest there. François Mauriac argued, using an ambiguous sentence spoken by Gide just before his death and recorded by Dr. Jean Delay, that there was the possibility that Gide had been struck by divine grace in his last moments.[36] Martin du Gard, who supposedly never entered a controversy, could not let this argument pass unchallenged, and published a note in the *Figaro littéraire* of January 5, 1952, taking strong exception to Mauriac's interpretation. He attempted to demonstrate that a "pious legend" was in the process of formation, and he hoped that there was still time to halt its propagation. Carefully going over the events of Gide's last days, he argued that there was absolutely no justification for attributing a religious meaning to Gide's words. The "historical truth" lay elsewhere: "Gide died, under the eyes of his family, his friends, in a state of the most assured, the most conscious agnosticism; certainly not without regrets, but without hope and without fear. Whether one deplores it or not, it is fitting to accept honestly the *fact*." [37]
This was Martin du Gard's last public utterance on the subject of religion.

It is quite striking that Martin du Gard began to concern himself publicly with contemporary political events just at the

[35] *O.C.*, II, 1,423 (italics his). One could argue that Gide arrived at a quite successful resolution of the final crisis in the life cycle described by Erik Erikson, that of ego integrity versus despair, and that Martin du Gard had much more difficulty, perhaps never attaining such a resolution. See Erik H. Erikson, *Childhood and Society* (New York: W. W. Norton, 1950), pp. 231–233.
[36] For details, see François Mauriac, "Notre Guerre de religion," *Le Figaro littéraire*, August 30, 1958, pp. 1, 8. The sentence is "Yes, it is always this struggle between what is reasonable and what is not."
[37] "Sur la Mort d'André Gide," p. 1 (italics his).

time that he was passing through the serious literary crisis which followed his auto accident of January 1, 1931, during which he was wrestling with the new plan of *Les Thibault*. The German scholar Jochen Schlobach has discovered in *Notre Temps* a manifesto Martin du Gard signed on January 18, 1931, "Against the Excesses of Nationalism, for Europe and for the Franco-German *Entente*." With Romain Rolland he signed an antiwar manifesto in June 1932,[38] and André Gide wrote thanking him for signing a petition in support of a Grand Congrès Mondial contre la Guerre, to be held in Amsterdam in August of 1932.[39] Gide recorded in his *Journal* for April 10, 1933, that Martin du Gard had enthusiastically supported a project to bring Einstein to the Collège de France.[40]

The year 1933 also saw the publication of *Vieille France*, first serialized in the leftist weekly *Marianne*, and then published in book form by Gallimard. *Vieille France* is surely the most radical of all Martin du Gard's works; one Communist writer sees it as literature "in the pure revolutionary tradition." [41] In it Martin du Gard is caught up by the "fever of the accuser." [42] Through an analysis of this long novella, and of an open letter he wrote in its defense (thus defying the

[38] Both references given in the bibliography of Scholbach's *Geschichte und Fiktion in "L'Eté 1914" von Roger Martin du Gard* (Munich: Wilhelm Fink Verlag, 1965), p. 276.

[39] André Gide, *Littérature engagée* (Paris: Gallimard, 1950), p. 16. In this collection of documents, there are many indications that Martin du Gard maintained an active correspondence on questions of current events and ideological positions during these years. See especially pp. 177–178.

[40] *Journal, 1889–1939* (Paris: Gallimard, Bibliothèque de la Pléiade, 1951), p. 1,162.

[41] Antun Polanscak, "Roger Martin du Gard et *Les Thibault*," *Studia Romanica et Anglica-Zagrabiensia*, December 1960, pp. 113–114.

[42] Robert de Saint-Jean, "La Vie littéraire—*Vieille France*, par Roger Martin du Gard," *La Revue hebdomadaire*, March 25, 1933, p. 485.

dictum of *Devenir!*, often taken to be his own: "Literature, go ahead and produce it if you want to, but for God's sake don't talk about it!") [43] we shall see how close he came at this time to following Gide into the Communist movement.

Vieille France is a savage satire of country life, an account of one hot summer's day in the imaginary and typical village of Maupeyrou. Through the device of having the postman Joigneau make his rounds, a classical unity of time, place, and action is maintained. Joigneau is an extraordinarily evil person, who regularly steams open any interesting-looking mail, who has persuaded his wife not to have children so that the mail service will not be disrupted, who like a great spider has spun a web of intrigue throughout the whole town, which in many ways he controls.[44] Decadence and depravity are rampant; the townspeople are materialistic in a groveling, petty, unimaginative way.[45] For the most part the church is deserted; only a few married women and old maids remain practicing Catholics, of the crudest variety, lacking any genuine religious spirit. In one home even the flies have died of *ennui*. The three war "heroes" are no better than anyone else, and the "war widows" are a sad lot, too, working at

[43] *O.C.*, I, 21.

[44] Robert Gibson points out that Martin du Gard had used animal imagery to describe some of the lesser characters in *Les Thibault;* in *Vieille France* this use is much more systematic. "Joigneau, the arch-schemer, is likened to a spider spinning a web; Loutre, the market-gardener, has a neck like a chicken; Mademoiselle Ennberg, the schoolmistress, has the jaws of a pike" (*Roger Martin du Gard* [London: Bowes and Bowes, 1961], pp. 102–103). Almost every character is so treated, including "Madame Flamart, who keeps a roadside café, has nostrils like a heifer, while her frequently cuckolded husband has every bull-like attribute except potency" (another emasculated character in Martin du Gard's work).

[45] Cf. *O.C.*, II, 1,040: In this ancient countryside everyone "thinks only of himself, of his little commerce, of his little security. . . . workers for little profit, whom greed ravages like a cancer."

home so that they can keep their pensions, terrified at the thought of losing them.

With a marvelous realism, and a surprising richness of detail and intricacy of plan for such a short work, Martin du Gard describes this universe of greed, pettiness, hypocrisy, and brutality, and of continual senseless agitation.[46] The young people, who are disgusted with country life, and whom Martin du Gard seems to regard as among the few bright spots in his somber picture, plan to leave for the city.

Three of the major characters emerge from the inhuman mass and are given a rather favorable treatment by Martin du Gard. The old *curé*, who now, like Candide, spends most of his time cultivating his garden, was once an idealistic young priest, who sincerely tried to revive the spirit of Christianity in his avaricious, envious, calculating parishioners. But to no avail: "Little by little a generalized indifference won out over his courage and his patience,—over his health." [47] At the end of the day, the Abbé Verne makes a powerful prayer, which remains unanswered. Martin du Gard ironically inserts the prayer between the half-mad meditations and the salivations of the pathetic M. de Navières and some stupid remarks by the *curé's* despotic sister, who controls him and the church activities. He begs God's forgiveness for his lack of courage, but he feels that he is suffocating in the spiritual aridity of his community. He asks God's assistance in aiding him to love this race of atheists, who have banned Him from their hearts, who act as though they were immortal and have no comprehension of the precipice awaiting them. He knows that he has

[46] "From morning to evening, the men are active. . . . Indefatigably the males, a worried frown on the forehead, run without rest . . . and the women, like obstinate ants [more animal imagery] run ceaselessly back and forth" (*ibid.*, p. 1,062).

[47] *Ibid.*, p. 1,040.

no right to be more severe than Christ, who forgave His executioners: "I ought to pity them; I only know how to condemn them—and to hate them!" [48] In Maupeyrou, then, even a deep religious faith is not enough. The *curé* cannot find love in his heart for his parishioners; he cannot find the reflection of Divinity which should be in each of them.

The two schoolteachers, the thin and pale M. Ennberg and his equally thin and pale sister, do a little better. They take the principle of compulsory secular education seriously, and are both dedicated social reformers, indignant at the conditions surrounding them. Ennberg acts as secretary for the mayor, M. Arnaldon, and suffers when the fatuous Arnaldon repeats the hollow rhetoric of democratic formulas: "And this was, for Ennberg, the worst wound: that which he could not pardon all the Arnaldons of France—being the derisory incarnation of a political ideal for which tomorrow, he, Ennberg, would stoically get himself killed on the barricades of a civil war." [49]

This school year, like the preceding ones, will finish with general indifference to and lack of encouragement for the Ennbergs' efforts. In Mlle Ennberg's seven years of teaching, the one student who had shown intelligence and potential character had been taken out of school by her parents, despite the teacher's pleas and offer of free tutoring. This particular evening Mlle Ennberg ventures to ask her brother whether it is the same in all the communes of France. She gets no answer. "There are certain thoughts which one must systematically reject if one is to conserve one's courage intact." [50] In a scene which reflects back upon the *curé*'s prayer, and which appears to contain an element of hope not found there, Mlle

[48] *Ibid.*, p. 1,099.
[49] *Ibid.*, p. 1,064.
[50] *Ibid.*, p. 1,102.

Ennberg meditates on her solitude, on the life of the village, "on that animal humanity which still grovels in the swamplands":

"Why is the world as it is? Is it really the fault of society? . . . ." And the terrible question which she had already often posed to herself [and which, it will be remembered, also tormented Jacques Thibault and quite possibly his creator, too] obsessed her once again. "Could it not be the fault of man? . . ." But in her heart she retained such a need for confidence, and such an ingenuous fervor, that she never resigned herself to doubting human nature. No! no! . . . Let the reign of a new society finally come—better organized, less irrational, less unjust, and we shall finally see, perhaps, what man can give! [51]

Vieille France would stand alone as a powerful indictment of much that is traditional in French life.[52] However, Martin du Gard went even further and sent a very revealing letter to Marcel Arland of the *N.R.F.*, which was published in the June 1933 issue. (Given Martin du Gard's long and loyal association with the *N.R.F.*, it is inconceivable that the letter could have been published without his permission.) Arland had reviewed *Vieille France* in the May issue and had been generally quite favorable, though he found it an incomplete portrayal of French country life. Arland argued that Martin du Gard did not want to see anything but the evils, and that this short work, though exact in its descriptions, lacked the roundness, the more universal truth of *Les Thibault*. This was

[51] *Ibid.*

[52] In an article entitled "Les Ennemis de la paysannerie à l'honneur," a reactionary paper, *La Production française* (December 19, 1937, p. 3), summarized Martin du Gard's portrayal of a French village and concluded: "It is for having written these horrors about our peasants that this fellow named Roger Martin (du Gard) [*sic;* i.e., he does not in their view merit the title] was made a millionaire by the sadists of Stockholm."

enough for Martin du Gard to compose a long reply, which has a strikingly Marxist tone.

He begins by registering surprise that his little book has stirred up so much resistance, that people have found in it hate rather than despair. "Evidently I showed myself without indulgence for the little people of the French countryside; for those whom I shall call broadly the *peasants*, in opposition to the little people of the suburbs, of the factories, whom I shall call, also simplifying, the *workers*." [53] Martin du Gard continues by stressing that people tend to base their opinions of peasant life on some happy vacation memory, or on an exceptional wartime friendship, or on the "generous poeticizings" of a Ramus or a Giono. (Publicly commenting on another writer in this fashion is also rare with Martin du Gard.) He admits that there are exceptions, but asserts that as a general rule one cannot discover the slightest spark of humanity in this "accursed race," the peasants.

What I ought to have made clear is that I have, on the contrary, much hope for the people of the cities, the *workers*. Yes, there, despite defects, there are immense possibilities of disinterestedness, of fraternity, of spiritual *élans*. Let a society come about in which the division of wealth will be less arbitrary, less unjust; in which every worker will have some leisure, the luxury of a little joy, the time to think of something other than his "croûte,"—then, as my schoolteacher in Maupeyrou believed, we shall doubtless finally see what the man of the people can give! I would like to write one day a *Jeune France* [never published, if he did write it] which would permit me to bring to my bituminous tableau some of the light that I had not been able to put there, whose lack has caused me to be so severely blamed. [54]

---

[53] Cited in Marcel Arland, "Chronique des romans," *N.R.F.*, June 1933, p. 985 (italics in original).

[54] *Ibid.*, pp. 985–986 (italics in original).

The reason for his choice of the title *Vieille France*, which has brought many attacks upon him, is, Martin du Gard explains, his belief that the conditions described in his "documentary film" are well on the way to disappearing: "At present, the formation, the conditions of life, the character of these ancient rural populations, is growing closer to the formation, to the life of the workers. The *peasant* is giving up his place: agricultural industry, in becoming universal, will make out of the rural population a nation of *workers*.[55]

So, in 1933, as Martin du Gard was preparing to face the enormous task of writing *L'Eté 1914* and *Epilogue* and grafting them onto the trunk of *Les Thibault*, he was looking toward the future and toward social change with a certain degree of optimism and was willing to make his views public. By 1934, after the February 6 riots, he went further, put aside the scruples he had shown in his 1933 letters to Francis Jourdain and signed a manifesto to the workers from the intellectuals in the Comité d'Action Antifasciste et de Vigilance. Some of the other signers were Alain, Julien Benda, J.-R. Bloch, Gide, and the Joliot-Curies. The manifesto reads as follows:

[55] *Ibid.*, p. 986 (italics in original). Martin du Gard's very Marxian predictions of the development of a universal agricultural proletariat seem today overly idealistic. The reasons for the persistence of traditions in agricultural France are still intriguing and challenging social scientists. Laurence Wylie points out that the French farmers realize the irrationality of their system, although they cling to it. The peasants in the village of Chanzeaux were not at all surprised at a rumor about the redistribution of their land into four large farms. For years, proposals to reorganize French farming on the model of the kolkhoz or the kibbutz, to break away from a *vieille France* which still in many ways resembles Martin du Gard's of 1933, have been circulated, considered, and even tried. See Laurence Wylie, "Social Change at the Grass Roots," *In Search of France* (Harvard University Press, 1963), p. 199.

United, above all divergences, before the spectacle of the fascist riots of Paris, and of the popular resistance which alone faced them, we declare to all the workers, our comrades, our resolution to join them in the struggle. . . .

We shall not permit the anger which the financial scandals brought to the surface to be turned against the Republic by the banks, the trusts, the cannon merchants.[56]

There is no evidence of any public statements by Martin du Gard in 1935 and 1936 until the publication in November 1936 of *L'Eté 1914*, with its strong pacifist message. From his correspondence with Marcel Lallemand it is now known that he was becoming discouraged about the prospects of communism and more and more entrenched in an unyielding pacifism. In words which are repeated in part by Jacques in *L'Eté 1914*,[57] and which suggest the loss of the hopes expressed in *Vieille France* and in the letter to Marcel Arland—a turning away from the idealism of the young teacher toward the pessimism of the old *curé* of Maupeyrou—Martin du Gard writes:

Am hard like iron *for neutrality*. Principle: anything, *rather than war! Anything, anything!* Even fascism in Spain! And do not press me, for I would say: yes . . . and "even fascism in France! . . ." It would be necessary to have totally forgotten *what war is* for a people: the supreme evil, suffering for the *n*th power. Nothing, *no trial*, no servitude, can be compared to war and all that it engenders. Do you have such a short memory? Does the "partisan" in you smother the "human"? *Anything,* Hitler, rather than war! (And besides, war would also be civil war, possible triumph of communism after years of blood, of

[56] Given in Léon Pierre-Quint's *André Gide* (Paris: Stock, 1952), pp. 534–535. Martin du Gard probably also signed a petition for the liberation of the German Communist Thaelmann and a telegram in the summer of 1936 supporting the Republican government in Spain.

[57] Cf. above, p. 139.

ruins, of unnamed trials.) And really the regime of the U.S.S.R. tempts me less and less, after the infamous Moscow trial. Man is man, with his adject essence.[58]

Shortly before receiving the Nobel Prize in November 1937, Martin du Gard, together with Gide, Mauriac, and Duhamel, sent an appeal to the Negrin-Prieto government in Madrid, which was reproduced in *Le Populaire*.[59] They demanded free trials and the privileges of defense for political prisoners—not, as Gide pointed out, because the writers had deserted the Republican cause but because of their loyalty to it and their hope that the Republicans would not resort to Francoist methods.[60] Later, after the Republican defeat, Martin du Gard became a member of the Comité d'Aide aux Intellectuels Espagnols. Through the efforts of this committee a number of Spanish intellectuals were able to leave the concentration camps which the French government had set up for refugees, to move to houses rented for them on the outskirts of Paris, and eventually to emigrate to South America.[61]

In some ways the winning of the Nobel Prize and Martin du Gard's activities at that time can be seen as the culmination of his involvement in political actuality. After 1937, and especially after 1940, he came to feel more and more *dépassé par les événements* and to feel that he had lived beyond his time,

[58] R. M. G., "Lettres à un ami," *N.N.R.F.*, December 1958, p. 1,150 (italics his).

[59] "Un Appel d'intellectuels français pour les garantis juridiques des accusés politiques en Espagne," October 27, 1937, p. 3.

[60] Gide, *Littérature engagée*, pp. 195–199.

[61] *Ibid.*, p. 201. In an unpublished letter of January 22, 1939, Martin du Gard wrote Félix Sartiaux of his great apprehension about Spain. "What a lot of naïveté I need to pursue my work, to tell my little stories." This sentiment, which sometimes seems to develop into a severe feeling of guilt over the fact that he is now old and safe from most of the danger and suffering of the age, is a recurrent theme in his later correspondence and in *Souvenirs*.

that he had no real sympathy for or comprehension of the new age, and that he had nothing to say to the younger generation.

Just after the announcement of the Nobel Prize (for obvious reasons on Armistice Day, 1937), the reporter Lucien Vermont caught up with Martin du Gard, by chance or by patience, and tried to interview him. At first Martin du Gard graciously refused,[62] but he did go on to admit his great pleasure at the honor granted him and his "secret hope" that the Nobel Prize would help the distribution of *L'Eté 1914*, in which he had tried, according to his abilities, "to work for peace, in drawing upon the example of the past, in resuscitating those days of anguish which preceded mobilization, in showing the absurd inertia of the pacific masses confronted with the menace of war." [63]

When he arrived in Sweden, he put himself freely at the disposition of the Stockholm journalists, and participated wholeheartedly in the festivities.[64] His Nobel Prize speech, which he knew would be widely circulated, has been viewed as a "confession." [65] Besides a discussion of his literary principles, which especially stresses his debt to Tolstoy, his speech

---

[62] He drew a parallel with his four-year-old grandson, who had wanted to follow him into the bathroom so that he could see him climb into the tub naked (Lucien Vermont, "Roger Martin du Gard Prix Nobel 1937 nous dit . . . ," *Les Nouvelles littéraires*, November 20, 1937, p. 1.

[63] *Ibid.*

[64] This information is from the detailed account by Elsa Thulin, "Roger Martin du Gard à Stockholm," *Les Nouvelles littéraires*, December 18, 1937, p. 1.

[65] R. Cheval, prefatory note to R. M. G., "Discours de Stockholm," *N.R.F.*, May 1959, p. 956. The speech itself is reprinted on pp. 957–960. Cheval comments on the parallel with Albert Camus's Nobel Prize speech exactly twenty years later, in which Camus deals very precisely with what has happened to Jean-Paul's generation—for which Antoine had so much hope. See Albert Camus, "Discours à

contains a fervent statement of his pacifism. Building from
what he told the reporter Lucien Vermont, Martin du Gard
suggests that one of the reasons for his having been chosen
may well have been the title of his most recent work, *L'Eté
1914*.

I have tried to resuscitate the anguished atmosphere of Europe,
on the eve of the mobilizations of 1914; I tried to show the
weakness of the governments of that time, their hesitations, their
imprudence, their unconfessed appetites; I tried especially to
make perceptible the stupefying inertia of the pacific masses, in
the face of the approach of the cataclysm which would claim
them victims, and which was to leave behind *nine million* men
dead, *ten million* men mutilated.

The Nobel jury, he further suggests, may also have made
this choice, which would automatically increase the prestige
and distribution of *L'Eté 1914*, because it felt the book capable "of defending certain values which are once again men-
aced, and of struggling against the disastrous contagion of the
forces of war." [66] As a son of the Occident, where the sound
of arms is once more threatening, he finds satisfaction in the
thought that his work can serve the cause of letters and, even
more, the cause of peace.

In these months of anxiety which we are living through; when,
already, blood is being shed in two extremities of the globe;
when already, almost everywhere, in an atmosphere poisoned
by misery and fanaticism, passions are fermenting, around lev-
eled cannon; when, already, too many indices reveal to us the
return of that cowardly fatalism which, alone, permits wars; in

l'Académie suédoise," *Les Prix Nobel en 1957* (Stockholm: Imprimerie
Royale P. A. Norstedt et Söner, 1958), pp. 47–50.
[66] "Discours à l'Académie suédoise," *Les Prix Nobels en 1937*
(Stockholm: P. A. Norstedt et Söner, 1938), p. 69 (italics his).

this exceptionally grave moment which humanity is traversing, I wish—without vanity, but with all my heart, which is gnawed with uneasiness—that my volumes on "L'Eté 1914" will be read, discussed, and that they will recall to everyone (to the old who have forgotten it, as to the young who are ignorant of it), the pathetic lesson of the past.[67]

Sometime before September 1939, Martin du Gard came to believe that the "pathetic lesson of the past" no longer provided an adequate guide for present action, and came to see war with Nazi Germany as inevitable, doubtless partly because of his visit to Germany during his return trip from Sweden. Yet in July 1938, he was far from abandoning the pacifism of his Nobel Prize speech. The Rassemblement Universel pour la Paix asked him for a declaration supporting its campaign, and he responded with a strong condemnation of war, which was published in *La Dépêche socialiste*. And, in a striking example of how politics can move into the domain of art, the condemnation is repeated almost verbatim in *Epilogue*, in a discussion of the horrors of war involving Antoine, Jenny, Daniel, and others. In both cases the word *monstrueux* is several times repeated. Both manifesto and novel express the notion that it is absurd to condemn the extensions of armed conflict—bombing of civilian populations, for example—if one accepts the necessity and justice of war in general. After all, women, children, and elderly people are no more "innocent" than the sons and husbands and fathers on the front lines. In the words of the manifesto, "Ce qui est

[67] *Ibid.*, pp. 69–70. In a letter of January 4, 1938, to Marcel Lallemand, Martin du Gard indicates clearly the great value he placed on this speech: "I did all that it was necessary to do, all that was expected of me. I think that my stay in Sweden has had an effect, and in the sense that I wanted" ("Lettres à un ami, *N.N.R.F.*, December 1958, pp. 1,154–1,155).

monstrueux, c'est la guerre tout court"; [68] according to *Epilogue*, "Ce qui est monstrueux, ce n'est ceci ni cela: c'est la guerre tout court!" [69]

The manifesto also describes as *monstrueux* the European masses' having let themselves, once again, after twenty short years, be brought to the brink of war. Their having permitted the sabotage of the efforts to create European unity through a genuine international tribunal, disarmament, and all the rest is equally *monstrueux*. What is most *monstrueux* of all is to observe public opinion "coldly analyzing 'total war,' submarine, aerial, and chemical warfare, treating a possible conflict as a sort of cosmic disaster independent of human wills [sometimes in *L'Eté 1914* Martin du Gard himself seems to hold this view]." The public has foolishly forgotten that "a war is a social event, whose realization in the last resort depends upon the consent or refusal of the mobilized masses."

And yet more monstrous is the fact that in this Europe unanimously terrified before the approach of the cataclysm, the instinct of conservation is not strong enough to provoke finally the liberating leap; the peoples of Europe have not been able to regain self-control, to arrive at understanding and union in spite of those who govern them, in order to create, against any war, no matter where it comes from and whatever be the pretexts, the vast movement of fraternal defense and cooperation which, alone, can assure common salvation.[70]

Within a year Martin du Gard came to change his mind. He told Jacques Brenner in 1951 that after the outbreak of hostilities in 1939, a number of young people who had read *Les*

---

[68] "Condemnation de la guerre," *La Dépêche socialiste,* July 30, 1938, p. 2.

[69] *O.C.,* II, 872.

[70] "Condemnation de la guerre," p. 2.

Thibault asked him if they should desert. "There, I thought, that is my influence on the young. Alas!, the war for some time [*depuis un certain temps*] had seemed to me to be inevitable, and I hoped that Nazi Germany would be defeated as rapidly as possible." [71] Another correspondent reports that Martin du Gard came to suspect that what he had said in *L'Eté 1914* had not been opportune. Circumstances in 1939, Martin du Gard felt, were not the same as in 1914, so that to ask what Jacques Thibault would have done in 1939, as people did, was to some degree irrelevant. "Nevertheless," he told Jean Heber-Suffrin with great seriousness, "at that particular moment I greatly regretted having written *L'Eté 1914*." [72]

The excerpts from his *Journal* which Martin du Gard published in his *Souvenirs* do not provide much detail about his activities during the Second World War. From time to time he remarks on the passionate, sometimes terrified, interest he has in events and on how this interest keeps him from concentrating on his literary projects.[73] Other sources show, however, that he maintained an impeccably correct attitude during the Occupation, an attitude which went beyond observation to an actual, if limited, participation in Resistance activity. This happened despite his rapid evolution toward an almost total pessimism after the more active and hopeful period of about 1932–1938, and despite ill health and advancing years.[74]

[71] Cited in Jacques Brenner, "L'Eté 1939," *N.N.R.F.*, December 1958, p. 1,055.

[72] Recorded in Jean Heber-Suffrin, "Roger Martin du Gard," *La Grive*, October–December 1958, p. 15.

[73] See especially *O.C.*, I, c, cxix, passages containing the phrase "*actualité* devours," and cxxi.

[74] By June 1942, he had lost more than forty pounds, and his health was, as a result, generally mediocre (*ibid.*, p. cvii). In Martin du Gard's unpublished correspondence with Félix Sartiaux, there is a fairly detailed account of his activities and attitudes during these

The literary supplement of *Le Figaro* (in its Lyons edition, because of the Occupation) published a questionnaire in October 1940. The central theme was the shape and scope of literature of the future. The inquiry also asked whether French literature before the war had been on a "wrong track" and if a great "reappraisal" was needed. Martin du Gard saw fit to reply, and most of his response was printed:

I have some difficulty in considering literature as an enterprise which can be steered in one direction or another. The expression of contemporary thought evolves with that thought, according to mysterious and historical laws which do not depend on our own wills. French literature follows its "route" (as the questionnaire very improperly says), which is neither true nor "false," which is, very simply, its route. One can like or not like its manifestations, but to me it seems illusory to want to direct its orientation, and puerile to attempt its "recovery" [*redressement*]. Were a young and powerful genius to appear tomorrow, our entire literature could be influenced in a direction which our critics have not predicted, nor indicated, nor wished. I think that the role of the critic is to follow and to comment, rather than. . . . But I am perhaps in error, and we may be moving toward a time when the literature, like the economy, will be "*dirigée*"? . . . As for the "role" of the writer in "public life," do you not think that it has always been the same in all historical epochs? The role of writers of first rank has al-

---

years. His letters are in a uniformly apocalyptic vein. He has no hope for a liberal democratic resolution of the war, and has come to believe that either fascism or communism will win out, that any sort of individualistic ideology will be doomed, and thus much, if not all, he values. He cannot believe, as do many around him, that there will be a return to order with the cessation of hostilities; he predicts a long period of social upheaval. "Are we not moving toward an epoch when *all will be forbidden to the individual* . . . ," Martin du Gard wrote to his architect friend on November 4, 1941 ("Lettres à l'architecte," *Cahiers du Sud*, January 1959, p. 338, italics his).

ways been considerable, and it will always be so, as long as . . .[75] [three lines have been deleted by the censor].

Word reached America in 1942 that Martin du Gard was living in the South of France and not "collaborating."[76] In the same year he made a bad guess about Pétain in a letter to Gide (Gide admits that he held the same view, but that they both soon revised their opinion). Martin du Gard suggested that the man had a certain natural nobility, that there was a "Pétain enigma," that Pétain might conceivably be at bottom "the most 'Gaullist' of us all."[77]

When the German occupation of the "Free Zone" of Southern France began in 1943, Martin du Gard's friends provided him with a false identity card as a protection. His scrupulousness was so extreme and his horror of false situations so strong, that almost immediately after he was given the card he destroyed it, "to regain his liberty of spirit."[78] After a meeting with the critic Georges Sadoul, in the spring of 1943, Martin du Gard gave his full adherence to the clandestine Comité National des Ecrivains.[79] Sadoul, today an internationally recognized and respected writer on the cinema, gives some details on Martin du Gard's courageous actions during this period. While his wife was working with the Swedish Red Cross preparing soups for undernourished children,[80]

[75] "Réponse," *Le Figaro*, Edition de Lyon, October 19, 1940, p. 3.

[76] From a "Biographical Note," *Accent*, Spring 1942, p. 130. The same issue contains the English translation of *Confidence Africaine*.

[77] Cited in Gide, *Journal, 1942–1949*, p. 19.

[78] Henri Chaperon, "Roger Martin du Gard (Souvenirs)," *Bulletin de la Société Littéraire des P. T. T.*, June 1959, p. 10.

[79] Georges Sadoul, "Rencontres, sous l'occupation, avec Roger Martin du Gard," *Les Etoiles*, June 19, 1945, pp. 1, 3.

[80] From an unpublished letter of Martin du Gard to Félix Sartiaux, March 13, 1944. His wife appears to have been an admirable woman, whose devout Catholicism did not have adverse effects on a long and happy marriage, which lasted until her death in 1949.

Martin du Gard hid an old friend, a Jewish professor from the University of Budapest, in his apartment. The Gestapo finally caught him, despite all Martin du Gard's efforts. Georges Sadoul adds: "I know that he made for this man, and for a hundred others, whom he did not always know, a hundred efforts, always ready as he is to devote himself to his fellow men. But he doesn't like this to be repeated, and doubtless he will reproach me for having spoken of it." [81]

Warned by friends in the Resistance that his name was on a list of suspects who would be arrested by the Germans in the event of an Allied landing in Provence, Martin du Gard and his wife left Nice in April 1944. They waited out the war in the department of the Lot, near Figeac, where his daughter's family had taken refuge.[82]

In the immediate postwar years, Martin du Gard's feeling of remoteness from contemporary events grew ever stronger. There is, however, an interesting note by Martin du Gard on the Académie Française, which was first published by Jacques Brenner in 1961. The context of the note shows clearly that it dates from the postwar period, and it casts light both on Martin du Gard's attitude during the war and on the reasons why he never pressed his candidacy to the Academy, though he surely would have been elected had he done so.[83] He asserts that he would take no pride in belonging to a group of

[81] "Rencontres," p. 3.

[82] From the chronological index at the beginning of the *Oeuvres complètes*. There are references to this move in Martin du Gard's correspondance, and it is reported in various biographical accounts, including Georges Sadoul's.

[83] Cf. Pierre Descaves, "Roger Martin du Gard, écrivain de race," *Erasme*, September 1946, p. 370. Descaves writes that Martin du Gard's friends would like to see him enter the Academy, and cites the precedent of Claudel, who was elected without actually submitting his candidacy. He hopes this precedent will work in favor of Martin du Gard.

whose wartime conduct he disapproved, since the Academy, without really compromising itself, had adopted a "passive attitude" which would have disappointed him, had he retained any illusions about it."

The silence of writers who were isolated, muzzled, at the mercy of torturers, was legitimate. That of the Academy was not. One expected from it a vibrant collective protest, which would have been as resounding, and would have had as much spiritual effectiveness, as that of the Belgian bishops, as that of the Dutch bishops. It was the Academy's duty to make its voice heard with dignity throughout the world, in the defense of the cause of suppressed thought and ridiculed justice. The individual courage of some of the members is known to me. But precisely the fact that this rebellious minority was not able to bring about a public censure launched by the entire Academy, by the Institute of France in its totality, proves how small in number the *Résistants* were among its ranks. This is not the brotherhood I wish for myself.[84]

The feeling of remoteness already described, and a concomitant sense of the incoherence of the present and the dangers of the future [85] were strong in Martin du Gard in these postwar years. Still, he did not retreat into complete isolation, though his public appearances were nonpolitical. They were primarily for the benefit of his favorite charity, an organization to provide books for sanatoria, which were especially overpopulated as a result of the privations of the war.[86] In

[84] Photocopy reproduced opposite p. 129 of Jacques Brenner's *Martin du Gard*.

[85] Cf., for example, an unpublished letter of June 21, 1947, to Mme Sartiaux: "Our colonial policy is incoherent, like all the rest. Wherever one looks, storms are gathering on the horizon."

[86] Cf. Descaves, "Roger Martin du Gard, écrivain de race," for details of a large charity sale at which Martin du Gard was present.

1949 Martin du Gard published an article in homage to his old friend Jacques Copeau, and a translation from English of Dorothy Bussy's novel *Olivia*.[87] Then in 1950 a note on Maupassant appeared.[88] The same year Martin du Gard accepted an honorary presidency of the Société des Amis de Léon Blum. This appears to be a politically significant act, though it must be specified that the main aim of this group, which has been largely accomplished, was to provide wide access to Blum's work through an extensive publishing venture.[89]

The controversy over Gide's death and the preparation of the *Notes sur André Gide* must have demanded a good portion of Martin du Gard's energy and attention, and there is no record of a public pronouncement on a political subject in 1951 or 1952. But at the time of the Rosenberg trial in 1953 Martin du Gard joined a number of distinguished French intellectuals, including Louis Aragon, Camus, and Simone de Beauvoir, in sending a telegram to the President of the United States demanding that Ethel and Julius Rosenberg be saved.[90]

From 1938 to 1953 he was president of the group, La Lecture au Sanatorium. In a little journal the organization published, Martin du Gard wrote a number of notices, and a longer article in *Le Figaro*, "La Grande Misère des bibliothèques des sanatoriums," May 29, 1946, p. 1.

[87] "Hommage à Copeau," *Les Nouvelles littéraires*, February 10, 1949, p. 1; and Olivia [Dorothy Bussy], *Olivia* (London: The Hogarth Press, 1949), R. M. G., tr. (Paris: Stock, 1949).

[88] "Que pensez-vous de Maupassant," *Les Nouvelles littéraires*, August 3, 1950, p. 1.

[89] Information from Le Parti Socialiste S. F. I. O., *En Hommage à Léon Blum—Troisième anniversaire de sa mort; "L'Action des Socialistes en 1936"* (Arras: Société d'Editions du Pas-de-Calais, 1953), p. 24.

[90] Reprinted in "Pour Ethel et Julius Rosenberg," *Les Lettres françaises*, June 18–25, 1953, p. 1.

This act could be seen as a reply to Georges Duhamel's published request of December 1952 that his friend make known his views on the dark problems of the age.[91] After the Rosenbergs were executed, Martin du Gard joined in another manifesto which praised the judges who had not accepted the death sentence and demanded that "every possible step be taken to assure the prompt rehabilitation of the parents of Michael and Bobby Rosenberg, heirs of their honor." [92]

Periods of ill health, an occasionally expressed wish for a quick, painless death, a progressive withdrawal from the world, and a sense that he was gradually emptying himself of his personality—"soon only the envelope, the appearance will remain" [93]—marked the decade of the 1950's for Roger Martin du Gard. The protests over the Rosenberg case were, nonetheless, not his final public acts. He joined the two other living French Nobel Prize winners, Camus and Mauriac, in an October 1957 telegram to Hungary's Premier Kadar, requesting the immediate release of the writer Tibor Déry and certain other imprisoned intellectuals.[94] Martin du Gard was deeply upset by their imprisonment and let himself be drawn into signing the telegram, under Camus's prodding,[95] even though he believed, as he had in the 1930's, that such inter-

[91] See above, n. 13.

[92] Reprinted in "L'Honneur des Rosenberg, pour la réhabilitation," *Les Lettres françaises,* July 2–9, 1953, p. 1.

[93] R. M. G., "Lettres à l'architecte," *Cahiers du Sud,* January 1959, p. 354. The letter was begun April 2, 1955, and completed April 4.

[94] "For Tibor Déry," Paris: The Tibor Déry Committee, 1959, p. 15 (a pamphlet giving full details on the case and reproducing various relevant documents).

[95] Martin du Gard's respect for Albert Camus was great enough for him to write an article of homage at the time of the younger man's Nobel Prize: "Personne n'est moins dupé: personne plus indépendant," *Le Figaro littéraire,* October 26, 1957, p. 1.

ventions tend to exasperate those in power and, if anything, to worsen the condition of prisoners.[96] Déry was set free in 1960.

The rule of the *bagarreurs*[97] (difficult to translate—perhaps "uncouth squabblers") seemed to Martin du Gard to be one of the prime characteristics of the 1950's, and an intellectual's plea could obviously have no effect on a *bagarreur*. Yet he was sufficiently shocked and revolted to sign a solemn petition to the President of the French Republic, René Coty, concerning one of the most somber incidents in the somber episode of the Algerian War. *L'Humanité* reprinted it on the front page of its edition of April 17, 1958:

> The undersigned:—
>
> —protest against the seizure of Henri Alleg's book, *The Question*, and against all the attacks against liberty of opinion and expression of ideas that recently preceded this seizure.
>
> —Ask that the facts reported by Henri Alleg be disclosed publicly and with complete impartiality.
>
> —Call on the Administration, in the name of the Declaration of the Rights of Man and of the Citizen, to condemn unequivocally the use of torture, which brings shame to the cause that it supposedly serves.
>
> —And call on all Frenchmen to join us in signing this "per-

[96] "For Tibor Déry," p. 16 (photocopy of an undated letter of Martin du Gard to a Hungarian refugee friend).

[97] In contrast with his joy at the news of Camus's Nobel Prize, Martin du Gard writes of "these mournful autumn days, when men of my age feel the shadows thicken around them, and are tempted, every morning a little more, to detach themselves from a world of *bagarreurs*" ("Personne n'est moins dupé," p. 1). The word is repeated in a letter of July 2, 1958, to Mme Sartiaux, cited below in n. 98.

sonal petition" and sending it to the League for the Rights of Man. . . .

Signed . . .

André Malraux

Roger Martin du Gard

François Mauriac

Jean-Paul Sartre.[98]

Martin du Gard died on August 22, 1958, and his last public act, the signing of the petition, was the one most frequently mentioned in obituary articles. Jean Tortel, one of the many who thought that this was the only time Martin du Gard had broken his rule of silence, found it remarkable "that the last gesture as a writer of this *taciturne* was to give his signature. For many, . . . his name beside the three others confirmed something which is a hope, or rather the true image of a

[98] This is the translation reprinted in the American edition of *The Question*, John Calder, tr. (New York: George Braziller, 1958). The book was first published by the Editions de Minuit in 1957, and during its two weeks of open sale sold 150,000 copies. It was then suppressed, the first book to be seized and burned in France since the eighteenth century. After the signing of the Armistice on March 18, 1962, which ended the seven-year Algerian conflict, the book again became available in France, with the petition to the President of the Republic reprinted on the back cover. Alleg, his health damaged by the almost incredible tortures he endured, escaped from a prison hospital in the fall of 1961, and is now back at his old job of editing *Alger républicain*. Martin du Gard's own private comment on his signing the petition was that it was a "histoire de fous." Having the Nobel Prize, having a book highly valued in Sweden, did not seem to him to have much to do with "the redoubtable military justice." He adds that the greatest advantage of De Gaulle's regime was that no one would miss the "collection of nearsighted clowns" that he replaced. "Yes, it was a close call! But let us not deceive ourselves, it's not finished; and the rule of the *bagarreurs* is, throughout the world, one of the characteristics of the new age" (unpublished letter of July 2, 1958, to Mme Sartiaux).

French intellectual tradition, which had apparently been brutally destroyed." [99]

It is a comment not only on the caliber of the man, but also on the times, that such a writer as Martin du Gard, with such a strong lifelong predisposition against public expression of his political and ideological convictions, could have broken his own rule of silence so frequently. At the same time, there is no denying that he did not speak out on many issues, and he dedicated himself more wholeheartedly to literature, and to literature alone, than have other important French novelists—for example the three who signed the Alleg petition with him. Perhaps Jean Rostand best characterizes Roger Martin du Gard's role when he speaks of him as "one of those tutelary consciences, whose simple presence, even when wishing to be silent, is sufficient to make the atmosphere of a nation less stifling." [100]

[99] "Roger Martin du Gard," *Cahiers du Sud*, November 1958, p. 261.
[100] "En Toute Cause offensée il voyait une cause à défèndre," *Le Figaro littéraire*, August 30, 1958, p. 8. This contradicts Rostand's previously cited assertion, made in the same article, that Martin du Gard "never refused the prestige of his name." Clearly Rostand is closer to the truth here.

CHAPTER VII

The "Failure" of Maumort

"Sometimes I have the feeling that creative writers who are my contemporaries have nothing but dead wood left in their reserves. One does not construct with dead wood." [1]

Epilogue was published in January 1940; Roger Martin du Gard died in August 1958. We have seen that in this eighteen-year period he spoke out from time to time on political matters, published a number of homage articles and other brief notes, a translation, and the more extensive *Notes sur André Gide*. It is not necessary to stress further the depth of his pessimism in these years; all the available documentation bears witness to his discouragement, even despair, and to his sense of his own decline.[2] Yet there is another element of Martin du Gard's activity in these last years, which has here-

[1] Unpublished letter of January 4, 1944, to Félix Sartiaux; by permission of Mme Félix Sartiaux.

[2] In addition to previous references, mention should be made here of the photocopy of a very pessimistic letter to an unknown correspondent, given as an epigraph to the memorial edition of the *N.N.R.F.*, December 1958. André Chamson has written that he at first believed Martin du Gard's despair during the German occupation to be the result of historical circumstances. "I never really understood what his pessimism was until very recent years, and I think I have never known anyone so fundamentally without hope [*désespéré*]" ("Je vous parle de l'autre rive," *N.N.R.F.*, December 1958, p. 1,000).

tofore been neglected and which must now be discussed. This is Martin du Gard's final great literary effort, *Le Journal du Colonel de Maumort.*

Martin du Gard's friends knew that he was working on another vast novel. There are references to his project in the unpublished Sartiaux correspondence and elsewhere, and in the spring of 1943, Georges Sadoul already noticed a large manuscript sitting in one corner of Martin du Gard's apartment in Nice.[3] One could assume that Martin du Gard would attempt to integrate the tragedy of the generation of 1940 into a novel. Such a work would seem a natural and fitting climax to his career; he had already dealt with three other great crises of the French conscience. By 1950 people began to wonder why he had as yet published nothing:

Why, given his taste for difficult subjects, and preoccupied as he is with the dual opposition of fanaticisms and of generations, has he not yet tried to call forth new dramatic actions, under the fires of the apocalypse which we are now living through? New problems, just as grave, more brutally imposed than the old ones, yet which are nevertheless made to his measure [*à sa taille*].[4]

At the same time, it was conceivable that such a venture would pose enormous difficulties for Martin du Gard, less because of his age than because of his lack of sympathy for the ideologies of the new epoch. When he met Martin du Gard in September 1944, Georges Sadoul felt instinctively that his friend was pleased with what he had been writing. Sadoul did not believe him when he said, "It's not a novel, it's a

---

[3] Georges Sadoul, "Rencontres, sous l'occupation, avec Roger Martin du Gard," *Les Etoiles*, June 19, 1945, p. 1.

[4] Pierre Dominique, "Martin du Gard," *Dictionnaire des Contemporains*, ed. Jean Galtière-Boissière (*Crapouillot*, 1950), p. 133.

posthumous work." Martin du Gard was terribly distressed by the news of the massacres and deportations, and was among the first Frenchmen to read the full dossier on the shooting of the twenty-seven hostages of Châteaubriant by the Germans. He told Sadoul with emotion, "All this will pass into my work.[5] This anecdote illustrates one of the most difficult literary problems Martin du Gard faced; his habit of dispassionate, careful observation did not equip him to deal with his new feelings. In a letter of April 13, 1945, to Mme Sartiaux, he spoke of his obsession with the prodigious and rapidly paced events going on around him:

It's the second time my generation has witnessed the collapse of an empire. . . . Whatever relief one may feel, this pathetic spectacle does not take place without causing a sort of anguish: it is not on the human scale. . . . One would like to be able to contemplate it with a serene eye. But one has too much rancor, too much hate in his heart. *Hate.* . . . This is the sentiment of which I did not believe myself capable. I have lived sixty years without having the slightest experience of it. But I know it now, and it is atrociously bitter.[6]

Martin du Gard did not possess the gift he so admired in his friend Camus, an "immediate perspicacity," [7] an ability to see clearly the significance of contemporary events, to capture and interpret them without falling into mere *reportage.*[8] Camus did not need the cushion of objectivity provided only

[5] Sadoul, "Rencontres," p. 3.
[6] Unpublished; by permission of Mme Félix Sartiaux (italicized words are underlined in the original).
[7] R. M. G., "Personne n'est moins dupé: Personne plus indépendant," *Le Figaro Littéraire,* October 26, 1957, p. 1.
[8] Cf. the important passage in the *Souvenirs* in which Martin du Gard criticizes his fellow authors who "lower" themselves to become what might be termed "incompetent political journalists" (cited in Chapter VI, above, pp. 178–179).

by the passage of time, and in Martin du Gard's opinion, he could "explain, judge the events of yesterday with the freedom, the breadth of view, the impartiality which one hopes future historians will have." [9]

The mystery surrounding Martin du Gard's literary intentions was cleared up in 1955, with the publication of his *Souvenirs* in the Pléiade edition of the *Oeuvres complètes*. Almost half of the *Souvenirs* deal with what Martin du Gard terms "the journal of the *Journal de Maumort*." [10] Included in the *Souvenirs* are letters to André Gide and some of Gide's replies, as well as selected notations from Martin du Gard's own *Journal*. There are some observations on the contemporary scene and a few biographical details, but the main emphasis is on a painfully lucid and moving account of a literary failure.[11]

The original idea for the *Journal de Maumort* was an ingenious one, born directly out of the crisis of 1940. Its elabora-

---

[9] R. M. G., "Personne n'est moins dupé," p. 1. The term Martin du Gard uses for this gap in time is *recul*. Cf. Louis Martin-Chauffier's remark that Martin du Gard was incapable of viewing events "without *recul*" ("L'Homme qui fuyait la renommée," *Livres de France*, January 1960, p. 4). In commenting on the work of a younger colleague, Martin du Gard was very critical of the "document d'époque" element he found in it. Political polemics date quickly, he added, and he had his own unhappy experience with *Jean Barois*. Many pages which won him "enthusiastic support in 1914, have become unreadable!" This occurred despite the advantage of his having had *recul* when he wrote *Jean Barois* ("Conseils à un jeune écrivain, deux lettres inédites à Roger Ikor," *Livres de France*, June–July 1961, p. 5).

[10] R. M. G., *Souvenirs*, O.C., I, xcix.

[11] This view is shared by André Rousseaux in his analysis of the *Souvenirs*, "Le Livre que Martin du Gard n'écrira pas," *Littérature du vingtième siècle* (Paris: Albin Michel, 1958), pp. 55–66. Rousseaux points out correctly that the key difficulty for Martin du Gard was the lack of time. The simple fact of his aging meant that he could not live long enough to place himself in the proper perspective.

tion can be traced out in the *Souvenirs;* by May 1941, Martin du Gard had put aside several other plans and was concentrating more and more upon his project, which he began to envision as a truly great work, a sort of testament. He became deeply enthusiastic about his new novel, by April 1942 conceiving it as a "livre-somme": "the totality of a life and an experience (that of Maumort); the utilization of a thousand *fiches* which I have been accumulating for forty years; the testament of a generation, on the eve of a complete division between two ages of humanity." [12]

Briefly, the basic plan was as follows: An elderly colonel, retired to his country property (Martin du Gard's own Le Tertre), finds his estate occupied by the invading Germans in June 1940. Just before the arrival of the enemy, in a moment of excessive prudence, the colonel destroyed a journal he had been keeping for forty years. He isolates himself in one wing of his château, leaving the rest to the Germans. Soon he begins a new journal, "a journal of his voluntary 'captivity' and of his daily reactions to events. But, inconsolable at having so precipitously burned the notebooks in which he had consigned, from day to day, the slightest episodes of a rather eventful existence, he gives in to the temptation to repair, as much as possible, this loss, by evoking, letting his pen run freely, at the mercy of his fantasy and his memories (that is to say without chronological order), a thousand details of his past." [13]

The broad potentialities of this device are apparent, both for individual character analysis and for commentary on historical events. Martin du Gard planned the work so that Colonel de Maumort would be able to speak with complete

[12] *Souvenirs, O.C.,* I, cvii.
[13] *Ibid.,* p. cii (note of July 16, 1941).

frankness; his wife was to have died, and his two sons were to have been killed in the First World War.

Despite the highly promising aspects of the plan, Martin du Gard sensed very early what was to his mind a potential danger. Maumort must not blend into Martin du Gard, and the use of the first person in the narrative could but aggravate this tendency. Martin du Gard therefore took pains to make Maumort a distinct individual, very different from himself through his education, his aristocratic background, and his military career. Even such precautions proved inadequate; though Martin du Gard carefully assembled his historical documentation and made an extensive study of the newspapers of June and July 1940 (the projected hinge period of the novel), he found by 1942 that he was substituting himself more and more for his colonel. He therefore gave himself another preparatory task, that of fabricating a complete biography of his colonel, from birth to his seventieth year. Then, "I shall have behind me the weight of a life *different from my own*, and that will prevent me from deviating, from unconsciously substituting my personality for that of Maumort." [14] Later he added similar biographies of the principal characters who were to play a role in the colonel's life. One definitely has the impression that Martin du Gard was manufacturing extra difficulties for himself, possibly because he really did not want ever to finish *Maumort*.[15]

---

[14] *Ibid.*, p. cv (italics his).

[15] This impression is supported by a note of May 15, 1942. Martin du Gard has a sense of peace in the vastness of his project; it is a work which can grow and perfect itself indefinitely, one which will be never finished for him, "and which nevertheless can be, at any moment whatever, interrupted by [his] death. A few ellipsis dots and a note of the editor will be sufficient: '*Here ends the manuscript of the Colonel de Maumort, struck down during the night of* . . .'" (*ibid.*, p. cviii; italics his).

Although Martin du Gard constantly encountered new problems, many of them technical in nature, the manuscript kept growing, and he was working with a real *élan*. He suggested in a letter to Gide of August 30, 1942, that this was partly due to a conviction, whether justified or not, "of creating a posthumous work," and this gave him "an exciting *liberty*; that which one has when one thinks in the intimacy of self alone." [16] It is curious that Martin du Gard already had this feeling in 1942; Georges Sadoul would probably still have doubted him in 1944, even had Sadoul known of this letter.

The war passed. New difficulties with the manuscript arose. Martin du Gard decided that he had been too much under the influence of the defeat of 1940 [17] and set about revising his chronology entirely. The colonel was to begin his *Journal* in 1945 instead of in 1940, and was to have been born in 1870 instead of in 1866. These changes required an infinitely complicated reshuffling, and again one feels that Martin du Gard was deliberately being overly careful. Perhaps this is an example of the negative effects of his education at the *Ecole des chartes*—his documentation now overwhelmed him and consumed most of his energies. Still, the novel progressed, and in 1948 Martin du Gard read some pages to Gide, the only person to whom he showed the manuscript. Gide felt that it was the finest writing his friend had produced.[18] This reassurance

[16] *Ibid.*, p. cxii (italics his).

[17] In his review of the *Souvenirs*, Emile Henriot notes that it is impossible for the Colonel de Maumort "to remain apart from the events which are throwing the contemporary world into upheaval; the risk was to fall by excess of actuality into *reportage*" ("Roger Martin du Gard vu par lui-même," *Le Monde*, December 28, 1955, p. 7).

[18] R. M. G., *Souvenirs, O.C.*, I, cxxiv. A year later, Gide was of the same opinion, telling his friend that he could continue to work in peace, that he had never written anything "so solid and so personal" (*ibid.*, p. cxxviii).

was not enough; the final item in the *Souvenirs* is a letter to Gide of May 1950, indicating a growing discouragement, and Martin du Gard ends with a quotation from Buffon: "Life begins to be extinguished long before it is entirely extinguished." [19]

Posthumous publication of the work has been arranged, and Gallimard will release it as soon as certain difficulties involving Martin du Gard's heirs are resolved. It is our guess that Gide was justified in his praise of the work, and that Martin du Gard was wrong when he wrote that his colonel would have interested only readers of 1910.[20]

A number of reasons for this "failure" have been suggested. (*Maumort* will always remain a failure in one sense, in that its creator could neither finish it nor make it public during his lifetime.) Martin du Gard's own sense of distance from the rapidly changing and confusing post-1940 world is clearly a factor. He tried to write *Maumort* as another novel of transition, but perhaps he was not sure in this case whether the transition came in 1940 or in 1945. The significance of 1914 had been much clearer to him in the 1930's when he was finishing *Les Thibault*, and when he had the necessary *recul*. Consciousness of a new situation, however, is not the same as acceptance of it or adaptation to it, even if, as one writer has asserted, Martin du Gard's entire work is a "ferociously lucid statement," and nowhere in it can one find "the slightest claim in favor of what is dying." [21] For many reasons—age,

[19] *Ibid.*, p. cxl. In a footnote Martin du Gard adds that he made another attempt to rewrite the work, this time as an epistolary novel rather than as a journal. This attempt failed, too, and in 1955 the work remained, if his assertion is to be believed, in scattered pieces.

[20] *Ibid.*, p. cxxvi.

[21] Jean Morand, "Roger Martin du Gard: *Oeuvres complètes*," *Comprendre*, September 1956, p. 127. Morand is certainly correct as far as Martin du Gard's published work is concerned, and even in his correspondence there is very little nostalgia for what has passed. In

class background, nationality, literary method—he could go no further than an artistic description, in nineteenth-century terms, of the immense importance of the break and shift in European development marked by the summer of 1914. Such a description may lead to a kind of transcendence, as Camus has argued.[22] Jean Guéhenno, noting the epigraph of *Jean Barois*—"A sick consciousness, there is in the theatre of modern fatality"—suggests that the study of this sickness has been the aim of Martin du Gard's work. There is much of the doctor in Martin du Gard, and "if the modern consciousness is sick by a sort of fatality, one cannot cease being affected by this, and one must employ all his forces to discover every path of this fatality, since only through lucidity can one re-create a sort of liberty." [23] Such a notion, the belief that triumph over one's condition is possible if one has laid bare its innermost truths, is not far from Flaubert's attitude toward his hated nineteenth century, although Martin du Gard lacks the bitter cynicism of the hermit of Croisset.[24]

Morand's opinion, Martin du Gard's attitude opens the door to "all the possibilities of the future."

[22] In *Le Mythe de Sisyphe*, Camus describes literary creation as "the moving *témoignage* of the sole dignity of man: the tenacious revolt against his condition, perseverance in an effort recognized as sterile" (*Le Mythe de Sisyphe* [Paris: Gallimard, 1942], p. 156). And on p. 158 he writes, "To create is to give a form to one's destiny." Jean-Paul Sartre makes the same point, with even more revolutionary implications: "To name is to show and to show is to change" (*Situations, II* [Paris: Gallimard, 1948], p. 129).

[23] "Le Sens d'un certain honneur," *N.N.R.F.*, December 1958, p. 1,038.

[24] Cf. a letter to George Sand: "And you beg me not to notice human folly, and to deprive myself of the pleasure of depicting it!" (*The George Sand-Gustave Flaubert Letters*, Aimee L. McKenzie, tr. [New York: Boni and Liveright, 1921], p. 85, letter of December, 1867). Cf. also "To dissect is to take vengeance" (*ibid.*, p. 29, letter of November, 1866).

Martin du Gard always claimed that he refused all partisan ideologies; he clung to his individualism, admitting its bourgeois origins. He thought that all uniqueness, all private initiative, would be forbidden in the new collectivist world he foresaw.[25] He felt in July 1944 that the *bourgeoisie* was condemned to perish, despite certain good qualities.[26] Perhaps the younger generation would adapt; he already saw signs of this.[27] In any case he had no dynamic solutions to offer; he was ready to pass the challenge on to others.

There is at least one contemporary of Martin du Gard's who had much more than "dead wood" in his reserves. In fact, Thomas Mann, who was born in 1875, six years before Martin du Gard, was able to produce in 1947 one of the major novels of the mid-twentieth century, a novel which deals very specifically with the 1933–1945 epoch in Germany—*Doctor Faustus*. There are definite parallels between Mann's technique in *Doctor Faustus* and Martin du Gard's in *Maumort*, as he describes it in the *Souvenirs*. Mann's enlightened humanist narrator, Serenus Zeitblom, begins his biography in 1943

[25] Cf. R. M. G., "Lettres à l'architecte," *Cahiers du Sud*, January 1959, p. 339, letter of November 4, 1941.

[26] He told Félix Sartiaux in a letter of July 18, 1944, that he thought the *bourgeoisie* of the nineteenth and twentieth centuries would inevitably disappear, "despite certain merits which will win for it a generally respectful judgement from history."

[27] He wrote to F., his architect friend, on October 10, 1947, "It's very moving, at my age, when one is preparing to pick up his funeral shroud in the cloakroom, to discover that the film is 'continuous,' and that the show will continue after you. . . . I would like to be certain that the young people I see coming into the world will have a happy and free life. It's quite possible: the young adapt to anything, and men have already found an equilibrium in societies completely different from the one that I knew, and which I watch disappear with a naive stupefaction" ("Lettres à l'architecte," p. 347).

(one year before Thomas Mann actually began the novel). Comments on the contemporary situation are interspersed with the narrator's re-creation of the life of Adrian Leverkühn, the *Meister,* and of his own life as it relates to Leverkühn's tortured, sick, destructive, yet mysteriously productive, existence. In fact, on one level Leverkühn's life experience is Germany's historical experience, and his pact with the devil is Germany's pact with the devil. Leverkühn's final renunciation and his collapse into insanity are closely linked with German history after 1933.[28] A similar complex triple time scheme would have existed in *Le Journal du Colonel de Maumort* (begun by Martin du Gard in 1941), as the old colonel tried to reconstruct the *Journal* he had destroyed at the moment of the Nazi invasion of 1940.

The reasons why Mann succeeded and Martin du Gard failed are many and complicated, and only a few of them can be suggested here. One is surely the fact that Mann was a German and therefore attained historical consciousness much sooner than did Martin du Gard. As early as 1924, with the publication of *The Magic Mountain,* Mann was fully aware of the immense chasm produced by the 1914 war and the 1918 defeat. Also, Mann was in exile after 1933, and thus he was able to look more objectively at the terrifying experience which his native country was undergoing. Georg Lukacs feels that Mann was able to continue to write because he remained completely objective toward socialism and was resigned to its ultimate victory. Mann, Lukacs argues, never went beyond a "critical realism," a description of the bourgeois world he knew, and did not try to describe a socialist character from

[28] There is a suggestion, when the narrative has not yet proceeded beyond 1910, that Adrian Leverkühn's musical theory "reflects Germany's experience as a nation" (H. T. Lowe-Porter, tr. [London: Secker and Warburg, 1959], p. 193).

the inside, as did Martin du Gard in what Lukacs calls his "heroic failure"—*L'Eté 1914*.[29] Mann's great genius obviously is a factor, and it is also significant that the narrator in *Doctor Faustus* and the brilliant musician hero-villian are two different people. This separation must have spared Mann many of the difficulties Martin du Gard encountered with his Colonel de Maumort.

Although, since the Second World War, there have been a number of important novels besides *Doctor Faustus* which

[29] *La Signification présente du réalisme critique*, Maurice de Gandillac, tr. (Paris: Gallimard, 1960), p. 154. Cf. also pp. 111–112, 114–115, 175–176, 182. Lukacs may be correct about Mann; one passage from *Doctor Faustus* is especially illustrative: "As a moderate man and son of culture I have indeed a natural horror of radical revolution and the dictatorship of the lower classes, which I find it hard, owing to my tradition, to envisage otherwise than in the image of anarchy and mob rule—in short, of the destruction of culture. But when I recall the grotesque anecdote about the two saviours of European civilization [Mann never mentions their names but always uses a circumlocution], the German and the Italian, both of them in the pay of finance capital, walking together through the Uffizi Gallery in Florence, where they certainly did not belong, and one of them saying to the other that all these 'glorious art treasures' would have been destroyed by Bolshevism if heaven had not prevented it by raising them up—when I recall all this, then my notions about classes and masses take on another colour, and the dictatorship of the proletariat begins to seem for me, a German burgher, an ideal situation compared with the dictatorship of the scum of the earth. Bolshevism to my knowledge has never destroyed any works of art. That was far more within the sphere of activity of those who assert that they are protecting us from it" (pp. 339–340). However, Martin du Gard may well be much closer to "critical realism" than the Marxist critic Lukacs would admit. In fact, we would argue that Martin du Gard was the most important representative of this tendency in France. It will be remembered that Jacques Thibault himself was never a real socialist and always retained many bourgeois qualities. Lukacs is thus unfair when he criticizes Martin du Gard for trying to portray a socialist character.

have been very long, no writer who could be described as following directly in the line of Martin du Gard has achieved real success. And this might be expected, given his precise "datedness," of which he was so conscious. Paul Nizan, whose work has largely fallen into obscurity,[30] might have risen to the first rank, had he not been killed early in the Second World War. Nizan, who won the Prix Interallié in 1939 for his *La Conspiration,* greatly admired Martin du Gard and wrote two valuable reviews of *L'Eté 1914.*[31] It was thought that he had drawn much of the inspiration for his novel from *Les Thibault.*[32]

Roger Ikor, whose admitted *maître* is Roger Martin du Gard,[33] received the Prix Goncourt in 1955 for *Les Eaux mêlées,* the part of *Les Fils d'Avrom* which deals with the period from 1914 to the 1930's. Yet there is little evidence of Martin du Gard's influence in Ikor's work. In *Les Fils d'Avrom* there are perhaps similarities—in length, in the concentration on an individual family, and in doctrine. Ikor is a humanitarian leftist with no particular political affiliation. These are superficial similarities, however. Ikor's novel does not open out onto history, or does so only in very limited

[30] The French Communist Party made a determined effort to blot out his memory, after his defection in September 1939. His early work, *Aden Arabie,* has recently been republished with an interesting preface by his old friend Jean-Paul Sartre. It is possible that Nizan's reputation will undergo a certain rehabilitation. Cf. Sartre's *Avant-Propos* to *Aden Arabie* (Paris: François Maspero, 1961), pp. 9–62.

[31] "Roger Martin du Gard: *Eté 1914,*" N.R.F., January 1, 1937, pp. 95–99, and "*Eté 1914,* par Roger Martin du Gard," *L'Humanité,* January 7, 1937, p. 8.

[32] On this question, cf. Léon C. Marcontonato, "Roger Martin du Gard et le Prix Interallié," *Cahiers du Sud,* June 1939, pp. 515–521.

[33] Roger Ikor, cited in the number of *Livres de France* dedicated to his work (June–July 1961), p. 10. The fact that Ikor has had an issue of *Livres de France* devoted to him is in itself an indication that he has gained some prominence.

sense, with the death of the grandson, Jean-Claude, in the Resistance. The focus is always inward toward the familial plane, much as in Duhamel's *La Chronique des Pasquier.* *Les Fils d'Avrom* is the story of the emigration and adaptation of a Russian Jewish family to France. Ikor has a rich humor and writes in a vigorous style; many of the adventures are comic or tragicomic, and he presents much fascinating sociological detail. The Mykhanowitzki family is very large, and none of the characters, except the hero Yankel and perhaps his father Avrom, is as deeply analyzed as are Martin du Gard's central figures. They could not possibly be treated in depth, for Ikor deals with an immense family over a fifty-two year period, from 1898 to 1950, in six hundred pages. The class and religious backgrounds of these people are very different from those of Martin du Gard's bourgeois characters. One thinks more of Zola than of Martin du Gard in reading Ikor, who has a fairly simple and fundamentally optimistic biological theory. A sort of regeneration will come from the mixing of races—thus the title *Les Eaux mêlées.*[34] At present Ikor is working on a novel series, *Si le temps,* several volumes of which have appeared.[35]

One other novelist merits brief mention here. Jean Davray

[34] See *Les Fils d'Avrom: La Greffe du printemps, Les Eaux mêlées* (Paris: Albin Michel, 1955), p. 458: "The bloods must renew themselves, otherwise the race will perish."

[35] There have been other novels which can be compared with individual volumes of *Les Thibault,* but none of them is of real importance. Pierre-Henri Simon reviews two representative novels of this school in his column, "La Vie littéraire," *Le Monde,* September 27, 1961, pp. 8–9. The novels are *La Mort du Pantin,* by Pierre Moustier, and *Les Passants,* by Jacques Chauviré. Simon concludes that these novels remind one of *Les Thibault,* especially of *La Mort du père,* with one very important difference. Martin du Gard, as a great artist, "possessed almost always the secret of opening the most objectively observed reality, and even ideology, onto a background plan of intuition and emotion which already belong to poetic truth."

has written a four-volume series, *Le Bruit de la vie* (1957–
1960). Davray follows much the same method as did Martin
du Gard in *Les Thibault;* he treats a series of short time spans
with intensity (February of 1934, October of 1936, 1938, and
1939 until just after the outbreak of war and the death of the
hero). The major characters are upper-bourgeois, and the
focus is on one family, the Leroy-Sautiers. Martin du Gard
even figures in the novel; he supposedly sends a note to the
younger brother, Bruno, who has just published a precociously
brilliant novel.[36] There is a diplomat friend of the family,
M. de Cambrecère, reminiscent of Martin du Gard's Rumelles,
who provides "professional" commentary on major happen-
ings. Davray's over-all aim in *Le Bruit de la vie* is quite
similar to that of Martin du Gard in *Les Thibault.* Through
the actions and reactions of his characters (Martin du Gard's
technique), Davray makes an effort to integrate into the
novel political developments in France and elsewhere in
Europe during the bitter years 1934–1939. He also follows the
method used by Romains and, to some degree, by Sartre of
alternating analysis of fictional characters with the presentation of real historical figures such as Paul-Boncour and Da-
ladier. Literary personalities such as Bergson and Gide also
find their way into the novel. In our opinion Davray does not
succeed in uniting the fictional and the historical, and in any
case his work has not gained wide recognition. Despite the
broad similarities in method, and despite the generous political
liberalism also found in Roger Ikor, Davray's basic philosophical approach is very different from that of Martin du Gard.
There is a much stronger emphasis upon, and greater value
given to, eroticism. For Davray, love is the ultimate solution
to the difficulties of the human condition, a way for some

[36] II: *Le Matin vient et la nuit aussi* (Paris: Plon, 1958), pp. 67–68.

characters, at least, to drive away *le bruit de la vie*,[37] while Martin du Gard in his novels is fundamentally pessimistic about the possibility of any valid and continuing love relationship.[38]

Even if there are no novelists of major importance following in a direct line from Martin du Gard, is it valid today to dismiss *Les Thibault*, as R. M. Albères did just after the Second World War, as "a great success which has remained isolated and without influence, except on some novels of an inferior genre"? [39] Is there perhaps a line of literary evolution leading from Martin du Gard to some of the French writers who, since the War, have turned toward political and social subjects in their novels? Albères pointed out in 1945 that France seemed to have turned toward a very "personalist form" of the novel and away from the "social form." Jules Romains and Martin du Gard had no disciples, and it took a foreign writer, Ilya Ehrenburg, to portray the fall of Paris in 1940.[40] Yet by 1949, Jean-Paul Sartre, whom Martin du

---

[37] Cf., for example, the reaction of a minor character when she is abandoned by the hero: "The sounds of life which had been menacing for so long, and which, with François, had been transformed into a hymn of joy, regained, in one instant, all their aggressiveness" (I: *Le Bruit de la vie* [Paris: Plon, 1957], p. 207). She is alone and without hope: "She had returned to the cage of her life" (*ibid.*, p. 208). When François finally finds genuine love with Claire, his brother's wife, just before the beginning of the conflict in September 1939, death becomes unimportant to them: "Events no longer had the strength to destroy their happiness" (IV: *Les Astres meurent* [Paris: Plon, 1960], p. 382). "They were going to part strengthened with a happiness which would conquer even the war" (*ibid.*, p. 395).

[38] Cf. above, p. 80.

[39] *Portrait de notre héros—Essai sur le roman* (Paris: Le Portulan, 1945), p. 208.

[40] *Ibid.*, p. 115. As far as Sartre is concerned, Albères mentions only *La Nausée*, which came out before the Second World War. Obviously, at the date of Albères's writing, the much more histori-

Gard had described in 1943 as "one of the most authentic promises of the generation which follows us,"[41] had completed three volumes of *Les Chemins de la liberté*. The third volume dealt very specifically with the fall of Paris. And in the same year Louis Aragon began to publish *Les Communistes*, a novel centering on the defeat of France in 1940.[42]

Clear parallels have already been pointed out between individual incidents in *Les Thibault* and *Les Chemins de la liberté*.[43] Jacques Brenner finds Martin du Gard very different from other novelists of the 1930's—Mauriac, Malraux, Julian Green, Georges Bernanos—but argues that with Sartre one witnesses a return to a more classic conception of the novel. The differences between Martin du Gard and Sartre are less striking, Brenner claims, than those between Martin du Gard

---

cally oriented first two volumes of *Les Chemins de la liberté* (1945) had not been published. The novel by Ilya Ehrenburg, *La Chute de Paris* (Paris: Éditions hier et aujourd'hui, 1944), won the Stalin prize in 1942. It is a good novel of the second rank, covering the period 1935–1940 and the fall of France, an interesting and forceful account employing the techniques of socialist realism. Ehrenburg manages to capture some of the tragic sense of the collapse of France in 1940, and his own strong emotional commitment to France and the city of Paris adds force to his novel.

[41] Unpublished letter of July 31, 1943, to Félix Sartiaux.

[42] It is curious that neither Sartre nor Aragon has completed his project. Sartre stopped with three volumes, Aragon with six.

[43] See above, Chapter V, nn. 58, 62, 71. Alfred Grosser comments on the vast difference between the heroic behavior of Jacques Thibault in *L'Eté 1914* and the behavior of Sartre's Philippe, the cowardly conscientious objector in *Le Sursis* and *La Mort dans l'âme*, "a little hooligan who is afraid of being slapped" ("Une Morale sans métaphysique, l'oeuvre de Roger Martin du Gard," *L'Esprit*, October 1958, p. 529). For Grosser the difference in behavior indicates a fundamental difference between the two novelists, rather than Sartre's realistic comprehension of a new historical situation in which pacifism is no longer relevant. Martin du Gard, as has been shown, came to this realization before September 1939.

and most of the novelists of the period *entre deux guerres*.[44] Sartre seems to be facing and working toward the solution of problems which had confronted Martin du Gard in *Les Thibault*, in particular the problem of what course of action the individual should take when confronted with uncontrollable external historical forces. Everett Knight argues that "the questions posed by Antoine Thibault are those with which Gide was all his life preoccupied and to which Sartre will eventually offer very precise answers."[45]

An excellent example is the conclusion of *La Mort dans l'âme*, the third volume of *Les Chemins de la liberté* and the last that Sartre has published to date. The death of Mathieu Delarue during the German invasion of 1940, which can be fruitfully compared to Jacques Thibault's death in the summer of 1914, is not the final event in the volume. Mathieu's end is in itself a call to action, since he has been able to find true liberty only through death.[46] A sort of epilogue follows, which unlike Martin du Gard's, is open-ended and points toward the future and the necessity of strong political commitment (despite the fact that all the main characters have so horribly bungled their lives that they seem almost to deserve the misery which the Second World War has in store for them).

The future, at least as seen in 1940, lies with the Communist Brunet, a simple man with an absolute, doctrinaire faith which has never been shaken by the reasonings of his friend Mathieu

---

[44] *Martin du Gard*, p. 50.

[45] *Literature Considered as Philosophy* (London: Routledge and Kegan Paul, 1957), p. 101.

[46] Before the war, in 1930, when he was struggling to remain free by not committing himself, Mathieu came to believe, "I have emptied myself, sterilized myself, to become nothing more than an expectation [*une attente*]" (I: *L'Age de raison* [Paris: Gallimard, 1945], p. 45).

Delarue.[47] (Mathieu resembles Sartre quite closely, being a *lycée* professor of philosophy of about the same age as his creator.) Rather than continuing to fight like Mathieu, which would be suicidal, Brunet surrenders to the Germans after eight days of heroic combat, of no sleep and little food. He immediately thinks that "there will be much work to do,"[48] to organize resistance among his demoralized and exhausted fellow soldiers, who are marching, not even contemplating escape, in an almost unguarded column. Some of the prisoners must be Comrades, or at least "matériel," "récupérable."[49]

Brunet has an absolutely coherent, if limited, vision of what must be done. The remainder of the volume deals with his struggle to make the other prisoners comprehend that the Germans are their enemies, that they are not going to be permitted to return to their homes, that they will be imprisoned in Germany. Brunet is ultimately victorious. The men are taken from their temporary camp and put on a train heading east, and as cut-off after cut-off is passed, they begin to realize that they have been duped, that they are not going to be demobilized. His victory may be hollow; he may be crushed by the weight of his own solitude; he may fear the movement of hatred and revolt against the Germans which is

[47] Cf. *ibid.*, p. 46, the description of Brunet: "He never gave the impression of being a single man; he had the slow, silent life of a crowd." Brunet tells Mathieu that the Party doesn't need him. "But *you*, you need the Party" (*ibid.*, p. 122, italics his).

[48] III: *La Mort dans l'âme* (Paris: Gallimard, 1949), p. 202.

[49] *Ibid.*, p. 204. Cf. p. 213: Brunet realizes what must be done with these men: "It will be necessary to destroy one by one, patiently, their hopes, burst their illusions, make them see in all its nakedness their revolting condition, make them disgusted with everyone and everything, and to begin, with themselves." Brunet remarks on p. 254, when the Germans decide to let some families visit the prisoners, "Nothing to do; they are not yet miserable enough."

in some sense begun by him. Nonetheless, he has won a victory; the French finally realize, for the first time since hostilities began in September 1939, that they are truly at war. There may be no ultimate metaphysical significance to Brunet's acts, and, viewed objectively, he may even be wrong. The intellectual Schneider, in some ways a reborn Mathieu and thus a reborn Sartre, can argue powerfully against the Communist position, of which Brunet himself cannot be sure, since he has no liaison with the Party. But Schneider is still with Brunet, "so as not to remain alone." [50] And Brunet survives, unlike Mathieu Delarue, unlike Jacques and Antoine Thibault.

Louis Aragon's *Les Communistes* was intended as a continuation of his earlier and very successful *Le Monde réel,* which had appeared in four volumes between 1934 and 1944.[51] There is the same detailed concentration on historical events as in *L'Eté 1914.* The six large volumes of *Les Communistes* which Aragon has published cover the period February 1939– June 1940. Actual documents are frequently cited, lists of names of hostages shot by the Germans are given, and many real historical figures find their way into the narrative. Individual destinies are closely tied in both with the historical tragedy and with the possibilities of renewal which Aragon

---

[50] *Ibid.,* p. 266. Cf. Sartre's *Situations, II,* 16: Existentialist writers have the intention of producing "certain changes in the society which surrounds us." And though Sartre is not himself a materialist, he accepts the necessity of joining with those who are. He hopes that someday enough liberation will have taken place so that when a man wishes to find his liberty through choosing, through *engagement,* he will not find one of the choices to be death (as in *La Mort dans l'âme*). "We must arrange it so that man can, in every circumstance, choose life" (*Situations, II,* 28).

[51] Begun after Aragon had left his surrealist phase.

sees as resulting from the defeat. The lessons learned in the defeat will lead to resistance against the Germans, with the Communists in the forefront.

Even before 1949, a number of critics found parallels between Martin du Gard and Louis Aragon, critics from both the right and the left of the political spectrum. From the right, Henri Clouard sees Aragon as both similar to and continuing Martin du Gard.[52] From the left, Claude Roy in 1949 placed Aragon and Martin du Gard together as the greatest living French novelists.[53] The Marxist Pierre Daix, furthermore, writing in 1957, finds many parallels between the two novelists. He sees Martin du Gard's work as standing on the frontier of two ages—the second of course being the period of socialist construction in the U.S.S.R. Therefore, Daix feels, *Les Thibault* speaks to a much larger group of people than the *bourgeoisie* whose decline it documents. "I do not say that Roger Martin du Gard foresaw this evolution, or that he is pleased with it; those are other problems." [54] Daix finds a line of literary evolution moving from Romain Rolland's *Jean Christophe* to *Les Thibault* to *Les Communistes*. In his comparison he uses the rock of Sisyphus image, pointing out that Jean-Christophe is a solitary character, as is Jacques Thibault when he calls upon the masses to "raise up the rock." (Jacques

[52] Henri Clouard, *Histoire de la littérature française*, II: *De 1915 à 1940* (Paris: Albin Michel, 1949), 410.

[53] Claude Roy, *Descriptions critiques*, I (Paris: Gallimard, 1949), 147. Critics, regardless of their preferences, have seen a parallel between the two writers. Justin O'Brien finds that Aragon's work is a "pale imitation" of *Les Thibault* ("Families I Hate You!" *Saturday Review of Literature*, March 25, 1939, p. 10). Malcolm Cowley describes Aragon as the "most gifted by nature and in achievement the most uneven" ("Nobel Prize Novel," *New Republic*, January 5, 1938, p. 260).

[54] *Réflexions sur la méthode de Roger Martin du Gard* (Paris: Les éditeurs français réunis, 1957), p. 72.

is alone in the plane, since he cannot communicate with *le Pilote*, and after the crash, he is unable to speak a word to his captors.) With Armand Barbentane, one of the major characters in *Les Communistes*, there is a new dimension added to our history. Armand, who survives the battle of France and is destined to become a Resistance leader and an organizer of partisan groups, is merely one man among other men; if he falls, even if he is totally defeated, "others will raise up the rock." [55] This is an admirably concise statement of the theory of socialist realism, and at the same time one possible resolution to the dilemma posed by Martin du Gard.

In general, the critical reception of *Les Communistes* has been less favorable than that of Aragon's other novels—the earlier volumes of *Le Monde réel*, such as *Les Cloches de Bâle*, or the more recent *La Semaine sainte*. We would tend to agree with the critics, especially when the novel falls to the level of a fairly crude didacticism, even to straight political propaganda, as when one of the characters defends the Nazi-Soviet pact. [56] At times, furthermore, the young hero, Jean de Moncey, seems unbelievably naïve. [57]

Still, Aragon's power to evoke scenes is quite extraordinary, and this ability is apparent whenever humane indignation

[55] *Ibid.*, pp. 78–79.

[56] Louis Aragon, *Les Communistes*, I (*Février–Septembre 1939*) (Paris: La Bibliothèque française, 1949), 132, 180, and especially 183–184. Cf. also one character's view of the Soviet annexation of part of Poland after the Nazi-Soviet pact: "In truth it was merely a liberation of those parts of the Ukraine and White Russia which, with the aid of Weygand, the Polish soldiers annexed twenty years ago" II (*Septembre–Novembre 1939*) (Paris: La Bibliothèque française, 1950), p. 135. Or see the defense of Maurice Thorez' desertion from the French forces in the fall of 1939 (*ibid.*, pp. 268–269).

[57] Cf., for example, III (*Novembre 1939–Mars 1940*) (Paris: La Bibliothèque française, 1950), 91–94, where a friend is explaining syndicalism to him.

rather than party feeling dominates the novel.[58] The scenes in the upper-bourgeois *salons* are as masterfully written as those in the earlier volumes of *Le Monde réel*, and the intensive portrayal of the misery and monotony of camp life during the "Phony War" of September 1939–May 1940, is especially well done. The battle scenes in the last two volumes, which deal with the German blitzkrieg, the brief period from May 10 to June 9, 1940, can be compared with the great battle scenes in Jules Romains's *Verdun*. As the German breakthrough begins, Aragon, rapidly changing scene and jumping from one to another of the many characters, all somewhere at the Front, captures quite successfully the consciousness developing in the masses of the French army that they are hopelessly trapped. The scenes of the actual defeat are equally memorable, and a paroxysm of violence is reached in the account of the battle around Lille. Here the French forces put up a heavier resistance, which helped make possible the evacuation of Dunkirk. The impression of the black force of Nazi anger bearing down on the beleaguered city of Lille is vivid; vengeance is taken on areas which contain pockets of resistance. Of course the Communists are in the thick of the fray, and a number of them survive, including Armand Barbentane.

Aragon has turned to other projects and has never carried his narrative beyond June 1940. It is obvious that his Communist and Communist-sympathizer heroes would have become partisan leaders, and that their role in the liberation of France would have been stressed. They have been, theoretically at least, chosen at random, are not privileged heroes, but

[58] Cf., I, 15ff (the novel's opening scene at the Spanish frontier in February 1939, at the time of the Republican defeat); *ibid.*, pp. 211ff (the description of the stifling atmosphere of a great factory); III, 111–120 (a prison scene of brutal intensity).

anyone at all. Aragon's strong ideological commitment and his method of socialist realism thus seem to have permitted him to deal with the defeat of 1940 with at least partial success.

Some of the ways in which other writers have integrated the crisis of 1940 into their work have been discussed. This Martin du Gard could not do, despite his heroic effort to write *Le Journal du Colonel de Maumort*. What can be concluded, then, about Martin du Gard's future influence? It has been shown that he was not as isolated as he believed himself to be, that themes, methods, problems found in his work have been taken up by later writers. Professor Léon Roudiez, writing in 1960, admits that materialism does not mean communism, and that it would be absurd to relate Martin du Gard's future popularity to the success of one or another political regime. Still, Roudiez suggests that "Martin du Gard's fortune will probably be linked up with the evolution of broad intellectual currents." [59] This point is well taken, and it is possible to add another line of literary evolution to the one Pierre Daix proposes (Rolland—Martin du Gard—Aragon). This second line of literary development would run from Bergson through Proust and lead eventually to the *antiroman* school—perhaps ultimately to the worship of the object or the sterility of the blank page. This is much the same dichotomy that Georg Lukacs elucidates in the case of German literature, using as his prime examples Thomas Mann and Franz Kafka.[60]

It is our view that the school of fiction represented by

[59] "Situation de Roger Martin du Gard," *French Review*, October 1960, p. 24.

[60] Lukacs, *La Signification présente du réalisme critique*, pp. 86–168, section entitled "Franz Kafka ou Thomas Mann." In this schematic representation, writers like Camus and Sartre would stand independently somewhere between the two literary trends.

Martin du Gard and Thomas Mann will prove more fruitful in future potentialities.[61] This view is of course subjective, and the number of critical studies devoted to an author bears no necessary relation to his influence on the great literature of the future. Still, it is worth noting that, since 1955 and the appearance of Camus's Preface to the *Oeuvres complètes*, there has been a steadily growing interest in Martin du Gard's work in many parts of the world. The first published monograph was Clément Borgal's, which appeared in 1957. Martin du Gard was delighted with this book and expressed a strong desire to meet its author.[62] He was equally pleased with Pierre Daix's long essay, *Réflexions sur la méthode de Roger Martin du Gard*, also published in 1957. After Martin du Gard's death, Daix reprinted excerpts from a letter he had received concerning the *Réflexions*. Martin du Gard registered "stupefaction" that Daix's thoughts had been inspired by a work, *Les Thibault*, "which is neither ancient nor modern, which is now at the awkward age of conventional and indifferent esteem; and which I am in the habit of considering a respectable museum piece, without current utility." He con-

[61] We of course believe that Proust is the greater genius, though on this question cf. Daniel Fernandez, "Proust ou Martin du Gard," *N.N.R.F.*, December 1958, pp. 1,079–1,091. For Jean Larnac, Martin du Gard "drives into a distant past the puppets of Proust" (*La Littérature française d'aujourd'hui* [Paris: Editions sociales, 1948], p. 86).

[62] This information is from an obituary article by Pierre de Boisdeffre, "Le Dernier des naturalistes: Roger Martin du Gard," *Combat*, August 25, 1958, p. 1. Boisdeffre is the editor of the series, "Classiques du xxᵉ siècle," which published the Borgal study. With great discretion, knowing Martin du Gard's desire for privacy, M. Borgal had not written to him while he was preparing the work. M. Borgal informed me in person that a meeting had been arranged for the summer of 1958, just at the time of Martin du Gard's death. Thus Martin du Gard never met his first biographer.

tinues, "I would like very much for you to be correct, so that I can pass away with the thought that I am leaving behind a novel which—without my willing it, without premeditation, that is to say in the proper manner—will aid readers to 'enter into the history' of tomorrow." [63] We find satisfaction in the thought that Martin du Gard lived long enough to be aware of these developments.

[63] Cited in Pierre Daix, "Roger Martin du Gard," *Les Lettres françaises* (August 28–September 5, 1958), p. 1.

Selected Bibliography

The bibliography is designed to provide the reader with an introduction to the materials available on Roger Martin du Gard's life and work. Further information is given in the thorough bibliography of A. V. Paevskoi and N. M. Eischiskina, *Roger Martin du Gard* (Moscow: Publishing House of the All-Union Book Press, 1958). A more recent source is the annotated bibliography in Jochen Schlobach's *Geschichte und Fiktion in "L'Eté 1914" von Roger Martin du Gard* (Munich: Wilhelm Fink Verlag, 1965).

WORKS BY ROGER MARTIN DU GARD

Books

Oeuvres complètes. 2 vols. Paris: Gallimard, Bibliothèque de la Pléiade, 1955. Here abbreviated *O.C.*

L'Abbaye de Jumièges. Etude archéologique des ruines. Montdidier: Imprimerie Grou-Radenez, 1909.

Confidence africaine. Paris: Gallimard, 1930. In *O.C.*, II, 1,105–1,127.

Devenir! Paris: Ollendorff, 1908. In *OC.*, I, 1-203.

Dialogue. Paris: Collection Blanche, 1930.

La Gonfle. Paris: Gallimard, 1928. In *O.C.*, II, 1,165–1,237.

Jean Barois. Paris: Gallimard, 1913. In *O.C.*, I, 205-559.

Noizemont-les-Vierges. Liège: A la lampe d'Alladin, 1928.

Notes sur André Gide, 1913-1951. Paris: Gallimard, 1951. In *O.C.*, II, pp. 1,355–1,423.

Souvenirs autobiographiques et littéraires. Paris: Gallimard, 1955. In *O.C.*, I, xxix-cxl.

Un Taciturne. Paris: Gallimard, 1932. In *O.C.*, II, 1,239–1,353.

Le Testament du Père Leleu. Paris: Gallimard, 1914. In *O.C.*, II, 1,129–1,163.

Les Thibault. 11 vols. Paris: Gallimard, 1922-1940.
  I: *Le Cahier gris.* 1922. In *O.C.*, I, 579-674.
  II: *Le Pénitencier.* 1922. In *O.C.*, I, 675-813.
  III: *La Belle Saison.* 2 vols. 1923. In *O.C.*, I, 814-1,050.
  IV: *La Consultation.* 1928. In *O.C.*, I, 1,051–1,133.
  V: *La Sorellina.* 1928. In *O.C.*, I, 1,134–1,250.
  VI: *La Mort du père.* 1929. In *O.C.*, I, 1,251–1,394.
  VII: *L'Eté 1914.* 3 vols. 1936. In *O.C.*, II, 9–758.
  VIII: *Epilogue.* 1940. In *O.C.*, II, 759–1,011.

L'Une de nous. Paris: Grasset, 1910.

Vieille France. Paris: Gallimard, 1933. In *O.C.*, II, pp. 1,013–1,103.

Note on English translations: *Les Thibault* has been well translated by Stuart Gilbert (2 vols.; New York: Viking Press, 1937, 1941). *Jean Barois*, also translated by Gilbert, did not appear until 1949, while the *Recollections of André Gide* were published in 1953. The last major work to be translated was *Vieille France*, under the title of *The Postman*, in 1954. (All were published by Viking Press.) The very important Preface by Albert Camus to the *Oeuvres complètes* will be reprinted in 1967 by Alfred A. Knopf, Inc., in a collection tentatively entitled *Lyrical and Literary Essays*, translated by Philip Thody. Hamish Hamilton Ltd. will publish the work in England under the title *Lyrical and Critical*.

ARTICLES AND PUBLIC STATEMENTS

"Un Appel d'intellectuels français pour les garantis juridiques des accusés politiques en Espagne," *Le Populaire*, October 27, 1937, p. 3. Reprints a telegram.

Arland, Marcel. "Chronique des romans," *N.R.F.*, June 1, 1933, pp. 985-986. Reprints an important open letter concerning *Vieille France* and Martin du Gard's ideological position at this time.

"Des Nouvelles de Roger Martin du Gard," *Les Lettres françaises*, May 30–June 5, 1957, p. 1. Reprints a letter of Martin du Gard concerning antiracist action.

"L'Honneur des Rosenberg, pour la réhabilitation," *Les Lettres françaises*, July 2–July 9, 1953, p. 1. Reprints a telegram.

Martin du Gard, Roger. "Condemnation de la Guerre," *La Dépêche Socialiste*, July 30, 1938, p. 2. Reprints a letter.

——. "La Grande Misère des bibliothèques des sanatoriums," *Le Figaro*, May 29, 1946, p. 1.

——. "Hommage à Copeau," *Les Nouvelles littéraires*, February 10, 1949, p. 1.

——. "Influence morale de Loisy," *Europe*, April 15, 1927, pp. 561–562. Also printed in *La Chronique des idées*, July 1927, pp. 49-50.

——. *In Memoriam (Abbé Marcel Hébert)*. Paris: Grou-Radenez, 1921. In *O.C.*, I, 561-576.

——. "Lettre à Romain Rolland–25 août 1915," in Romain Rolland, *Journal des années de guerre, 1914-1919* (Paris: Albin Michel, 1952), p. 504.

——. "Mon Souvenir de M. Houtin," *La Chronique des idées*, October 1927, pp. 148-150. Reprinted in Houtin, Albert. *Mon Expérience, II. Ma vie laïque, 1912-1926*. Paris: Rieder, 1928, pp. 367-370.

———. "Notes sur *Jeanne d'Arc a-t-elle abjuré?*, par Marcel Hébert," *N.R.F.*, May 1, 1914, pp. 891–893.

———. "Personne n'est moins dupé: Personne plus indépend-ant," *Le Figaro littéraire*, October 26, 1957, p. 1. (On Albert Camus.)

———. "Projets de préface pour *Jean Barois*," *N.R.F.*, December 1, 1959, pp. 1,123-1,128.

———. "Que pensez-vous de Maupassant?" *Les Nouvelles littéraires*, August 3, 1950, p. 1.

———. "Réponse," *Le Figaro*, Edition de Lyon, October 19, 1940, p. 3. Reply to an inquiry, "Que sera demain la littérature?"

———. "Sur la Mort d'André Gide," *Le Figaro littéraire*, January 5, 1952, p. 1.

———. "Le Vieux-Colombier: Conférence de Jacques Copeau à la salle des Sociétés Savantes, 8 novembre 1919," *N.R.F.*, December 1, 1919, pp. 1,113-1,118.

Le Parti Socialiste S. F. I. O. *En Hommage à Léon Blum— Troisìeme anniversaire de sa mort; "L'Action des Socialistes en 1936."* Arras: Société d'Editions du Pas-de-Calais, 1953. Pamphlet giving information on Martin du Gard's membership in the Société des Amis de Léon Blum.

"Pour Ethel et Julius Rosenberg," *Les Lettres françaises*, June 18–June 25, 1953, p. 1. Reprints a telegram.

"Pour protester contre la saisie de *La Question* et demander que la lumière soit faite sur les tortures," *L'Humanité*, April 17, 1958, p. 1. Reprints a manifesto.

Les Prix Nobel en 1937. Stockholm: Imprimerie Royale P. A. Norstedt et Söner, 1938. Martin du Gard's Nobel Prize speech is on pp. 67-70. Also reprinted in *N.R.F.*, May 1959, pp. 956-960.

Schlumberger, Jean. *Madeleine et André Gide*. Paris: Gallimard, 1956. Relevant section, pp. 185-194, cites an extract from Martin du Gard's *Journal*.

Sernin, André. *L'Apprenti philosophe, roman d'un Khagneux.* Paris: Nouvelles Editions Latines, 1954. Reprints a letter of introduction by Martin du Gard on pp. 9-12.

Tibor Déry Committee. "For Tibor Déry." Paris: The Committee, 1959. Contains a photocopy of a letter of Martin du Gard and reprints a telegram he signed requesting Déry's release from prison.

PUBLISHED CORRESPONDENCE

Listed here are collections of the more extensive correspondence and a selection of articles containing important letters or fragments of letters from Martin du Gard to their authors. Several important collections will be published soon. Jean Delay is editing the *Correspondance Gide–Martin du Gard,* and Jean Schlumberger himself is preparing the *Correspondance Martin du Gard–Schlumberger.* Professor Maurice Rieuneau of the Faculty of Letters at Grenoble has gathered more than 4,000 items which will be included in the *Correspondance générale,* and he will edit this collection, to be published under the auspices of the C.N.R.S. (Centre national de la Recherche scientifique).

Charasson, Henriette. "Autour de Roger Martin du Gard," *La Dépêche Tunisienne,* September 20, 1958, p. 6. Quotes two letters of 1916 dealing with *Jean Barois.*

Daix, Pierre. "Roger Martin du Gard," *Les Lettres françaises,* August 28–September 5, 1958, pp. 1, 5. Reprints a letter concerning Daix's *Réflexions sur la méthode de Roger Martin du Gard.*

Ikor, Roger. "Martin du Gard, l'exemplaire," *L'Education nationale,* November 27, 1958, pp. 16-18. Contains a photocopy of a late, pessimistic letter of Martin du Gard.

Jourdain, Francis. "Sur Deux Lettres de Roger Martin du Gard," *Les Lettres nouvelles*, November 1958, pp. 496-505. Concerns political involvement.

Martin du Gard, Roger. "Conseils à un jeune écrivain (deux lettres inédites à Roger Ikor)," *Livres de France*, June–July 1961, pp. 4-5.

———. "Consultation littéraire: Lettres à Pierre Margaritis," *N.N.R.F.*, December 1958, pp. 1,117-1,135.

———. "Deux Lettres inédites à Louis Martin-Chauffier," *Livres de France*, January 1960, p. 8.

———. Letters and fragments of letters to Auguste Valensin, in Auguste Valensin, *Textes et documents inédits* (Paris: Aubier, 1961), pp. 342-348.

———. "Lettres à l'architecte," *Cahiers du Sud*, December 1958, pp. 1,137-1,161.

———. "Lettres inédites à Charles du Bos et lettre inédite à Mme Hougron-Desjardins," *Cahiers Charles du Bos*, May 1959, pp. 2-45.

———, and Jean Schlumberger. "Martin du Gard et Schlumberger se racontent leur guerre," *Le Figaro littéraire*, June 17–June 23, 1965, pp. 7, 8.

Schlumberger, Jean. Preface, in Roger Martin du Gard, *Les Thibault: I* (Paris: Imprimerie Nationale, 1960), pp. 1-10. Cites an important fragment dealing with *Epilogue* and Martin du Gard's preference for Antoine over Jacques Thibault.

———. "*Vieille France* et l'art," *N.N.R.F.*, December 1958, pp. 1,068-1,073. Quotes from a letter dealing with *Vieille France*.

TRANSLATION

Roger Martin du Gard, tr. *Olivia*, by Olivia [Dorothy Bussy] (London: The Hogarth Press, 1949). Paris: Stock, 1949.

WORKS ABOUT MARTIN DU GARD

FULL-LENGTH BIOGRAPHIES AND CRITICAL STUDIES.

Boak, Denis. *Roger Martin du Gard.* Oxford: Clarendon Press, 1963.

Borgal, Clément. *Roger Martin du Gard.* Paris: Editions Universitaires, 1957.

Brenner, Jacques. *Martin du Gard.* Paris: Gallimard, 1961.

Daix, Pierre. *Réflexions sur la méthode de Roger Martin du Gard.* Paris: Les éditeurs français réunis, 1957.

Gibson, Robert. *Roger Martin du Gard.* London: Bowes and Bowes, 1961.

Narkir'er, Fedor Semenovich. *Rozhe Marten diu Gar: Kritiko-biograficheskil ocherk.* Moscow: Goslitizdat, 1963.

Robidoux, Réjean. *Roger Martin du Gard et la religion.* Paris: Aubier, 1964.

BOOKS WHICH MAKE SIGNIFICANT REFERENCE TO MARTIN DU GARD

Albères, R.-M. *Portrait de notre héros: Essai sur le roman.* Paris: Le Portulan, 1945.

Blum, Léon. *Souvenirs sur l'Affaire.* Paris: Gallimard, 1935.

Brée, Germaine, and Margaret Guiton. *An Age of Fiction: The French Novel from Gide to Camus.* New Brunswick: Rutgers University Press, 1957.

Brodin, Pierre. *Les Ecrivains français de l'entre-deux-guerres.* Montreal: Editions Bernard Valiquette, 1942.

——. *Présences contemporaines*, II: *Littérature.* Paris: Editions Debresse, 1955.

Brombert, Victor L. *The Intellectual Hero: Studies in the French Novel, 1880-1955.* New York: J. B. Lippincott and Co., 1961.

Clouard, Henri. *Histoire de la littérature française*, II: *De 1915 à 1940*. Paris: Albin Michel, 1949.

Copeau, Jacques. *Souvenirs du Vieux-Colombier*. Paris: Nouvelles Editions Latines, 1931.

Cormeau, Nelly. *Physiologie du roman*. Brussels: La Renaissance du Livre, 1947.

Delhorbe, Cécile. *L'Affaire Dreyfus et les écrivains français*. Paris: Editions Victor Attinger, 1932.

Gide, André. *Journal, 1889-1939*. Paris: Gallimard, Bibliothèque de la Pléiade, 1951.

———. *Journal, 1939-1942*. Paris: Gallimard, 1946.

———. *Journal, 1942-1949*. Paris: Gallimard, 1950.

———. *Journal des faux-monnayeurs*. Paris: Gallimard, 1927.

———. *Littérature engagée*. Paris: Gallimard, 1950.

Houtin, Albert. *Un Prêtre symboliste, Marcel Hébert*. Paris: F. Rieder et Cie, 1925.

Lalou, René. *Histoire de la littérature française contemporaine*. Paris: Presses universitaires, 1953. Vol. II.

Larnac, Jean. *La Littérature française d'aujourd'hui*. Paris: Editions sociales, 1948.

Lukacs, Georg. *La Signification présente du réalisme critique*. Maurice de Gandillac, tr. Paris: Gallimard, 1960.

Madaule, Jacques. *Reconnaissances*, III. Paris: Desclée de Brouwer, 1946.

Magny, Claude-Edmonde. *Histoire du roman français depuis 1918*. Paris: Editions du Seuil, 1950. Vol. I.

Mallet, Robert. *Une Mort ambiguë*. Paris: Gallimard, 1955.

Martin du Gard, Maurice. *Les Mémorables, I (1918-1923)*. Paris: Flammarion, 1957.

Moeller, Charles. *Littérature du vingtième siècle et christianisme*. Paris: Casterman, 1957. Vol. II.

Peyre, Henri. *The Contemporary French Novel*. New York: Oxford University Press, 1955.

Prévost, Jean. *Problèmes du roman*. Lyons and Paris: Confluences, 1943.

Rim, Carlo. *Mémoires d'une vieille vague*. Paris: Gallimard, 1961.

Rousseaux, André. *Littérature du vingtième siècle*. Paris: Albin Michel, Vols. I (1938) and VI (1958).

Roy, Claude. *Descriptions critiques*. Paris: Gallimard, 1949. Vol. I.

Simon, Pierre-Henri. *L'Esprit et l'histoire: Essai sur la conscience historique dans la littérature du vingtième siècle*. Paris: Armand Colin, 1954.

——. *Histoire de la littérature française au xxe siècle, 1900-1950*. 2 vols. Paris: Armand Colin, 1957.

Sneyers, Germaine. *Romanciers d'entre deux guerres*. Paris: Desclée de Brouwer, 1941.

ARTICLES AND SHORTER PIECES

Abraham, Pierre. "Roger Martin du Gard," *Les Lettres françaises*, August 28–September 3, 1958, pp. 1, 5.

Agathon [Henri Massis and Alfred de Tarde]. "Leur Jeunesse: A propos de *Jean Barois*," *L'Opinion*, January 17, 1914, pp. 77-78.

Altman, Georges. "Les Livres: Histoires de familles bourgeoises," *L'Humanité*, April 29, 1929, p. 5.

——. "Sur *Les Thibault* de R. Martin du Gard—Histoires de famille," *Monde*, February 8, 1930, p. 3.

Bidou, Henri. "Le Mouvement littéraire," *Revue de Paris*, January 15, 1937, pp. 444-446.

——. "Revue littéraire—*L'Eté 1914*," *Journal des débats politiques et littéraires*, January 2–January 3, 1937, p. 4.

Camus, Albert. "Il aidait à vivre," *Le Figaro littéraire*, August 30, 1958, p. 1.

———. Préface, in Roger Martin du Gard, *O.C.*, I, vii-xxix.

Chaperon, Henri. "Roger Martin du Gard (Souvenirs)," *Bulletin de la Société littéraire des P.T.T.*, June 1959, pp. 9-11.

Crémieux, Benjamin. "*La Mort du père*, par Roger Martin du Gard," *N.R.F.*, July 1, 1929, pp. 256-262.

———. "*Les Thibault*, I: *Le Cahier gris*, par Roger Martin du Gard," *N.R.F.*, June 1, 1922, pp. 753-755.

De May, Glado. "*Les Thibault*, monument social," *Glanes*, November–December 1948, pp. 30-44.

"Les Ennemis de la paysannerie à l'honneur," *La Production française*, December 12, 1937, p. 3.

Fernandez, Daniel. "Proust ou Martin du Gard," *N.N.R.F.*, December 1958, pp. 1,079-1,091.

Giron, Roger. "M. Roger Martin du Gard, témoin irrécusable de son temps," *Toute l'Edition*, December 26, 1936, pp. 1, 6.

Giroud, Françoise. "Qui est donc ce Martin du Gard," *L'Express*, August 28, 1958, p. 11.

Grosjean, Jean. "Un Grand Hagiographe," *N.N.R.F.*, December 1958, pp. 1,036-1,041.

Hall, Thomas White. "A Note on the So-called 'Change in Technique' in *Les Thibault* of Roger Martin du Gard," *French Review*, December 1953, pp. 108-113.

Heber-Suffrin, Jean. "Roger Martin du Gard," *La Grive*, October–December 1958, pp. 14-15.

Hébert, Marcel. "Rassegna Bibliographica," *Coenobium*, December 31, 1913, pp. 78-79.

———. "Testament spirituel," *Coenobium*, March 31, 1914, pp. 32-34.

Heitz, Georges. "Deux Romanciers d'aujourd'hui: Roger Martin du Gard et Henry de Montherlant," *Le Monde nouveau*, January 15, 1925, pp. 15-26.

Henriot, Emile. "Roger Martin du Gard vu par lui-même," *Le Monde*, December 28, 1955, p. 7.

Ikor, Roger. "L'Humanité des Thibault," *Europe*, June 1946, pp. 28-47.

Kaiser, Grant E. "Roger Martin du Gard's *Jean Barois*, an Experiment in Novelistic Form," *Symposium*, Summer 1960, pp. 135-141.

Kanters, Robert. "Simple Adieu aux Thibault," *Cahiers du Sud*, September 1940, pp. 433-435.

Lacretelle, Jacques de. "Critique des livres: *Les Thibault*, VII: *L'Eté 1914* par Roger Martin du Gard," *L'Ami du peuple*, December 26, 1936, p. 4.

Lalou, René. *Roger Martin du Gard*. Paris: Gallimard, 1937. Pamphlet, a reprinting of an article which first appeared in the *Revue de Paris*, August 15, 1937, pp. 821-844.

Lanson, Gustave. "Mouvement Littéraire—Roger Martin du Gard, *Jean Barois*," *Le Matin*, December 24, 1913, p. 7.

Laulan, Robert. "Roger Martin du Gard et la formation chartiste," *Mercure de France*, March 1959, pp. 550-551.

Madaule, Jacques. "Chronique," *La Vie intellectuelle*, January 10, 1937, pp. 306-314.

——. "Roger Martin du Gard: *Les Thibault: Epilogue*," *Esprit*, November 1940, pp. 52-55.

Mantaigne, André. "Une Récompense et un homme," *La Lumière*, October 29, 1937, p. 6.

Marcontonato, Léon C. "Roger Martin du Gard et le Prix Interallié," *Cahiers du Sud*, June 1939, pp. 515-521.

Martin-Chauffier, Louis. "L'Homme qui fuyait la renommée," *Livres de France*, January 1960, pp. 3-6.

——. "Huit Jours chez Roger Martin du Gard," *Vendredi*, November 19, 1937, p. 1. Reprinted in *N.R.F.*, December 1, 1937, pp. 1,031-1,032.

Martin du Gard, Maurice. "Roger Martin du Gard," *La Revue des deux mondes*, October 1, 1958, pp. 463-474.

Massis, Henri. "Les Idées et les faits: Lectures—Du côté d'Agathon, II," *La Revue universelle*, January 15, 1935, pp. 217-223.

———. "Les Idées et les faits: Lectures—Du Prix Nobel et d'un écrivain pacifiste," *La Revue universelle*, February 1, 1938, pp. 354-361. Reprinted in Massis, *La Guerre de trente ans* (Paris: Plon, 1940), pp. 258-265.

———. "Le Romantisme de l'adolescence," *La Revue universelle*, September 15, 1922, pp. 750-760. Reprinted in Massis's *Jugements, II* (Paris: Plon, 1924), pp. 108–124.

Michaud, Régis. "Roger Martin du Gard," *Books Abroad*, Spring 1938, pp. 149-151.

Morand, Jean. "Entre la littérature et la vie: La solitude de Roger Martin du Gard," *Les Lettres nouvelles*, November 1958, pp. 507-515.

Nizan, Paul. "*Eté 1914*, par Roger Martin du Gard," *L'Humanité*, January 7, 1937, p. 8.

———. "Roger Martin du Gard: *Eté 1914*," *N.R.F.*, January 1, 1937, pp. 95-99.

O'Nan, Martha B. "Form in the Novel: André Gide and Roger Martin du Gard," *Symposium*, Spring–Fall 1958, pp. 81-93.

———. "The Influence of Tolstoy upon Roger Martin du Gard," *Kentucky Foreign Language Quarterly*, Spring 1957, pp. 7-14.

Pénard, Jean. "Aspects d'une amitié: Roger Martin du Gard et André Gide," *Revue des sciences humaines*, January–March 1959, pp. 77-98.

Perrin, André. "Roger Martin du Gard et *Les Thibault*," *Le Mois*, January 10, 1937, pp. 164-180.

Picon. Gaëtan. "Portrait et situation de Roger Martin du Gard," *Mercure de France*, September 1958, pp. 5-25.

———. "Roger Martin du Gard," *Paragone*, December 1958, pp. 79-83.

Pierre-Quint, Léon. "Roger Martin du Gard, le constructeur," *Monde nouveau*, June 1956, pp. 40-56, and July 1956, pp. 37-50.

Polanscak, Antun. "Roger Martin du Gard et *Les Thibault*," *Studia Romanica et Anglica-Zagrabiensia*, December 1960, pp. 103-124.

Porché, François. "Chronique littéraire," *L'Echo de Paris*, December 7, 1936, p. 4.

Poupet, Georges. "La Vie littéraire: Oedipe aussi était averti: à propos de *L'Eté 1914*, septième partie des *Thibault*," *Le Jour*, December 7, 1936, p. 2.

Prévost, Alain. " 'Vos Oeuvres nous aident à vivre,' écrit-on à Moscou à propos de Roger Martin du Gard," *Libération*, January 14, 1957, p. 2.

Prévost, Jean. "Comment Roger Martin du Gard a écrit *Les Thibault*," *Les Nouvelles littéraires*, December 5, 1936, p. 1.

"Prizewinner," *Time*, November 29, 1937, p. 69.

Rain, Pierre. "L'été 1914," *Sciences politiques*, March 1937, pp. 32-41.

Rice, Howard C. *Roger Martin du Gard and the World of the Thibaults: A Biographical and Critical Estimate.* New York: Viking Press, 1941. Pamphlet.

Rostand, Jean. "En Toute Cause offensée il voyait une cause à défendre," *Le Figaro littéraire*, August 30, 1958, pp. 1, 8.

Roudiez, Léon S. The Function of Irony in Roger Martin du Gard," *Romanic Review*, December 1957, pp. 275–286.

——. "Situation de Roger Martin du Gard," *French Review*, October 1960, pp. 13-25.

Rousseaux, André. "La Vie littéraire," *Le Figaro*, November 28, 1936, p. 6.

Roux, François de. "Les Livres de la semaine," *L'Intransigeant*, December 14, 1936, p. 2.

Roy, Claude. "Roger Martin du Gard ou le Massif Central," *Libération*, February 28, 1956, p. 2.

Sadoul, Georges. "Rencontres, sous l'occupation, avec Roger Martin du Gard," *Les Etoiles*, June 19, 1945, pp. 1, 3.

Schlumberger, Jean. "*Jean Barois*, par Roger Martin du Gard," *N.R.F.*, January 1, 1914, pp. 147-151.

——. "Roger Martin du Gard," *Livres de France*, January 1960, pp. 10-12.

——. "Sur Roger Martin du Gard, Prix Nobel de littérature pour 1937," *Toute l'Edition*, November 20, 1937, pp. 1, 3.

Severac, J.-B. "*La Mort du père*, par Roger Martin du Gard," *Le Populaire*, May 22, 1929, p. 4.

——. "*Les Thibault*, IVme et Vme parties: *La Consultation* et *La Sorellina* par Roger Martin du Gard," *Le Populaire*, June 27, 1928, p. 4.

Simon, Pierre-Henri. "Un Grand Roman de la famille: *Les Thibault*," *Pour la vie*, March 1955, pp. 44-55.

Sneyers, Germaine. "Revue littéraire—*L'Eté 1914*, par Roger Martin du Gard," *La Revue générale*, January 15, 1937, pp. 112-117. Belgian periodical.

Souday, Paul. "Les Livres," *Le Temps*, January 7, 1914, p. 3; August 17, 1922, p. 2; November 22, 1923, p. 3; June 7, 1928, p. 3; April 11, 1929, p. 3.

Stéphane, Roger. "Roger Martin du Gard," *France observateur*, August 28, 1958, p. 13.

Thulin, Elsa. "Roger Martin du Gard à Stockholm," *Les Nouvelles littéraires*, December 12, 1937, p. 1.

Vermont, Lucien. "Roger Martin du Gard Prix Nobel 1937 nous dit . . . ," *Les Nouvelles littéraires*, November 20, 1937, p. 1.

Weber, Eugen. "The Secret World of Jean Barois," in John

Weiss, ed., *The Origins of Modern Consciousness* (Detroit: Wayne State University Press, 1965), pp. 79-109.

Zweig, Stephan. ". . . 1914 et aujourd'hui," Bracke [A. M. Desrousseaux], tr., *Le Populaire*, December 20, 1936, p. 4. Available in German in Zweig's *Zeit und Welt* (Stockholm: Bermann-Fischer Verlag, 1943), pp. 353-362.

Index